DISCIPLINES & DISRUPTION
Projects Catalog of the 37th Annual Conference of the Association for Computer Aided Design in Architecture (ACADIA)

EDITORS
Joel Lamere, Cristina Parreño Alonso

COPY EDITING
Pascal Massinon, Mary O'Malley

GRAPHIC DESIGN
Rebekka Kuhn

PRINTER
IngramSpark

PUBLICATION EDITOR
Anastasia Hiller

COVER IMAGE
Maroula Bacharidou

Conference hosted by Massachusetts Institute of Technology School of Architecture + Planning, Department of Architecture.

ISBN 978-0-692-96501-6

PROJECTS

Projects Catalog of the 37th Annual Conference of the
Association for Computer Aided Design in Architecture

Massachusetts Institute of Technology, School of Architecture
+ Planning, Department of Architecture

———

Edited by Joel Lamere, Cristina Parreño Alonso

acadia

PROJECTS

6   **Introduction**
       Joel Lamere, Cristina Parreño Alonso

8   **Keynotes & Awards**
   10   **Thomas Heatherwick**
         ACADIA Design Excellence Award & Keynote

   12   **Jonathan Chemla**
         Keynote

   14   **Ben Fry**
         Keynote

   18   **Neri Oxman**
         Keynote

   22   **Jessica Rosenkrantz & Jesse Louis-Rosenberg**
         Keynote

   26   **Lisa Iwamoto & Craig Scott**
         ACADIA Digital Practice Award of Excellence

   30   **Bob Martens**
         ACADIA Society Award of Excellence

   34   **Bartlett School of Architecture, B-Pro Program**
         ACADIA Academic Program Award of Excellence

   38   **Heather Roberge**
         ACADIA Teaching Award of Excellence

   42   **Wesley McGee ·**
         ACADIA Innovative Research Award of Excellence

46   **Exhibition Projects**
   48   **Gabriella Carolini**
         The Missing Financial Architecture of Urban
         Development: Exploring the Critical Geography of
         Urban Property Tax Potential in African Cities

   50   **Rania Ghosn, El Hadi Jazairy**
         Blue Marble Circus

   52   **Mariana Ibañez, Simon Kim**
         RolyPolygon: Confessional

   54   **Lauren A. Jacobi**
         Renaissance Spaces of Money

   56   **Joel Lamere, Cynthia Gunadi**
         Grove

   58   **Takehiko Nagakura, Woongki Sung**
         AR Mail from Harbin

60   **William O'Brien Jr.**
       Other Masks

62   **Cristina Parreño Alonso**
       Tectonics of Transparency

64   **Skylar Tibbits**
       Programmable Materials: Active Auxetics

66   **Sarah Williams, Jacqueline Klopp, Peter Waiganjo**
       Wagacha, Dan Orwa, Adam White
       Digital Matatus

68   **Peer Reviewed Projects**
   70   **Chandler Ahrens, John Carpenter, Aaron Sprecher**
         Fracture, Parallel States of the Abstract and the
         Physical

   76   **Masoud Akbarzadeh, Mehrad Mahnia, Ramtin**
         Taherian, Amir Hossein Tabrizi
         Hedracrete: Prefab, Funicular, Spatial Concrete

   82   **Amin Bahrami, Raana Dorneshan**
         Non-Modular Muqarnas: A Design Tool for Creating
         Non-Modular Muqarnas Using Topological-Based
         Computation

   88   **Nathan Bishop, Pooya Baktash, Ivan Vasyliv**
         Ceiling Pressurized Ocular Diffusers (POD's)

   94   **Stephanie Chaltiel, Maite Bravo**
         Monolithic Earthen Shells & Robotic Fabrication

   100   **David Costanza**
         Taut: Tensioned Surface Morphologies in the
         Production of Textile Composites

   106   **Scott Crawford, Stephen Van Dyck**
         Collaborative Parametric Design of a
         Theatroacoustic System

   112   **Dana Cupkova, Colleen Clifford, Thomas Sterling**
         Migratory Landforms

   118   **Ricky del Monte, Jo Kamm**
         Smallest Parts: How a Design of Great Complexity
         Can be Completed with Great Simplicity

   122   **Marcella Del Signore, Cordula Roser Gray**
         DATAField

   128   **Shelby Elizabeth Doyle, Erin Linsey Hunt**
         IM_RU

TABLE OF CONTENTS

134 Wendy W Fok, Michael Koehle
Ownership/Authorship In Three-Dimensional
Photographic Reproductions

138 Andrei Gheorghe, Robert Vierlinger, Philipp
Hornung, Manora Auersperg, Sigurd Reiss
Architecture Challenge 2016: "Robotic Contouring"

144 Ryan Goold, Daniel Fougere, Tsz Yan Ng, Wes
McGee
Concrete Lattice- Unitized Architecture of
Assembly

150 John Granzow, Catie Newell, Kim Harty
String Section

156 Nicholas Hoban, Jay Chenault, Alessandro
DellEndice, Matthias Helmreich, Jesus Medina
Ibanez, Pietro Odaglia, Federico Salvalaio,
Stavroula Tsafou, Philipp Eversmann, Fabio
Gramazio, Matthias Kohler
House 4178 – A Robotic Pavilion

162 Alvin Huang, Anna M. Chaney
Data Moiré: Optical Patterns as Data-Driven Design
Narratives

168 Damjan Jovanovic
Platform Sandbox, A Pedagogical Design Software

174 Julie Larsen, Roger Hubeli
The Production of Thinness: A Fabricated
Concrete Pavilion

180 Dr. Julian Lienhard, Dr. Christian Bergmann,
Dr. Riccardo La Magna, Jonas Runberger
Textile Hybrid

186 Adam Marcus
Signal / Noise: Code and Craft in Architectural
Drawing

192 Nono Martínez Alonso
Suggestive Drawing Among Human and Artificial
Intelligences

198 Seth McDowell, Rychiee Espinosa
Unfindable Objects for BIM

204 Ashish Mohite, Mariia Kochneva, Toni Kotnik
Surface Ornamentation as Byproduct of Digital
Fabrication

210 Tsz Yan Ng, Wes McGee
Thermoplastic Concrete Casting

216 Trevor Ryan Patt
Punctual Urban Redevelopment in Informal Urban
Contexts

222 Felix Raspall, Carlos Bañón
(ultra) light network

228 Benjamin Rice
Expressive Robotic Networks

232 Uwe Rieger
LightScale II- arc/sec Lab

238 William Sharples, Christopher Sharples, Sameer
Kumar, Andrea Vittadini, Scott Overall, Clinton
Miller, Victoire Saby, John Paul Rysavy
Wave/Cave

244 José Pedro Sousa, Pedro de Azambuja Varela,
Pedro Martins
The CorkCrete Arch

250 Ming Tang, Mara Marcu
Augmented Coral: An Installation Using Digital
Fabrication and Mixed Reality

256 Filip Tejchman
Motivational Rock: Entropy in Architecture

262 Daniel Tish, Dr. Lars Junghans, Dustin Brugmann,
Geoffrey Thün
Latitudo Borealis

268 Kenneth Tracy, Christine Yogiaman
Kaleidoscopic Monolith

274 Yuan Yao, Yuhan Li, Yang Hong
HEXY: Soft Self-Organization Robot

280 Lei Yu
Arachne: A 3D-Printed Building Façade

286 ACADIA 2017 Credits

288 ACADIA Organization

290 Conference Management & Production Credits

292 Peer Review Committee

294 ACADIA 2017 Sponsors

Introduction

Joel Lamere
Assistant Professor, Department of Architecture, MIT
Principal, GLD Architecture

Cristina Parreño Alonso
Belluschi Lecturer, Department of Architecture, MIT
Cristina Parreño Architecture

In centering the 2017 ACADIA conference around the theme of "Disciplines + Disruption," we are foregrounding one predicament. Two parallel and contradictory forces are essential in advancing architectural agendas through computation: the long-standing disciplinary research interests that guide incremental progress, and the flux of disruptive forces that undermine the clarity of those trajectories. We embrace both, and see in the current moment a particularly urgent need to do so. As we graduate from a phase of computational adolescence, during which we've seen many of the early pioneers' visions become commonplace reality, the question of *where we go from here* is less certain than ever. The previous generation has succeeded, insofar as digital tools are ubiquitous in architectural design and integral to all stages of the process, from design education to building construction. The *digital project* no longer needs explicit champions, because it is everywhere. But recent global developments remind us that progress along disciplinary axes does not equate to progress generally. The vision of a future augmented by advanced computational technology has arrived, and it leaves much to be desired. The contributors to this conference seek to expand that vision, in some instances through continued hard-won research within a specific lineage. Others transgress inherited disciplinary boundaries, suggest visions of alternate futures, and respond in previously unimaginable ways to previously unimaginable problems. These others offer disruptions with the potential to renew and reroute the discipline. Jointly, these disparate strategies—the *disciplinary* and the *disruptive*—actively shape what is to come.

As ever, the ACADIA conference values many modes of contribution in the field of computational design, all of which are instrumental in the production and dissemination of knowledge. Two separate volumes of Proceedings are produced with each conference, recognizing the breadth of those contributions. This volume is dedicated to Peer-Reviewed Projects while the complementary publication presents the Peer-Reviewed Papers that were selected this year. In both cases, the organization— arranged as a single group, ordered alphabetically—speaks to our vision of what a body of research or creative practice must do to merit its inclusion in this year's conference. Rather than reinforce disciplinary boundaries, sitting neatly within the confines of a single category of inquiry, projects and papers must cross-pollinate multiple lineages and coexist simultaneously in the three broad themes that the conference proposed this year.

This time, the themes work not so much as categories that bracket the work but as topics of relevance around which we can begin to establish productive discussions about innovative practices in computational architecture today. *Disruptions in Material/Construction* focuses on recent innovations in

PROJECTS

materials, fabrication and construction. *Disruptions in Design Tools/Information Processing* centers on questions of agency and authorship, through interrogating both design process and design tools. And finally, *Disruptions in Society & Cultures* addresses the social and cultural transformations that attend technological innovation.

This volume is organized in three parts: Award Winners and Keynote Speakers, Exhibition Projects, and Peer-Reviewed Projects. Each grouping contributes meaningfully to the conference agenda, through recipients, speakers and authors whose works exemplify *disciplinary* and *disruptive* ambitions. Keynote Speakers and Awardees are distinguished thinkers and practitioners, invited to reflect the current state of the discipline. All are long-time participants in the discourse, either directly through their scholarship or because their work is central to how we perceive the relationship between computation and design. The Exhibition Projects offer a window into the host institution's role in the larger conversation. At MIT, where many of the computational tools we take for granted today were born, this relationship has a long and complex history. As such, for *Optimism in Three Acts*, the curators have decided to focus on how current MIT faculty critically deploy technological tools toward diverse aims through agency, memory and empathy.

The bulk of this volume is devoted to Peer-Reviewed Projects. If there is an argument for the work presented in this conference to be inclusive and challenge the boundaries of the discipline, in the case of the Projects, this proposition becomes of paramount importance. Projects are manifestations of design research whose outcomes are objects in the world, in specific cultural contexts, which deploy innovative materials and construction systems, or experimental design processes, all *simultaneously*. This is not to say, of course, that Papers cannot be so inclusive, just that Projects *must* be, whether explicitly or implicitly. Projects exist at the messy locus between the bracketed bounds of pure research and the many contingencies that define the production of realized architectural artifacts. They necessarily defy efforts at neat subcategorization. We acknowledge and amplify this resistance to delineation, and reject the fragmented disciplinary bounds that once defined project-based research. Instead, we simply present these Projects as a single collective, accepting the breadth of their interests and concerns. In merely listing them rather than sorting them, we are advocating *disruptive* connections over *disciplinary* fragmentation.

DISCIPLINES + DISRUPTION

KEYNOTES & AWARDS

Thomas Heatherwick

ACADIA 2017 Design Excellence Award & Keynote

Bio

Thomas Heatherwick, Founder and Design Director of Heatherwick Studio, is a British designer whose prolific and varied work over two decades is characterised by its ingenuity, inventiveness and originality. Defying the conventional classification of design disciplines, Thomas founded Heatherwick studio in 1994 to bring the practices of design, architecture and urban planning together in a single workspace.

Thomas leads the design of all Heatherwick Studio projects, working in collaboration with a team of 200 highly-skilled architects, designers, and makers. The studio's unusual approach applies artistic thinking to the needs of each project, resulting in some of the most acclaimed designs of our time. Based in London, Heatherwick studio is currently working in four continents. Following the success of the UK Pavilion for the Shanghai World Expo in 2010, Heatherwick studio has gone on to win exciting design briefs including the Learning Hub at Singapore's Nanyang Technological University, and the new Google campus in Silicon Valley and Google UK Headquarters in London. The studio has recently completed Zeitz MOCAA project in Cape Town and Bund Finance Centre in Shanghai, both completed in 2017.

Thomas has been appointed a Commander of the Order of the British Empire, a Royal Academician and in 2004 became the youngest Royal Designer for Industry.

1 Learning Hub, Singapore, Singapore, 2013. (Photo: Hufton + Crow)

2 Learning Hub, Singapore, Singapore, 2013. (Photo: Hufton + Crow)

3 Bombay Sapphire Distillery, Laverstoke UK (Hufton + Crow)

Jonathan Chemla

Keynote

Since the very early days of the Iconem project, our mission was dedicated to the preservation and transmission of our culture and history. Archaeological remains are the physical traces of our heritage, and their disappearance because of both human and natural factors has been our motivation to stand up. To do so, we focused on developing new technologies to precisely record archaeological sites in three dimensions, and provide ways to access and visit these digital copies. Our philosophy is to digitize heritage sites across the world in order to numerically preserve 3D copies freezing their state at one point in time, and to open access to this documentation for the scientific community as well as every human being. From a team of three to now more than ten people, we brought together the knowledge and know-how of researchers, architects, engineers and artists to respond to this challenge.

There are many causes for the disappearance of heritage sites: looting has reached dramatic scales in the past decades; natural causes such as floodings and earthquakes severely damage and destroy some sites; ideological destructions have also been used as a weapon by several groups to annihilate culture and tighten the control over populations; urbanization, expansion of cities and exploitation of mining resources are severe constraints for the physical preservation and documentation of these heritage sites.

The first projects have been carried out mostly in the Middle East - Afghanistan, Syria, Iraq where threats to heritage were immediate and archaeological teams had not much time on the terrain - and Europe - Pompei, Italy, or France. We are now working in more than 20 countries over the world, in the Middle East, Europe, Asia and North Africa, for institutions such as UNESCO, the World bank, United Nations, for Ministries of Culture, and for companies like Microsoft or Google. Because of an important understanding of the terrain, we adapt to each problem faced by teams on the ground, set up a practical solution, build high precision 3D digital copies of the sites and use them to conduct thorough analyses to answer these problems. Besides archiving the site in space and time with this "3D photograph", the model can be used to store in a same reference space all available layers of documentation of a site – old engravings, architectural drawings, photographs and 3D models at different instants in time. Using this multi-layered approach let us understand the degradation of sites by comparing them with archives photos in order to compel institutions to take action or point out the structural damages monuments have suffered. Using long range drones, we can even understand looting and ideological destructions on sites located on ISIS controlled territories.

The technology at the heart of our project combines recent algorithms - called photogrammetry - with the usage of drones to acquire quickly several thousand photos of the environment. Using powerful resources, we combine them in a 3D model which perfectly replicates the geometry and texture of the site. This makes possible the fast recording of the state of monuments - sometimes spread over a large site - under complex conditions - remote places, dangerous terrains and short time frames, areas not cleared of mines, etc.

1   Afghanistan -The Buddhist site of Mes Aynak is located on the second largest copper mine in the world, and is a vast religious and economic complex. Terra cotta sculptures cannot be easily moved without damages, and 3d scanning helps plan the excavations, archive the state of the site, and let archaeologists understand the past.

2   Syria -Krak des Chevaliers. With the technical support of the DGAM, ICONEM digitized the whole citadel which suffered structural and superficial damages during the Syrian conflict, with over 100.000 photos of both interiors and exteriors.

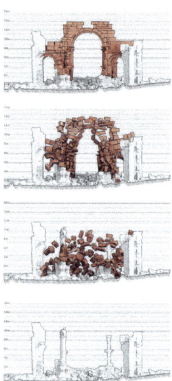

⑬   Palmyra. Simulation of the physics of the destruction of the monumental arch. Using the photogrammetric 3d model as a basis, which we acquired in April 2016 right after ISIS lost control of the city, we can use other sources of documentation to reproduce the pre-destruction state of the arch, and use the simulation to identify the original position of the blocks.

As Iconem CTO, my focus has been to set up, adapt and develop the whole 3D production pipeline which processes wide sites with millimetric precision. Delivering the processed data to archaeologists and cultural institutions in a unified set up, as well as imaging ways to explore these immersive environments in real time participate a lot in the work. New compression and streaming technologies indeed let anyone with any device explore the scanned environments in three dimensions. Scientists can therefore virtually explore the site - whether it is unreachable, not safe, or has changed state. My background is that of a scientist, research engineer, and hacker which specialized in image processing, machine vision and 3D computer graphcis and worked in the medical imaging field. I have always dedicated my work towards challenging technical problems with a strong impact, and found the opportunity to participate as a "heritage activist" very motivating. Gathering a talented team around that motivation, and seeing the full potential that we can achieve by combining our skills is very rewarding, day after day.

More recently, we have been using the data, intially dedicated to scientific purposes, for promoting heritage in immersive exhibitions in France, Canada - other projects are soon to be announced. The value of the work we carry out with scientists also lies in the potential to do exhibitions to bring people closer to our common heritage. The diffusion is finally an effective mean of conservation of the memory and of preservation and transmission to future generations.

Jonathan Chemla

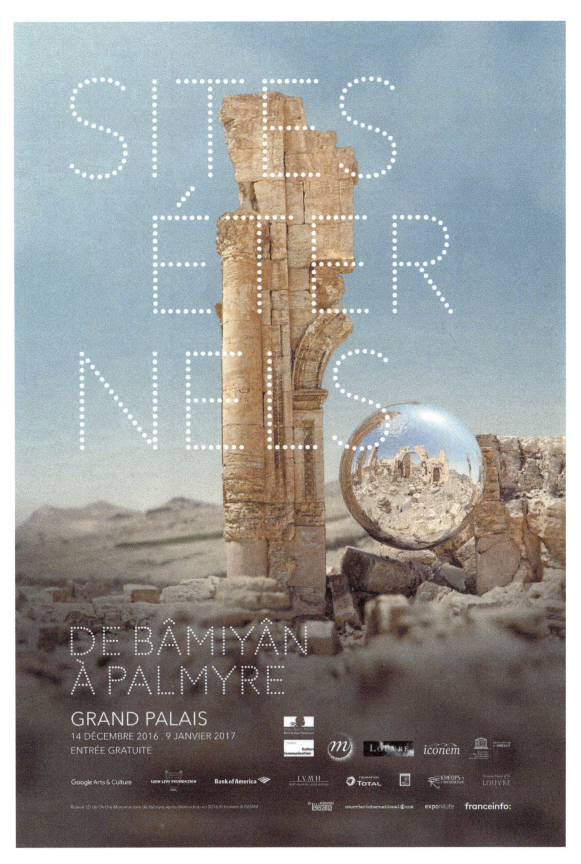

4   Poster of the "Sites Eternels" (Eternal Sites) exhibition at Grand Palais, Paris, which immersed the visitor within four iconic sites of Syria and Iraq - the Umayyad mosque in Damascus, the Krak des Chevaliers, Palmyra and Dur-Sharrukin.

Ben Fry

Keynote

Bio

Ben Fry is principal of Fathom, a design and software consultancy located in Boston. He received his doctoral degree from the Aesthetics + Computation Group at the MIT Media Laboratory, where his research focused on combining fields such as computer science, statistics, graphic design, and data visualization as a means for understanding information. After completing his thesis, he spent time developing tools for visualization of genetic data as a postdoc with Eric Lander at the Eli & Edythe L. Broad Insitute of MIT & Harvard. During the 2006-2007 school year, Ben was the Nierenberg Chair of Design for the Carnegie Mellon School of Design. At the end of 2007, he finished writing Visualizing Data for O'Reilly. In 2011, he won the National Design Award for Interaction Design from the Cooper-Hewitt.

With Casey Reas of UCLA, he currently develops Processing, an open source programming environment for teaching computational design and sketching interactive media software that won a Golden Nica from the Prix Ars Electronica in 2005. The project also received the 2005 Interactive Design prize from the Tokyo Type Director's Club. In 2006, Fry received a New Media Fellowship from the Rockefeller Foundation to support the project. Processing was also featured in the 2006 Cooper-Hewitt Design Triennial. In 2007, Reas and Fry published Processing: A Programming Handbook for Visual Designers and Artists with MIT Press, and in 2010, they published Getting Started with Processing with O'Reilly and MAKE. Processing 1.0 was released in November 2008, and is used by tens of thousands of people every week.

Fry's personal work has shown at the Whitney Biennial in 2002 and the Cooper Hewitt Design Triennial in 2003. Other pieces have appeared in the Museum of Modern Art in New York (2001, 2008), at Ars Electronica in Linz, Austria (2000, 2002, 2005) and in the films Minority Report and The Hulk. His information graphics have also illustrated articles for the journal Nature, New York Magazine, and the The New York Times.

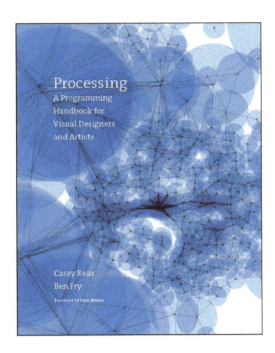

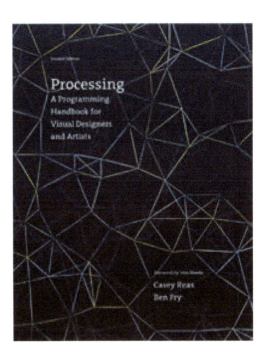

1   Processing, a Programming Handbook for Visual Designers and Artists.
     First Edition. Image credit: Ben Fry and Casey Reas

2   Processing, a Programming Handbook for Visual Designers and Artists.
     Second Edition. Image credit: Ben Fry and Casey Reas

3   Ben Fry, "Isometricblocks," 2004.
     Haplotype block diagram for the CFTR region of the human genome. Image credit: Ben Fry.

Neri Oxman

Keynote

Bio

Architect, designer and inventor Neri Oxman is the Sony Corporation Career Development Professor and Associate Professor of Media Arts and Sciences at the MIT Media Lab, where she founded and directs The Mediated Matter Group. Her team operates at the intersection of computational design, digital fabrication, materials science and synthetic biology; and applies that knowledge to design across scales and disciplines, from micro to building scale. Oxman's goal is to augment the relationship between built, natural, and biological environments by employing design principles inspired and engineered by Nature, and implementing them in the invention of novel design technologies. Areas of application include architectural design, product design, fashion design, as well as the design of new technologies for digital fabrication and construction.

Oxman coined the term, and pioneered the field of, Material Ecology, which considers form generation, manufacturing, the environment and the material itself as inseparable dimensions of design. In this approach, products and buildings are biologically informed and digitally engineered by, with and for, Nature.

Oxman work has resulted in more than 100 papers and patents and is included in permanent collections at the Museum of Modern Art (MoMA), the San Francisco Museum of Modern Art (SFMOMA), Centre Georges Pompidou, the Boston Museum of Fine Arts (MFA), Cooper Hewitt Smithsonian Design Museum, the Smithsonian Institution, the Museum of Applied Arts in Vienna (MAK), the FRAC Collection and the Boston Museum of Science, amongst others including prestigious private collections.

Since 2005, Oxman and her team have won numerous awards and has grown in international scope and acclaim at venues such as the World Economic Forum, where she is part of the Expert Network, and the White House. Among Oxman's awards are a Graham Foundation Carter Manny award (2008), the International Earth Awards for Future-Crucial Design (2008), the HOLCIM Next Generation award for Sustainable Construction (2008), a METROPOLIS Next Generation award (2009), a 40 Under 40 Building Design+Construction award (2012), the BSA Women in Design award (2014), the Vilcek Prize in Design (2014), an Emerging Voices award from the Architectural League of New York (2015), the Innovation by Design award from Fast Company (2015), and the Silicon Valley Forum Visionary Award (2017).

In 2008 Oxman was named "Revolutionary Mind" by SEED Magazine. In the following year she was named to ICON's "top most influential designers and architects to shape our future" and to Esquire's "Best and Brightest". In the following year, Oxman was selected to FASCOMAPNY's "most creative people" and the "10 most creative women in business". In 2014, Oxman was named to Carnegie's Pride of America. In 2015, she was named to ROADS' 100 Global Minds: the Most Daring Cross-Disciplinary Thinkers in the World, and in 2016 she was named a Cultural Leader at the World Economic Forum. Oxman appeared on the covers of FASTCOMPANY (2010), WIRED

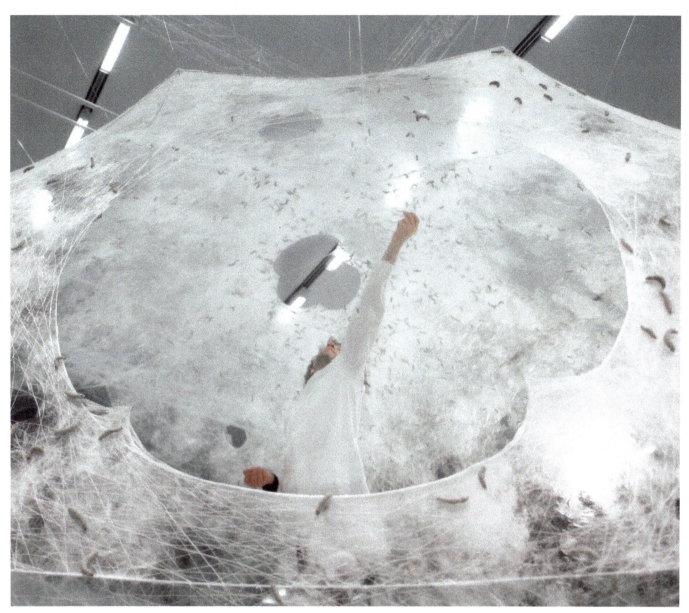

1   Silk Pavilion, 2012. By The Mediated Matter Group. Photo: The Mediated Matter Group.

2   Water-Based Fabrication, 2014. By The Mediated Matter Group. Photo: The Mediated Group.

3   GLASS II, 2017. By The Mediated Matter Group. Photo: Paula Aguilera, courtesy of The Mediated Matter Group.

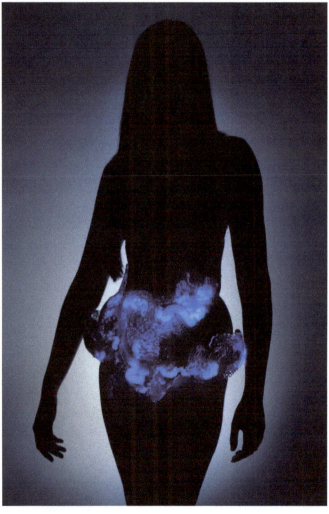

4   Digital Construction Platform, 2016. By The Mediated Matter Group.
Photo: The Mediated Matter.

5   Mushtari, 2015. By The Mediated Matter Group in collaboration with Stratasys.
Photo: Paula Aguilera, courtesy of The Mediated Matter Group.

Neri Oxman

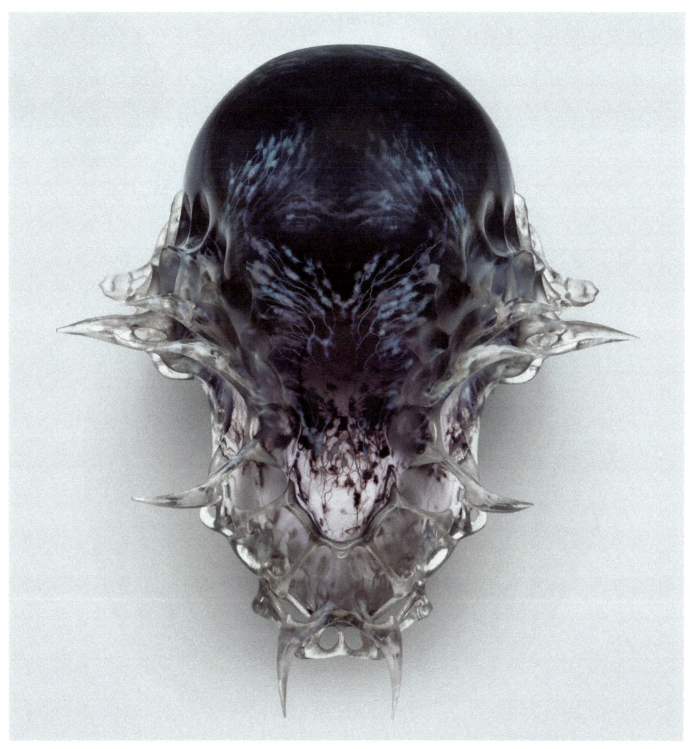

6   Vespers, 2016. By The Mediated Matter Group in collaboration with Stratasys. Photo: Yoram Reshef, courtesy of The Mediated Matter Group.

UK (2012), ICON (2013), SURFACE (2016), and more. She has been written about in The New York Times, The Wall Street Journal, WIRED, Fast Company, The Boston Globe and more.

Neri Oxman received her PhD in Design Computation as a Presidential Fellow at MIT, where she coined the term Material Ecology to describe her research area. Prior to MIT she earned a diploma from the Architectural Association (ARB/RIBA Part 2) after attending the Faculty of Architecture and Town Planning at the Technion Israel Institute of Technology, and the Department of Medical Sciences at the Hebrew University in Jerusalem.

Nervous System

Keynote

Bio

Nervous System is a generative design studio that works at the intersection of science, art, and technology. Designers Jessica Rosenkrantz and Jesse Louis-Rosenberg create using a novel process that employs computer simulation to generate designs and digital fabrication to realize products. Drawing inspiration from natural phenomena, they write computer programs based on processes and patterns found in nature and use those programs to create unique and affordable art, jewelry, and housewares.

Founded in 2007, Nervous System has pioneered the application of new technologies including 3D printing, webGL, and generative design. Nervous System releases online design applications that enable customers to co-create products in an effort to make design more accessible.

Our work at Nervous System combines scientific research, computer graphics, mathematics, and digital fabrication to explore a new paradigm of product design and manufacture. Instead of designing objects, we craft computational systems that result in a myriad of distinct creations. These forms are realized using computer-controlled manufacturing techniques such as 3D printing, laser cutting, and CNC routing.

We are fascinated by natural processes that produce complex forms from simple rule sets and local interactions. Our projects center around adapting the logic of these processes into computational tools; we do this by translating scientific theories and models of pattern formation into algorithms for design. We abstract a natural phenomenon into a set of rules that specifies discrete instructions for a computer to carry out. The design systems we encode are generative; they have no fixed outcome. Rather than thinking of them as mere tools, we consider them our medium. These systems are digital materials with inherent properties and behaviors.

KEY PROJECTS

Cell Cycle (2009)

Cell Cycle is our first project merging generative processing and 3D-printing to create affordable, customized products. It is both a web-based design app and a 3D-printed jewelry collection where anyone can co-create cellular jewelry for 3d-printing in plastic or precious metal inspired by the structures built by radiolaria. In the app, you sculpt a responsive physics simulation of a spring mesh, twisting, morphing and subdividing cells to transform a basic mesh into an intricate, customized structure. Cell Cycle was the first online tool for customizing 3d-printable products.

Hyphae (2011)

The Hyphae Lamps are a series of generative lamps inspired by how veins form in leaves. Each lamp is digitally grown in a computer simulation and fabricated with 3D printing. Every lamp is unique. Efficient LED fixtures illuminate the lamps, casting dramatic, aetherial shadows on the surrounding environment.

1   Kinematics Dress 1 (photo by Steve Marsel, 2014).

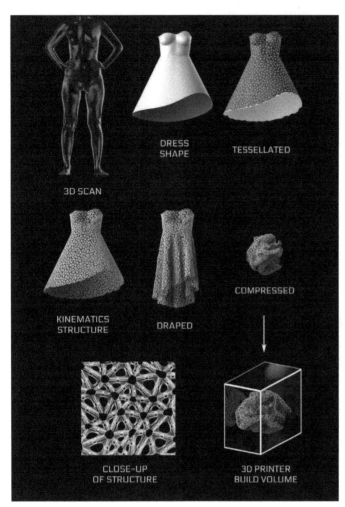

2   Kinematics System (2013).

3   Hyphae x Floraform Chandelier (photo by Jessica Rosenkrantz, 2017).

Kinematics Dress (2014)

Kinematics is a project that fuses fashion, software, and 3D printing to examine how digital fabrication and generative design can impact the way clothing is created. Composed of thousands of unique interlocking components, each dress is 3D printed as a single folded piece and requires no assembly. Kinematics uses 3D scanning to create custom fit garments, sculpted on the body by the customer, and applies a physics simulation to find an efficient configuration for fabrication. The Kinematics Dress represents a new approach to manufacturing which tightly integrates design, simulation, and digital fabrication to create complex, customized products.

New Balance Data-driven midsoles (2016)

Nervous System collaborated with New Balance to create running shoes with midsoles adapted to specific runners. Inspired by nature's variable density foams, Nervous System created a system that generates midsoles from runner's biometric data, creating variable density cushioning customized to how a person runs.

ABOUT NERVOUS SYSTEM

Jessica Rosenkrantz graduated from MIT in 2005 and holds degrees in architecture and biology. Afterwards, she studied architecture at the Harvard Graduate School of Design. She is currently a lecturer at MIT in the department of architecture. Jesse Louis-Rosenberg also attended MIT, majoring in mathematics. He previously worked as a consultant for Gehry Technologies in building modeling and design automation.

Nervous System's designs have been featured in a wide range of publications, including WIRED, the New York Times, the Guardian, Metropolis, and Forbes. Jesse and Jessica have given talks on their generative design process in many forums, including MIT, Harvard, SIGGRAPH, and the Eyeo Festival. Their work is a part of the permanent collection of the Museum of Modern Art, the Museum of Fine Arts, Boston and the Cooper-Hewitt, Smithsonian Design Museum.

Their studio is based in Somerville, Massachusetts.

4   Floraform collar (photo by Rachel Tine, 2015).

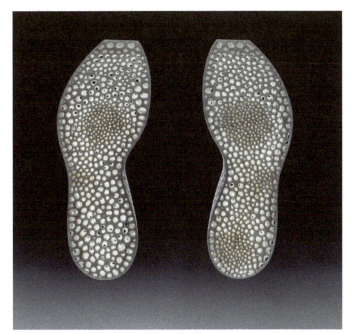

5   Data-driven midsoles (© New Balance 2015).

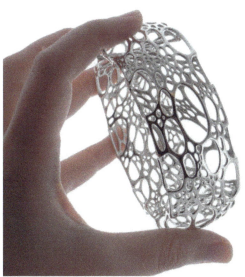

6   Custom cell cycle bracelet in sterling silver (photo by Jessica Rosenkrantz).

IwamotoScott Architecture

ACADIA 2017 Digital Practice Award of Excellence

Bio

IwamotoScott Architecture is a San Francisco–based architecture and design practice led by Lisa Iwamoto and Craig Scott. Since founding the partnership in 2002, they have maintained an experimental and design intensive office, evolving the conceptual nature of the practice together. The firm is committed to pursuing architecture as a form of applied design research and engages in projects at multiple scales and in a variety of contexts, encompassing full-scale fabrications, museum installations and exhibitions, theoretical proposals, competitions and commissioned design projects.

IwamotoScott has received numerous awards, including the Architectural League's Emerging Voices and Young Architects, Architectural Record's Design Vanguard, over twenty AIA Design Awards, a P/A Award and numerous other architecture and interior awards. Their work has been published in hundreds of journals and exhibited in over fifty museums and galleries. Lisa received her Master of Architecture degree with Distinction from Harvard University, and a Bachelor of Science degree in Structural Engineering from the University of Colorado. She is author of *Digital Fabrications: Architectural and Material Techniques*, published in 2009 by Princeton Architectural Press, and is Professor at the University of California Berkeley. Craig is Professor at California College of the Arts. He received his Master of Architecture degree with Distinction from Harvard, and his Bachelor of Architecture from Syracuse University.

Synthetic Wholes

In Michael Heizer's "Double Negative" from 1969, two voids—one, the edge of an existing canyon, the other, a machine-made cut—intersect to infer a third (the double negative), achieving what Marc Treib has called the "presence of absence." Since the time of its construction, Double Negative has inspired much theoretical discourse on the nature of the non-physical art object—in this case one that reinterprets a site-specific condition, the naturally occurring canyon, and the material, space, of which it is made. At an architectural scale, Robert Venturi's stair/fireplace in the Vanna Venturi House from 1962 architecturally grapples with a similar negative space making strategy. Here, the stair and window act as intersecting voids carved through the back of the fireplace. By introducing programmed space and light behind the fireplace, the traditional notion of the hearth—historically the grounded, solid center of the home—is redefined. By defying expectation in these ways, both projects achieve a transformation and de-familiarization of the commonplace.

The Double Negative serves as a touchstone for our work; we privilege the design of space and volume over syntax and surface. It is critical to us that buildings are neither completely foreign, nor simply "fit in" with their surrounds, but that site and building together form a hybrid or synthetic whole. Unlike earthwork sculpture however, architecture cannot rely upon the mere act of digging to unveil the magical and unified confluence of form, space and material. Instead, we grapple with how to create abstraction using formal geometry and common building materials. This is a pervasive question in our work.

Our practice is currently in a transitional moment. Two areas of investigation that founded the firm—material and digital fabrication research centered on one-to-one scaled installations, and formal/spatial

1   Pinterest HQ, San Francisco CA (photo: Bruce Damonte, 2016).

2   Voussoir Cloud, SCIArc Gallery, Los Angeles CA (photo: IwamotoScott, 2008).

3   Bloomberg Tech Hub, San Francisco CA (photo: Bruce Damonte, 2015).

exploration pursued through design competitions and speculative proposals—are now conflated and being tested at building scale.

Installations taught us to think about methods of making first, where material and structure generate the conceptual and formal premise of the work. Computational techniques and digital fabrication are used in tandem with analog production as a means to more fully engage material behavior in relation to geometry. The projects conflate structure and skin, and redefine relationships of part to whole. At the same time, the goal is always to suppress these qualities in favor of a certain formal abstraction. Materials are not there to simply reinforce the formal diagram, nor are they there to self-explicate fabrication, structural diagrams or computational techniques. We seek to reimagine structure and material assembly as a way to question and confound expectation.

At the other end of the scale, the speculative projects span the spectrum from large urban propositions to single buildings. The large projects allow us to computationally construct messy urbanisms,

where part to whole is redefined as a loose fit between program and infrastructure. Individual building designs focus on synthesizing space and form to create subtle architectural objects. Here, negative space making meets projective and prismatic geometry. This work explores relationships between two-dimensional representation and three-dimensional form, and again, seeks to find ways of making both the work and experience of it unexpected and unpredictable.

The convergence of these avenues of design research is now leveraged for brick-and-mortar work. Here, the realm of the everyday inspires us, where innovation is born out of necessity, context and constructional constraints. Creating volume and depth with standard materials, identifying moments for spatial richness through the intersection of negative space, and crystallizing geometric formal strategies in relation to site defines our work. This forms the research agenda—one that aims to create a synthetic whole where design is the search for a meaningful confluence of form, space, material, structure and site.

4   City View Garage, Miami Design District, Miami FL (photo: Craig Scott, 2015).

5   ONE Kearny Lobby (photo: Matthew Millman, 2010).

6   Goto House, Napa County CA (photo: Bruce Damonte, 2017).

Bob Martens

ACADIA 2017 Society Award of Excellence

A Perspective towards Open Access of CAAD-related Publications

The main goal that propelled the development of the Cumulative Index of Computer Aided Architectural Design (CumInCAD) was to build a "collective memory" from conference proceedings of CAAD associations and to make this memory unconditionally accessible to the scientific community as a web-based bibliographic repository.

The need for such a digital library was driven by issues of potential (partial) data loss on the one hand and limited utilization on the other. Access to previous proceedings is still rather limited due to a relatively small number of distributed printed copies. Publications such as conference proceedings are seldom stored in libraries as complete series, but remain mostly in the participants' bookshelves.

A web-based repository provides a "historical evolution," allowing readers/users to learn from previous efforts and drawing attention to older original publications that may have been ignored because they could not be retrieved on the internet.

It was Tom Maver who brought Ziga Turk (University of Ljubljana / Slovenia) and Bob Martens together in 1998. Soon after, a first prototype was made available: a free index of major publications related to CAAD. However, full access to recent conference papers (i.e., in the first two years after release) was limited to members of the donating CAAD associations. Furthermore, the aim was to handle maintenance on a shoestring budget.

During the initial stage of development (from 1998 on), the metadata of CAAD-related conference proceedings were compiled and published online, including all abstracts and approximately 50% of the full texts.

At this point, associations such as ACADIA, CAAD Futures and eCAADe were already in their second decade, whereas CAADRIA and SiGraDi had been newly founded to serve the regions of Asia and Latin America more effectively. While the conference proceedings can be regarded as the only tangible result of an association's activity, the previous paper-based publications of fewer than 250 copies were practically unavailable.

CAAD Futures was the only exception due to the fact that publishing and distribution of its proceedings were handled by a renowned publishing house, which led to high purchasing costs per conference volume.

It was clear from the very beginning that the success of a library like CumInCAD would strongly depend on its contents, i.e., the availability of a critical mass. Conference papers were provided by the above mentioned associations. They furnished digital datasets of the most recent conferences, and older publications were digitized (even retrospectively going back to the first conferences).

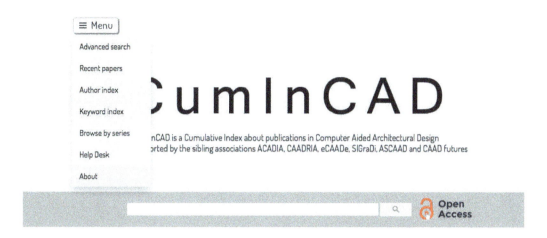

1a CumInCAD 2.0- Start page menu

1b CumInCAD 2.0: Smartphone

#	author	citation		select
1.	Johnson, Jason Kelly (2016)	**Foreword: Complex Entanglements** ACADIA // 2016: POSTHUMAN FRONTIERS: Data, Designers, and Cognitive Machines [Proceedings of the 36th Annual Conference of the Association for Computer Aided Design in Architecture (ACADIA) ISBN 978-0-692-77095-5] Ann Arbor 27-29 October, 2016, pp. 6-7 http://papers.cumincad.org/cgi-bin/works/Show?acadia16_6		
2.	Johnson, Jason Kelly; Cabrinha, Mark; Steinfeld, Kyle (2012)	**Synthetic Digital Ecologies** ACADIA 12: Synthetic Digital Ecologies [Proceedings of the 32nd Annual Conference of the Association for Computer Aided Design in Architecture (ACADIA) ISBN 978-1-62407-267-3] San Francisco 18-21 October, 2012), pp. 15-17 http://papers.cumincad.org/cgi-bin/works/Show?acadia12_15		

2a CumInCAD: ACADIA

≡ Menu

CumInCAD

CumInCAD is a Cumulative Index about publications in Computer Aided Architectural Design supported by the sibling associations ACADIA, CAADRIA, eCAADe, SIGraDi, ASCAAD and CAAD futures

 Open Access

id acadia12_15
authors Johnson, Jason Kelly; Cabrinha, Mark; Steinfeld, Kyle
year 2012
title Synthetic Digital Ecologies
source ACADIA 12: Synthetic Digital Ecologies [Proceedings of the 32nd Annual Conference of the Association for Computer Aided Design in Architecture (ACADIA) ISBN 978-1-62407-267-3] San Francisco 18-21 October, 2012), pp. 15-17
summary Why use the terms synthetic and ecology in the context of a conference dedicated to the field of digital architecture, computation and fabrication? How do we begin to unpack the synthetic union of diverse elements, processes, collaborators, and code underlying any single contemporary design or research project? What could our field gain by interrogating these diverse ecologies? What are the relationships and interactions between our design processes, including our various tools and techniques, and the multiple environments with which we routinely work, collaborate and make? It is these questions and more that we hope to address at this year's "Synthetic Digital Ecologies" conference. A quick scan of the papers and projects that will be presented at ACADIA reveals an extraordinary ecology of experimental research that emerged by working between messy labs, studios, workshops, hacker spaces and the like. In many ways today's so-called "digital architects" do not feel compelled to distinguish between what is digitally designed and what is not. They are leading the way through a promiscuous and synthetic mixing of skill sets, of pens and paper, hardware and

2b CumInCAD: ACADIA, Detailed record

Bob Martens

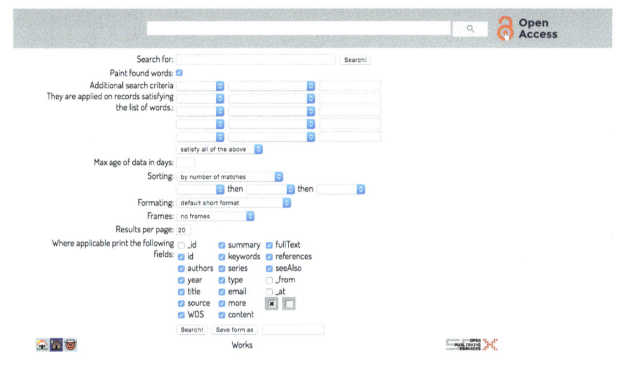

3 CumInCAD 2.0: Advanced search

In the period 2002–2004, the project underwent significant further expansion in the context of an EU project (www.scix.net), and the interface was re-engineered. In addition, a citation index of contained references was created.

CumInNCAD is not the first attempt to provide indexed information related to CAD/CAAD. Doug Noble and Karen Kensek indexed articles that appeared in ACADIA publications. Although the "ACADIA 15 Year Index 1981-1996" (http://www-rcf.usc.edu/~dnoble/author.html) is no more than a plain text list, it provides an overview and is often found by search engines.

CADline was a bibliographic service developed by Yehuda Kalay in cooperation with librarians at a time when no web-based services were available. A proprietary system does not attract users in the same way as a web-based interface, and it also requires more preparatory work. The collected information, nearly 1.000 entries, was subsequently donated to CumInCAD.

As of today, CumInCAD includes bibliographic information of over 13,100 bibliographic records predominantly

from CAAD-related conferences such as ACADIA, ASCAAD, CAADRIA, eCAADe, SiGraDi and CAAD futures.

All recorded entries include not only abstracts, but ideally also full texts (PDF), which are available for some 10,300 papers.

After years of successful support, the previous system interface (WODA) became outdated, and ongoing developments, such as Google Scholar, Scopus etc., offered novel opportunities. On top of this, the CAAD associations decided to abandon the previous approach of limited Open Access and are moving towards 100% Open Access (leading to enhanced visibility).

In 2015, the whole system environment was redesigned and relaunched (http://papers.cumincad.org). Again, the University of Ljubljana, represented by Tomo Cerovsek and his team, was the main IT partner. One of the improvements involved a substantial adaptation of the (WODA-) database management environment used for input and output (data entry and automatic index file preparation). Metadata (standard metadata suitable for indexing) were created and can now be indexed with Google Scholar.

Bartlett School of Architecture, B-Pro Program

ACADIA 2017 Academic Program Award of Excellence

Founded in 2011, the B-Pro – or Bartlett Prospective – is a family of three advanced postgraduate courses at the Bartlett School of Architecture, which share a unique approach to the future of design, architecture and the urban environment: MArch Architectural Design, MArch Urban Design and MSc/MRes Architectural Computation. B-Pro was founded by Professor Frédéric Migayrou, Chair of the Bartlett School of Architecture, who heads the programme together with deputy director Andrew Porter. Whilst Architectural Design students undertake advanced experimental research in computational design and fabrication, Urban Design students explore critical approaches towards urban design, defining creative strategies for global cities and communities. With more than 220 students, B-Pro is one of the largest post-graduate courses with an interest in experimental research. This year these programmes are joined by the established MSc/MRes Architectural Computation (AC, previously Adaptive Architecture and Computing), which engages with and advances the main technologies by which tomorrow's architecture will be designed and constructed.

The 12-month B-Pro courses welcome a diverse international student cohort, offering highly structured access to the realisation and application of research, and to the production of new schemes of conception and construction in architecture and urbanism. Throughout the year, B-Pro develops numerous seminars, workshops, lectures and public events, such as Plexus, to underpin these ideas and promote collaboration, discussion and inspiration.

Throughout the year, B-Pro tutors and students develop numerous seminars, workshops, lectures and public events to encourage collaboration and the discussion of ideas which further our understanding of the future of design, the urban environment and architecture.

B-Pro is structured in a series of so called Research Clusters, teaching units directed by two to three tutors, that develop their own briefs. They each define their own particular interpretation of the programme and its pedagogical approach. Each Research Cluster is also associated with a report tutor, who helps students develop a critical, theoretical and historical understanding of their design and research. Typically, projects in the B-Pro M.Arch AD and UD courses are developed over one year of collaborative research with groups of three to four students. Since 2011, Research Clusters have been led by a cross-section of experimental practitioners and researchers such as Alisa Andrasek, Daniel Widrig, Jose Sanchez, Guan Lee, Andy Lomas, Ruairi Glynn, Claudia Pasquero, Ulrika Karlsson, Kostas Grigoriadis, Enriqueta Llabres, Soomeen Hahm, Igor Pantic, Roberto Bottazzi, Daniel Koehler, Manuel Jimenez, Gilles Retsin, Daghan Cam, Stefan Bassing among others. The AD and UD programmes don't define an overarching brief, but allow the different clusters to experiment and define their research interests and directions. The latest technologies – robotics and AI, CNC fabrication, 3D printing, supercomputing, simulation, generative design, interactivity, advanced algorithms, extensive material prototyping, biotechnologies, and links to material science – and their many applications, are researched in great depth.

1   CURVOXELS: Tutors: Gilles Retsin, Manuel Jimenez Garcia, Vicente Soler Students: Hyunchul Kwon, Amreen Khaleel, Xiaolin Li

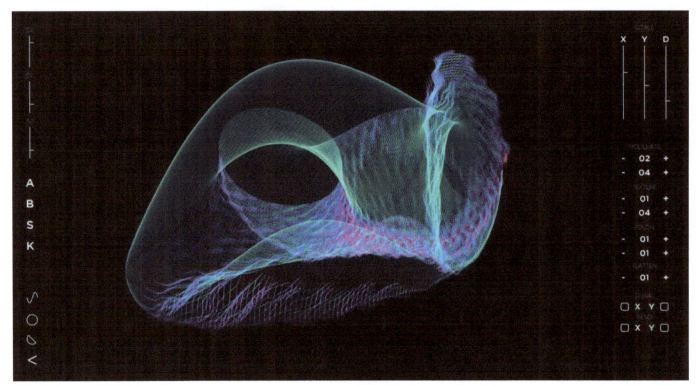

2   Project by student Fabio Galicia

A diverse array of projects carried out by students on the newly
relaunched Architectural Computation programme, challenge
the boundaries of what architectural computation can achieve.
Projects explored artificial intelligence; prototyped objects for
dynamic building components and wearable devices to assist
learning; and developed new interfaces between the real and
the virtual. The work of this group demonstrates the possibility
of becoming truly fluent in computational language, opening new
domains for research.

As we look to the future, B-Pro programmes will be further
enhanced by collaboration with the recently-launched MRes
in Architecture and Digital Theory, directed by Professor Mario
Carpo and Frédéric Migayrou, dedicated to the theory, history
and criticism of digital design and digital fabrication. Students
will also benefit from access to new opportunities for computational research and fabrication offered by a vast new studio
and workshop space in Hackney Wick, Here East B-Pro, entirely
devoted to creative design, will become even more of a nexus
of stimulating exchanges between history and theory, design
and technology. Through a shared vision of creative architecture,
B-Pro is an opportunity for students both to participate in a new
community and to affirm the singularity of their individual talents.
These programmes are not only an open door to advanced architectural practice but also form the base from which each student
can define their particular approach and architectural philosophy,
in order to seek a position in the professional world.

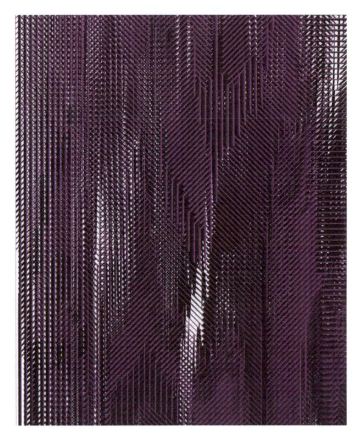

3   ABUNDANCE

Tutors: Alisa Andrasek, Daghan Cam, Soomeen Hahm, Andy Lomas

Students : Eleni Chalkiadaki, Jingwen He, Mikaela Psarra

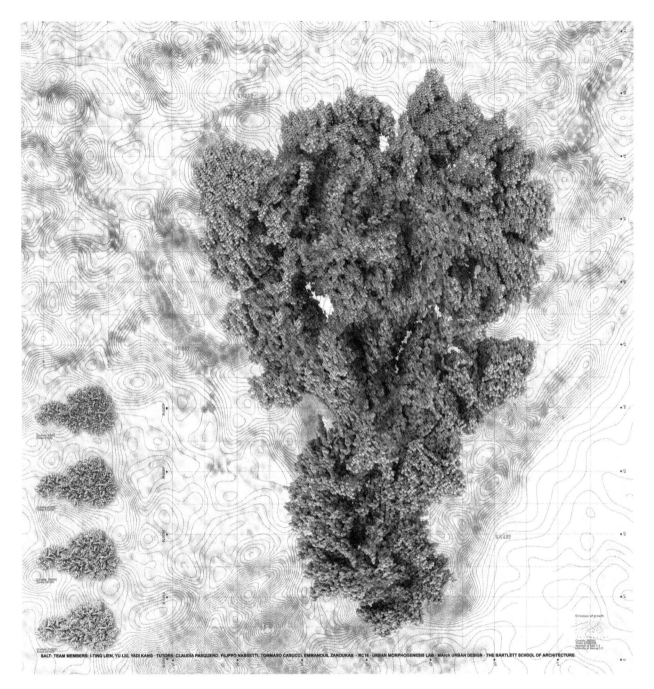

4   SALT

Tutors: Claudia Pasquero, Filippo Nasssetti, Tommaso Casucci, Emmanouil Zaroukas

Students: I-Ting Lien, Yu Liu, Yadi Kang

Heather Roberge

ACADIA 2017 Teaching Award of Excellence

Inventing Problems – Architectural Inquiry between Tradition and Technology

Frequently overheard and on display in academic corridors is the proclamation "the digital turn is over" and the cheerful siren call of Post Modernism. After over a decade of exuberant technophilia, a new generation of academics is arguing for a return to history as a reaction to architectural pedagogy's long, and some would claim undertheorized, embrace of technology. Criticism of the digital turn is directed at two broadsided targets, the parametricist and the digital fabricator. Recent chronicles of disciplinary concerns like *Log 31: The New Ancients* or the Make New History theme at the Chicago Architecture Biennale argue for a return to architecture's disciplinary tradition. *Log 31* argues that architectural knowledge is most convincingly produced by the erudite scholar rather than the technician. History is posited as an antidote to technology. In short, the swing of the discursive pendulum appears to once again place tradition in opposition to technology. As a challenge to this position, I'd like to cast doubt on the validity of the polarity in the first place, opening the space for a position that incorporates the instrumentality of both at once. Rather than embrace tradition or technology, my research and teaching argues for the importance of "a problem" as a nexus of inquiry around which analysis, technique and insight from both tradition and technology are gathered.

"The problem" connotes a disciplinary issue that has been thoroughly articulated by historians and academics and thus has an established place in disciplinary tradition. In contrast, "a problem" assumes that disciplinary knowledge is ever expanding and thus makes possible the incorporation into the discipline of problems that have not yet been recognized as such, problems about which we may currently know little. Architectural knowledge follows the articulation of many such problems. After all, "the" problem was first simply a problem. Problems are pervasive, often originating outside of the discipline and typically from forces wildly outside a designer's control. A problem of geometrical description might be resolved mathematically before it is resolved through a drawing invention or a new digital tool. Only after work on "a problem" can the scholar write this discovery as architectural knowledge. Often a problem migrates from outside to inside the discipline, and for this reason architectural inquiry is often productively caught between technology and tradition.

It is the invention of a problem that produces acts of architecture, occasions for disciplinary expansion, and new assertions on their way to becoming new traditions. Problems are at once put in relation to tradition and are of the present. In the space between tradition and technology, intelligent and comprehensive acts of architecture renew, swerve, and produce disciplinary debate.

This presentation will elaborate on three problems explored in the context of graduate teaching at UCLA Architecture and Urban Design that embrace the productive interdependence of tradition and technology. The first research studio, Genealogies of the Column, constructs eight genealogies of the column with acts of writing, curation, and design, culminating in speculative design proposals for a new Arts Library at UCLA. The work seeks to understand the various manners in which the articulation of the column contributes to disciplinary notions of space. The column is

1   Augmented Perception: Reinvigorating Field of View – Askos Problem, 2016

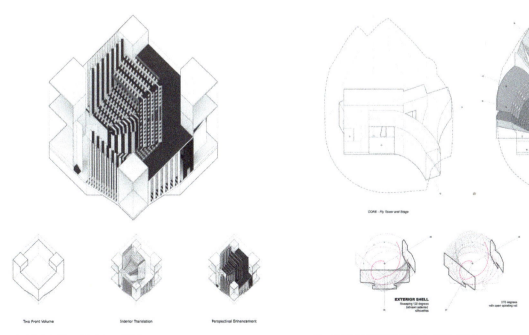

Two Front Volume   Interior Translation   Perspectival Enhancement

CORE - Fly Tower and Stage   PERIPHERY - Seating

EXTERIOR SHELL   30 degrees

2   Augmented Perception: J. Salunga, 2016   3   Augmented Perception: L. Choi, 2016

4 Exercises in Plasticity: F. Mui, K. Moore, and A. Rickett, 2014

deeply connected to spatial, tectonic, and material orders, and as such embodies theoretical positions regarding these orders. From excessively massive to improbably slender, distributions of material as columns articulate theories of space.

The second research studio, Augmented Perception, speculates on architecture's possible responses to existing and emerging scopic regimes. Visual perception is rapidly transforming as a consequence of changes in field of view, which is the extent of the observable world that is seen at a given moment. Shaped by emerging lenses, the contemporary scopic regime is at once panoramic and immersive while also fragmented and magnified. Today the camera-outfitted drone, the GoPro camera, Google Cardboard, and Oculus Rift expand the limits of human perception. These technologies, when considered together, effectively expand the possibilities of perception by redefining, multiplying, and combining fields of view. How might these new vantage points transform how we conceive of architectural constructs?

The third course, a technology seminar titled Exercises in Plasticity, challenges the identical repetition associated with cast objects, developing ingenious molds that propose non-uniform seriality as an objective of casting. Despite the promise of rapid prototyping technologies, casting continues to produce three-dimensional copies more quickly, economically, and durably than rapid prototyping. Beyond the known advantages of serial production—the interchangeability of standardized parts and the durability of continuous surfaces—casting, and its required tooling, have received little academic attention despite their central roles in the production of seriality.

Each of these courses invents a problem, mines its history and contemporary conditions, and directs its possible architectural futures. The histories studied in each reveal insights into the relationships of technology, material, and culture, informing speculations that learn from and contribute to design research.

Heather Roberge

5   H. Roberge: En Pointe, SCI-Arc Gallery, 2015

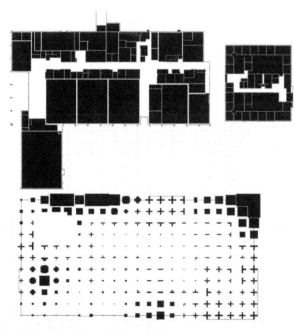

6   Genealogies of the Column: E. Price, 2015

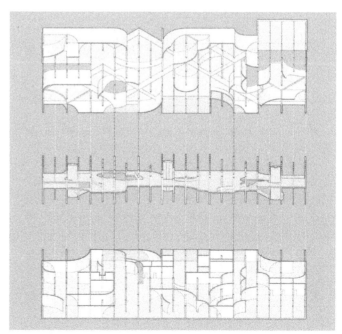

7   Genealogies of the Column: K. Moore, 2015

Wes McGee

ACADIA 2017 Innovative Research Award of Excellence

BIO

Wes McGee is an Assistant Professor in Architecture, Director of the FABLab at the University of Michigan Taubman College of Architecture and Urban Planning, and a Principal at Matter Design. He received a Bachelor of Science in Mechanical Engineering and a Masters in Industrial Design from the Georgia Institute of Technology. His work revolves around the interrogation of the means and methods of material production through research focused on developing new connections between design, engineering, materials, and manufacturing processes as they relate to the built environment. With the goal of seamlessly integrating critical feedback between fabrication constraints and design intent, the work spans multiple realms, including algorithmic design, computational modeling of material behaviors, industrial control technologies, and the development of novel production processes that utilize industrial robots as bespoken machines of architectural production.

Wes founded the studio Matter Design in 2008 with Brandon Clifford; today, their work spans a broad range of scales and materials, always dedicated to reimagining the role of the designer in the digital era. In 2013 Matter Design was awarded the Architectural League Prize for Young Architects & Designers, as well as the Design Biennial Boston Award. In 2012 his work was featured in the Venice Architecture Biennale (in collaboration with Supermanoeuvre), and in 2017 Matter Design participated in the Seoul Architecture Biennale.

Design, Technology, and Collaboration

"The future is already here — it's just not very evenly distributed." -William Gibson

While this quote may approach the cliché, it aptly describes the disparity between the means and methods of production employed in the building construction sector and those employed in other "high-tech" industries like aerospace. Today there is an increasingly widespread investment of design thinking into the possibilities created by direct access to advanced processes of production, and a reinvention of the technologies that we employ to design and fabricate the built environment. The adaptation of advanced manufacturing technologies to the service of the building construction sector has not been a simple task. With the expanding availability of robotic fabrication and algorithmic design techniques, I (along with many others) have undertaken the development of customized fabrication processes and design tools for the production of complex building components and construction systems. The underlying premise of this work has been that as advanced manufacturing technologies become increasingly integrated into the building construction process, it becomes critically important for designers and architects to engage and interact with the complete process spanning from design through construction, creating new workflows that enable closed-loop feedback amongst the various performative aspects of the system.

Fundamental change cannot occur in a vacuum. The complex relationship among design, technology, craft, and production is a critical aspect of architectural discourse today. The adoption of digital design and fabrication techniques by architecture has led to increased specialization in the

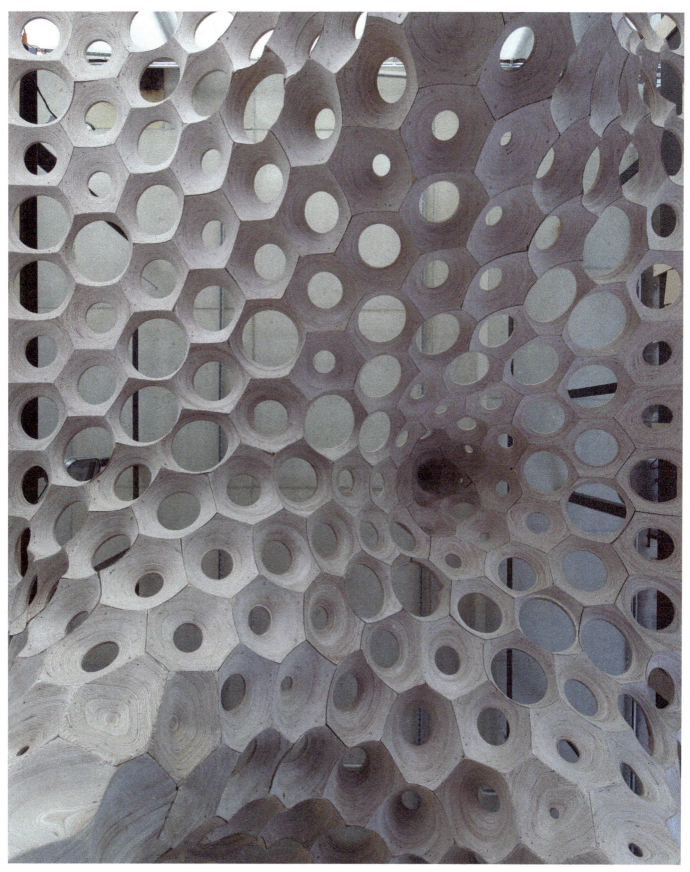

1   "La Voute de Lefevre," *Matter Design* (image credit Brandon Clifford, 2012)

2 "Periscope," *Matter Design* (image credit Brandon Clifford, 2010)

3 "Cannabilistic Architecture," *Matter Design* (image credit Brandon Clifford, 2017)

discipline, and this comes with a price. Architects and designers are not inherently suited to inventing entirely new modes of production, and thus have been forced to collaborate with an increasingly broad cohort of specialists, from manufacturing engineers to materials scientists to computational design experts. This investment in collaboration has the potential to payoff greatly, as it places architecture at the crossroads of design and technology.

This dedication to collaboration was an underlying motivation for founding Matter Design with Brandon Clifford in 2008. Our shared interests in design and making contrasted with our diverse training, spanning from engineering to architecture. The success of the studio has motivated us to continually expand this approach by involving a growing network of collaborative researchers across multiple disciplines. These collaborations have helped to shape the direction of my research, and reinforced the goal of developing software and hardware tools that enable designers to engage efficiently with advanced fabrication technologies. This research has gradually expanded to include

not only the development of new tools and techniques, but also to develop and implement reusable frameworks that are transportable across different processes, including both hardware control systems and software interfaces that seamlessly connect to "designer friendly" software packages. These frameworks have been applied in a diverse range of projects, from kinetic, deformable surfaces to adaptive and responsive fabrication techniques. The hypothesis proposed by this work is that the integration of user-driven software and hardware tools within a closed loop computational environment will allow critical design feedback to be analyzed, while simultaneously enabling performance optimization to occur continuously throughout the design and manufacturing process, and expanding the range of possibilities that these technologies produce.

On behalf of all my collaborators, I thank the ACADIA board for selecting me to receive the Innovative Research Award of Excellence. None of this research would have been possible without the support of my family, friends, colleagues, students, and administrators.

Wes McGee

4   "Microtherme," *Matter Design* (image credit Brandon Clifford, 2015)

5   "Round Room," *Matter Design* (image credit Brandon Clifford, 2014)

6   "Robotic Waterjet cut carrera marble," (image credit Wes McGee, 2008)

DISCIPLINES + DISRUPTION

EXHIBITION PROJECTS

The Missing Financial Architecture of Urban Development

Gabriella Carolini
Department of Urban Studies and Planning, Massachusetts Institute of Technology

Exploring the Critical Geography of Urban Property Tax Potential in African Cities

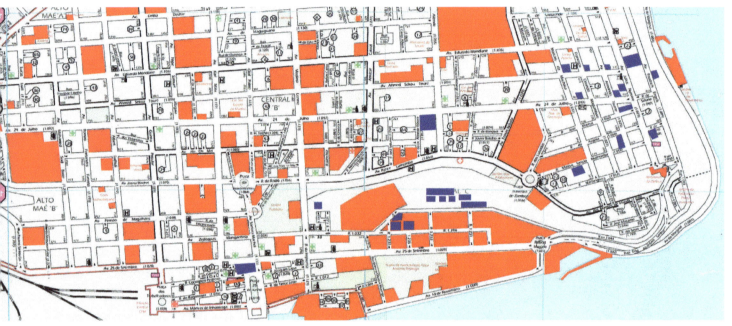

1   Map of Maputo, Mozambique: close up of map on right, highlighting in blue, tax-exempt residential luxury condos built since 2012.

This research project seeks to contribute to the knowledge frontier on understanding both the explicit and implicit role that property tax revenue systems play in shaping the financial architecture of key urban infrastructures in booming African cities. The central premise of this work is that the financial and related managerial architecture behind urban infrastructure projects, such as those in the water and sanitation sectors, matters for equitable urban development and healthy urban communities. Relatedly, the distributive potential of infrastructure development tied to Africa's urban real estate boom depends on the strength of governments to socialize project benefits. Worldwide, the municipal property tax is widely recognized as a critical mechanism that holds the potential to effectively address this distributive challenge. Here we marry an explicit study of property tax potential and viable models of valuation and collection in African cities with an investigation of the implicit role that property tax systems play in determining how key infrastructure projects in cities are financed, and ultimately how this financing shapes who benefits from such projects. The central research question is: how can the revenue potential of the current urban real estate boom in African cities like Addis Ababa be better leveraged to finance key urban infrastructure that services the wide urban population – including the urban poor?

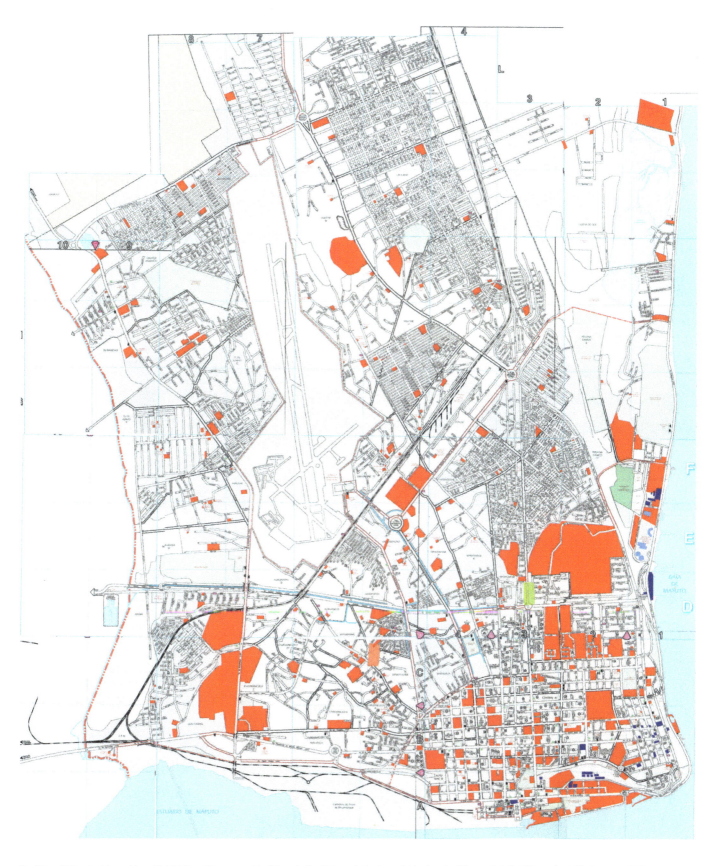

2   Map of Maputo, Mozambique highlighting all tax-exempt buildings in the high market-value neighborhoods of the capital city. We used satellite imagery of Maputo between 2012 and ground-truthing surveys of buildings to produce these images.

Blue Marble Circus

Rania Ghosn
DESIGN EARTH

El Hadi Jazairy
DESIGN EARTH

1   Blue Marble Circus, 2017

Blue Marble Circus is a monument to industrial humanity's plastic footprint, which—despite its planetary scale—remains outside our geographical imagination. The installation takes aim at the dissonance between our individual worries and the Earth's vast environmental transformations. The installation is a 1:10 miniature of the Pantheon, celebrated for its "architecture of the cosmos." The plywood structure peels off to make visible a 10 ft diameter sphere that fits under the dome. The white foam sphere is made of 32 polygon panels (12 pentagons and 20 hexagons), which were machined on a 5-axis CNC router for a curved profile on the outside and a polygonal cut inside. The geodesic sphere revisits the image of the "Blue Marble," the iconic symbol of the environmental movement. The materiality addresses the industrial applications of fossil fuels, such as the extruded polystyrene foam for thermal insulation. The plastic expression invites an alternative imagination now that greenhouse gases and greenhouse agriculture are at the forefront of planetary issues. The globe is also a camera obscura, an optical device that projects site-specific views of the surroundings into the chamber. Such a miniature of the world is hence an architectural invitation to re-learn, like Atlas, how to carry the world—and all there is above it—on our shoulders.

Sponsors: MIT School of Architecture and Planning Dean's Office; MIT Center for Art, Science & Technology Fay Chandler Faculty Creativity Seed Fund

PRODUCTION NOTES

Architect: Rania Ghosn, El Hadi Jazairy

Location: Design Biennial Boston

Date: 2017

Conceptual Design: Aaron Weller, Larisa Ovalles

Fabrication: Justin Lavallee, Christopher Dewart, Cristina Clow, Lex Agnew, Rawan Al-Saffar, Ching Ying Ngan, Marc Smith, Sabrina Madera, Michael Epstein, Paul Short, Jongbang Park, Xin Wen

Structural Engineer: Paul Kassabian, Simpson Gumpertz & Heger

Optics Consultant: Lee Zamir, Tom Gearty -

Autodesk BUILD Space: Athena Moore, Taylor Tobin, Adam Allard -

MIT Facilities and Support: Jim Harrington, Jennifer O'Brien, Seth Avecilla, Maria Moran

2   Blue Marble Circus, 2017

3   Blue Marble Circus, 2017

4   Blue Marble Circus, 2017

RolyPolygon: Confessional

Mariana Ibañez
Ibañez Kim

Simon Kim
Ibañez Kim

1   Carbon fibre, 2016

The Confessional is a single-person environment created by a frame and tensile fabric with a customized interactive system woven into its surface. The base frame, RolyPolygon, is a low-count polygon—a sphenoid hendecahedron—whose fabricated form and position are not prescribed but invented as it is being constructed. The underlying geometry is a unique polygon that allows for packing, allowing this pod to aggregate with others in a new, informal community.

Wound about a sacrificial frame, the carbon fibre (CFRP) shell is layered not only to produce efficacy in lightweight monocoque structures, but also for identity, pattern interference, and visual effects.

Stretched across the monocoque shell of the RolyPolygon, the Confessional is a soft cocoon that can be customized—in this case by a Robert Motherwell graphic. Stitched into its surface is a matrix of LED lights, flex sensors, and speakers controlled by a microprocessor.

For this prototype, the occupant may choose different interactive behaviors: to whisper their secrets and desires in anonymity, as often seen in the films of Wong Kar Wai, or to communicate with others. As they speak and gesture, the pods fill with light and their voices may broadcast wirelessly to other RolyPolygons, creating a community among clustered cocoons near or far away.

PRODUCTION NOTES

Architect: Mariana Ibañez, Simon Kim,
    A collaboration with Andrew John
    Wit, Assistant Professor, Temple
    University

Location: Tayler School of Art,
    Philadelphia

Date: 2016

Project Team: Aidan Kim, Joseph
    Giampietro, Dan Lau, Lyly Huyen,
    Han Kwon

Support: TCR Composites, Tyler
    School of Art

2   RolyPolygon Confessional, 2016

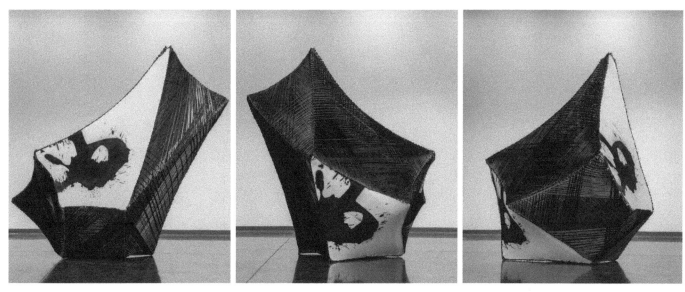

3   RolyPolygon Confessional, 2016

Renaissance Spaces of Money

Lauren A. Jacobi
Massachusetts Institute of
Technology

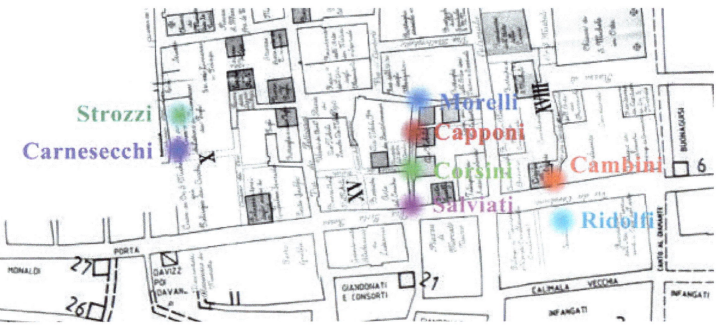

1   Schematic location of local banks, assembled from Guido Carocci's texts on Florentine history. Base maps: Guido Carocci, "Plan of Florence 1427," and Loris Macci and Valeria Orgera, *Architettura e civiltà delle torri: torri e famiglie nella Firenze medievale* (1994), p. 14.

These computer-aided designs are key to arguments I make in my book, *The Architecture of Banking in Early Modern Italy: Constructing the Spaces of Money* (forthcoming, Cambridge University Press). My broad ambition with the book is to give the spatial history of late medieval and Renaissance Italian banking and mercantile exchange a central role within urban and architectural studies and in other fields. Economic historians have long argued that over the course of the twelfth to the thirteenth centuries, European society confronted rapid re-monetization, which had an impact that extended well beyond that discrete temporal period. Exploring the wake of re-monetization, this book focuses attention on the location, places, and types of spaces that were used for banking in Florence and beyond. It also examines how buildings where banking activities took place were conceived and how they shaped the era's episteme. This project yields new insights into the early history of capitalistic practices, although medieval and Renaissance thinkers would have found that term unfamiliar.

The first illustration is a significant part of the book's first chapter. Contributing to a reassessment of the dialectical opposition between pre-modernity and modernity, the first chapter, "Networked Agglomerations," examines the spatio-structural reality of networks of banks in Florence and Rome in the fifteenth and sixteenth centuries as a means of challenging a conventional framing of the development of capitalism. By analyzing where and why international and local Italian Renaissance banks were situated topographically, the first chapter insists that agglomerations of banks, as well

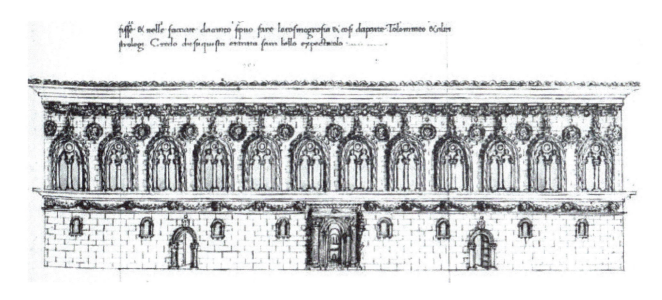

2   Filarete, Treatise on Architecture (Magliabecchiana Manuscript), book XXV, folio 192r, showing drawing of the façade of the Banco Mediceo in Milan, ca. 1462–64, Biblioteca nazionale centrale di Firenze.

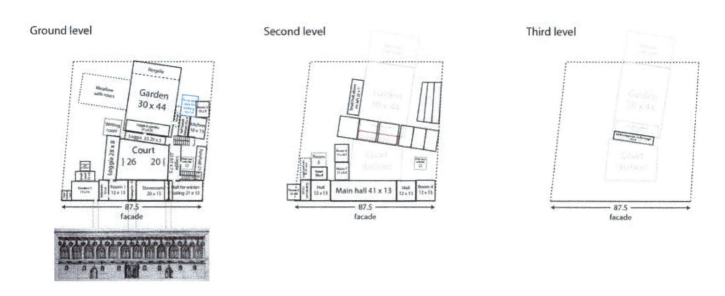

3   Schematic reconstruction of the Medici bank in Milan based on Filarete's description.

as how the body of the banker was managed within that setting, were ideological mechanisms actively used to counter the impingement of moral prohibitions on the generation of profit (Figure 1). In examining how the built form of the early modern city altered diachronically, I track how money was increasingly thought of in abstract terms. The illustration and the chapter demonstrates that as pre-industrial Italy became monetized, a mercantile building became critical to the reputation of banks and trade firms, local and international alike, arguably because of the contingency of money itself.

The final two images are key to the book's third chapter, "Across Economic Geographies: Banking and Trade Sites outside of Florence," which is the first comparative study of the location and architectural language of buildings used for banking and mercantile exchange outside of the Italian peninsula by Florentines in their extraterritorial nations. Computer-aided drawing enabled me to understand the layout of the Medici bank in Milan (Figures 2 and 3), which has contributed to a reassessment of the banks' design and program.

Grove

Joel Lamere
GLD, Massachusetts Institute of Technology

Cynthia Gunadi
GLD

1   Grove © Jane Messinger, 2015.

Grove is a temporary installation on the Rose Fitzgerald Kennedy Greenway, designed and built as part of the Design Biennial Boston 2015. Translucent balloon-like forms sit atop a white steel structure and seem to glow against a backdrop of the Greenway's horticultural parcel between Congress and Pearl Streets. From the outside the installation evokes a dense clustering of trees, formally reconceived. Inside, seen through nine viewing holes, the hollow form reveals an unexpected, airy interior of interconnected chambers.

Although the exterior resists legibility, Grove visitors discover and engage with viewing holes calibrated to various heights. Heads, but not bodies, enter the communal interior; visitors experience the dislocation of being in two spaces—acoustically, visually, atmospherically—at once. The booleaned intersections between pods create a surprising, cathedral-like enclosure. One might catch glimpses of (or overhear) others in this strangely intimate public space. Visitors become part of the installation itself, a spectacle for viewers who are farther away.

Grove imagines an alternate future for architectural production, eschewing wasteful massiveness for radical thinness. The installation instantiates this thinness by building off ongoing research into what we are calling cured-surface inflatables. Specifically, this body of work explores the use of inflatable molds for composite fabrication, where we are developing new construction methods, studying resultant spatial effects, and speculating on implicit architectural potentials.

PRODUCTION NOTES

Design: Joel Lamere + Cynthia Gunadi

Project Team: Sophia Chesrow, Grigori Enikolopov, Zain Karsan, Dohyun Lee, Elizabeth Galvez

Thanks: Caitlin Mueller, Steven O. Anderson, John Skibo, Matt Wagers, Chris Dewart, Christopher Gunadi

Dimensions: 14.5'(w) x 13'(d) x 13.5'(h)

Materials: Resin-infused fiberglass, steel

Location: Boston, MA

Date: 2015

2   Grove © Jane Messinger, 2015

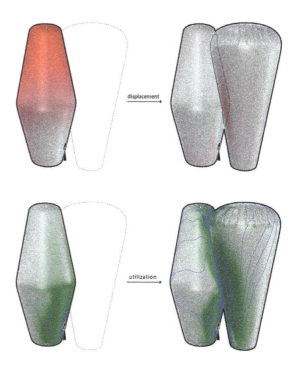

3   Grove diagram

Hybridizing the disparate fields of inflatables and composites capitalizes on their relative advantages. Inflatable structures are highly scalable, easily tailored to unique conditions, inexpensive to produce, and simple to erect. Composites, meanwhile, represent the forefront of material technology, offering longevity, high performance, and unparalleled structural capacity. By curing composite surfaces around sewn inflatable molds, our construction process marries the two, with strong formal implications. The geometries produced through inflation are compound-curvature volumes, ideal as surface-active shell structures, whose interior spaces are fashioned by sartorial techniques and material forces rather than conventional design figuration. The outcome is architectural form embedded with structural logic, not merely rationalized with structural elements.

Grove exhibits architectural possibilities inherent to this method. The installation presents an alien materiality and geometry; it retains the puffed quality of its inflated molds, but as stable form. The texture and patterning of the fiberglass bears traces of the fabrication process, akin to board-formed concrete, but is here transformed by thinness and translucency.

The design and making of Grove leverages cutting-edge computational tools and digital fabrication techniques. Its twelve individual pods were fabricated separately, then aggregated to form the whole. We developed processes within advanced computational design environments, allowing us to simulate the inflation of each pod, analyze its structural behavior, and calculate its intersections with neighbors. Vinyl sheet was cut with a CNC drag knife then sewn and inflated, with resin-infused fiberglass strips laid across the resultant balloon-like molds. After curing for twelve hours, each pod was cut along pre-inscribed intersection lines transferred from the mold, allowing for the extraction of the vinyl. Pods were fused together along those openings with an additional strip of fiberglass, producing an aggregate structure substantially more rigid than individual pods. The resultant form is only 2 mm thick, weighing less than 360 pounds total, yet incredibly strong.

This radical thinness challenges traditional notions of architectural enclosure, consolidating cladding and structure into a single surface that mediates between interior and exterior. Cured-surface inflatables use minimal means towards maximal ends, suggesting—especially as architecture continues to move towards more high-performance or "smart" materials—structural, environmental and atmospheric opportunities along its surface. This research envisions a lightweight future for architecture: rapid yet lasting, thin yet strong, expedient yet enduring.

AR Mail from Harbin

Takehiko Nagakura
Massachusetts Institute of
Technology

Woongki Sung
Massachusetts Institute of
Technology

1   A user lays out plans on postcards, and the photogrammetric 3D models augment them in the tablet.

1. INTRODUCTION

AR Mail from Harbin is a mobile application that enriches spatial experience and social interactions for visitors at cultural heritage sites. It combines augmented reality (AR) technology, captured photogrammetric 3D models, and traditional paper media.

The paper media used with AR Mail from Harbin is a set of architectural drawings printed on postcards. The AR system shows the captured 3D portion of Harbin's main church over the corresponding plan printed on a postcard, along with animated human figures on the ground. A combination of four postcards completes the plan layout of the church. Additionally, a postcard printed with an image of the dome is augmented with the roof model of the church, and another card printed with scissors can be used to cut a section of the 3D model from any desired angle (Figure 2).

2. USE SCENARIO

A scenario of the use case is as follows. A visitor to the city of Harbin goes to the St. Sophia Cathedral, a magnificent Russian Orthodox church built in 1907 that has since been converted to an architectural museum. After touring the site and the interior of the building, the visitor picks up a set of postcards. At the hotel, he downloads the associated AR application and uses his smartphone to see part of the church emerging as a 3D model on the corresponding plan printed on a postcard.

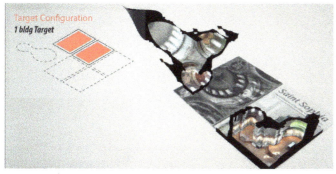

2   A user can freely arrange postcards and explore various types of digital content.

By combining the postcards of different parts of the church plan, he can study its design in a way not possible on the site. For instance, he can make a section model of the church, get a close-up of the roof details, and overlook the building placed in the central square of the city. He then can write some messages on the postcards and mail them to his family back in his home country. His family members read his messages, use their smart-phones to view the building in 3D on the postcards, and retrace his experience visiting the cathedral.

3. DEVELOPMENT AND EVALUATION

The 3D content of this application was prepared through a photogrammetric capturing expedition on the site one day during the summer of 2017. The AR tool was created using the Unity 3D platform and Vuforia AR library.

This application provides means for:

- Extending the experience of the visit through photogrammetric 3D models captured on the site;

-Conveying the experience to a person in a remote location by communicating through the conventional process of mailing postcards; and

-Bringing a sense of playfulness to a visit to an historical site.

This low-cost visualization method can be deployed for tourism centers and other locations of historic importance. The application can also be tailored to each site by adding annotations, playful graphics (such as digital figures), and audio recordings that provide additional information about the site.

4. ACKNOWLEDGEMENTS

This project was made possible in collaboration with Harbin Institute of Technology and Harbin St. Sophia Cathedral Museum. Thanks to Prof. Hongyuan Mei, Prof. Cheng Sun, Chief Curator Xingguo Su, Prof. Yu Shao, Prof. Kai Xing, Prof. Shouheng Chen, Dr. Yunsong Han, Dan Li, Xu Zhang, and all the students in HIT who participated in this project on site. A part of the development of the project and its travel cost has been supported by MIT-SUTD International Design Center Research Funding Program.

This project was presented at the VR Village of SIGGRAPH 2017 in Los Angeles.

Other Masks

William O'Brien Jr.
WOJR, Massachusetts Institute
of Technology

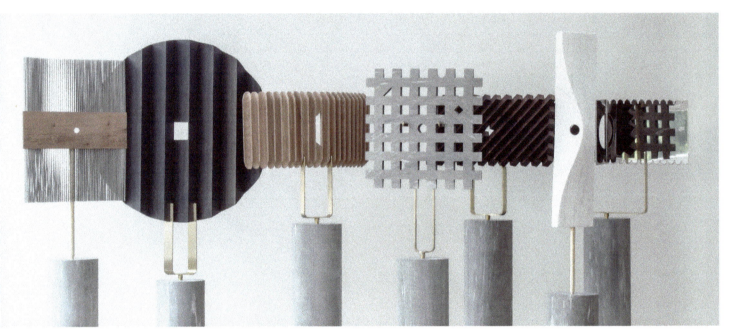

1 Family Masks

The body of work shown in the exhibition stems from an ongoing project which offers a grieving man a hidden space of refuge in the woods. Included in the exhibition is a range of artifacts that explore the periphery of architectural representation; while orthographic drawings and a scale model provide the work with an architectural center of gravity, pieces such as a stone bas-relief and seven sculptural masks engage the overlapping domain of art.

The work situates the artifact of the mask within the context of the discipline of architecture. A close reading of an artifact involves examination of all of its physical characteristics, including its figural, structural, material, and decorative features. This study is done not only with the aim of identifying the cultural significance of the particular object, but also with the broader aspiration of understanding the rituals and values of the users of the object, and those of its makers. The most curious of artifacts are those whose features invoke multiple, competing interpretations of their cultural significance.

For us, the making of architecture is the making of artifacts. To think about the design of a work of architecture as such is to regard the acts of making form and reading form as simultaneous and inseparable. Being attuned to architecture in this particular way has lead to a practice that is invested deeply, if not wholly, in the agency of architectural form as the medium through which cultural commentary is conveyed.

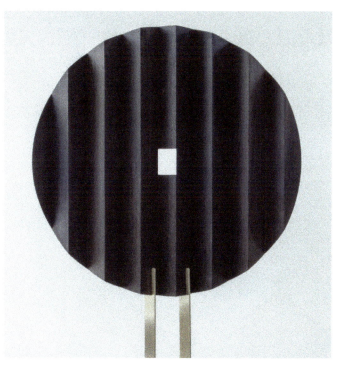

2 Bend Mask: The brass was first waterjet cut, polished and then went through a break and form process. Afterwards the piece was welded and eased to its final form. To create the mirrored finish the mask was polished once more and then electroless nickel plated.

3 Black Sun Mask: Strips of white oak from the same stock were planed, mitered and glued together to create an oversized blank by a master wood worker. The blank was then transferred to a digital process, CNC milling the blank into the circle on a custom fixture. A steel wool vinegar finish with a final coat of wax was applied to create the black stain texture.

4 Brush Mask: A 75 year old white oak column from Chicago was reclaimed. After flip milling using a CNC mill to size on a custom jig, a feature set toolpath strategy was used to drill 1200 holes on both sides with a friction-fit tolerance to fit the music wires. The wires were then inserted by hand.

5 Comb Mask- Plywood blanks were bent through a vacuum bagging process on milled thermoplastic molds. The flutes were then glued together on a custom jig and then mitered on a table saw. The piece was then hand finished, layers of natural paste wax was applied for the finished appearance.

Tectonics of Transparency

Cristina Parreño Alonso
Massachusetts Institute of
Technology, Cristina Parreño
Architecture

1   The Wall (left, © Jane Messinger, 2014; right, © John Horner, 2014).

"Tectonics of Transparency" is a research project that explores the notion of physical and phenomenal transparency in architecture. On the one hand, it looks at new potentials for materials in non-conventional assemblies, and on the other hand investigates light and transparency as triggers for new effects in community engagement and novel forms of cultural and social exchange between users and the environment. The format of the research allows for experimentation with technique and effect, at scales ranging from small-scale prototypes to large architectural installations.

Tectonics of Transparency is currently being developed through a series of interventions in public spaces where the prototypes become spatial, site specific and interactive, adding value to the public space.

"Glow" is a public art project for Hyde Square, an area of the city of Boston with a diverse population, including notable Latino, African American and Afro-Latino communities. The project—the result of a contest held by the City of Boston—aims to reconstruct the rotary at Centre, Perkins, and Day Streets in Jamaica Plain. Glow addresses the concerns of the community by using the relationship between art and architecture to promote the engagement of the local residents with the square, facilitating a recognizable space for congregation and expression while at the same time including a signature image for Hyde Square.

1   "The Wall"

Author: Cristina Parreño
Architecture

Structure: SGH

With the collaboration of: Sixto
Cordero, Haydee Casellas, Dohyun
Lee, Stefan Elsholtz and Nazareth
Ekmekian

Sponsor: HASS and IDC at MIT

"Glow" (not pictured)

Authors: Cristina Parreño + Amin
Tadjsoleiman

Structure: SGH

Client: City of Boston

2　The Tower (Photographs: © Jane Messinger, 2015).

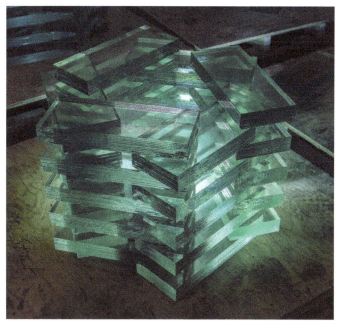

2　"The Tower"
　　Author: Cristina Parreño Architecture
　　Structure: SGH
　　Client: Design Biennial Boston 2015
　　Sponsors: CAST and Turner Construction

A series of four structures built of transparent 30-foot-tall acrylic transparent poles will provide shade and a sense of identity to the square, while serving as an indicator of the level of social activity in the public space. The poles, which hold a set of fiber optics, will also move with the wind and the touch of the user, generating a dynamic illuminated artificial landscape made of transparent reeds.

Each structure will be equipped with a set of sensors that detect the presence around the poles, producing varied levels of intensity in the illumination of the fiber optics inside of the poles.

During the day pedestrians will be able to pass through openings in the poles of "Glow" and experience an optical illusion that results from the translucent coloration of the material, the angle at which light falls on a given place within the structure and the place where a viewer might be standing or sitting.

Under the umbrella of Tectonics of Transparency, we have designed "The Tower" for the Design Biennial Boston 2015, in the Rose Kennedy Greenway and "The Wall" at the International Design Center at MIT. These prototypes explore the relationship between formal design, spatial perception, structural efficiency and systems of fabrication. They also introduce the variant of the glass medium, which contributes by offering a completely new set of parameters and thus requires new means and methods of aggregation, joinery, and stabilization.

The prototypes aim to use high compressive strength as a vehicle to produce new spatial environments that are specific to glass in the hopes of enabling an interpretative mode of participation. The ambiguity of the artifacts raises issues of perception, privacy, transparency, light and opacity and thus facilitates the possibility of multiple readings among users. The project has earned funding support from the International Design Center at MIT, the HASS Award, Turner Construction, and the Center for Arts, Science and Technology at MIT.

Programmable Materials: Active Auxetics

Skylar Tibbits
Self-Assembly Lab,
Massachusetts Institute of
Technology

1   Photographs of a planar rectangular grid made of programmable bilayer struts, depicting gradual shape change due to local auxetic behavior along one of its rows and columns when exposed to ambient heat.

When a material is being stretched, it usually becomes thinner in the axis perpendicular to the direction of the pulling force. However, contrary to common materials, when pulled, auxetic materials expand in all directions, or when compressed they shrink in all directions.

Heat-Active Auxetic Materials, developed at MIT's Self-Assembly Lab, are materials that exhibit auxetic behavior when exposed to heat. Compared to traditional auxetic materials, heat-active auxetic materials demonstrate autonomous performance, environmental response, easy customization, and greater possibilities for the design and fabrication of material properties.

Auxetic materials paint a picture for the future of customizable foams, crash protection, packaging materials, clothing or various other applications that rely on material stretch and compression. Imagine if these materials could be designed to transform autonomously based on temperature, moisture or light with unique stretch or compression properties that are unheard of in today's traditional materials.

PRODUCTION NOTES

Team: Athina Papadopoulou,
Hannah Lienhard, Maggie Hughes,
Schendy Kernizan, Jared Laucks &
Skylar Tibbits

Date: 2017

2 Photographs of a three-dimensional lattice made of programmable bilayer struts, depicting gradual shrinking due to auxetic material behavior when exposed to the ambient heat of an infrared heat lamp.

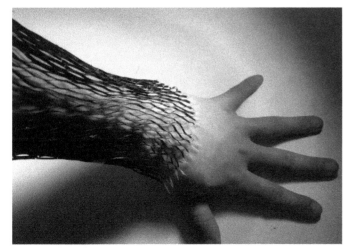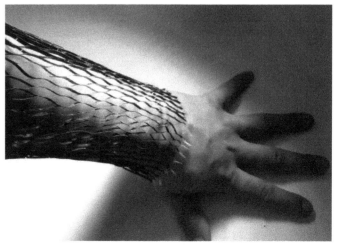

3 Photographs demonstrating a temperature adaptive sleeve made of programmable bilayer struts. The sleeve's apertures open up when exposed to high temperatures to allow for breathability.

Digital Matatus

Sarah Williams
Massachusetts Institute of Technology

Jacqueline Klopp

Peter Waiganjo Wagacha

Dan Orwa

Adam White
Digital Matatus Lead Research Team

1 University of Nairobi Student collecting data on Matatu system using an application developed the Civic Data Design Lab. (Photo Credit: Adam White, 2014)   2 Matatu Sign Painter in Kibera. (Adam White, 2014)

Access to data is essential for generating urban plans for rapidly developing cities in the global south, but it is often challenging to acquire. This is because it either does not exist or is tightly controlled by those in power. However, data does exist—locked away in records of everyday interactions such as cell phones and credit card transactions. My research team, Digital Matatus, set out to test whether it is possible to capture this data by leveraging the ubiquitous nature of mobile technologies in developing countries, to collect data on an essential infrastructure, and open that data up for anyone to use. The results show that developing strategies that allow the public to interact with data through the creation of civic tools and visualizations helps to improve civic life while also helping to generate new planning strategies.

Focusing on Nairobi's semi-formal bus system, or Matatus, as they are commonly known, the project was not only successful in generating data, but also in transforming it into tools that could be acquired by civic actors to develop urban change. Distributed using the open data standard GTFS, the local technology community used the data to develop mobile phone routing applications. Non-governmental organizations (NGOs) used it to develop Bus Rapid Transit Plans (BRT) plans. The downloadable paper transit map allowed Nairobi's residents and the government to visualize, for the first time, the comprehensive system that serves their city, which generated a debate about its future amongst the various stakeholders. The implications of the research go beyond Kenya, as it shows how we can leverage the power of "Big Data" to generate urban change through active data

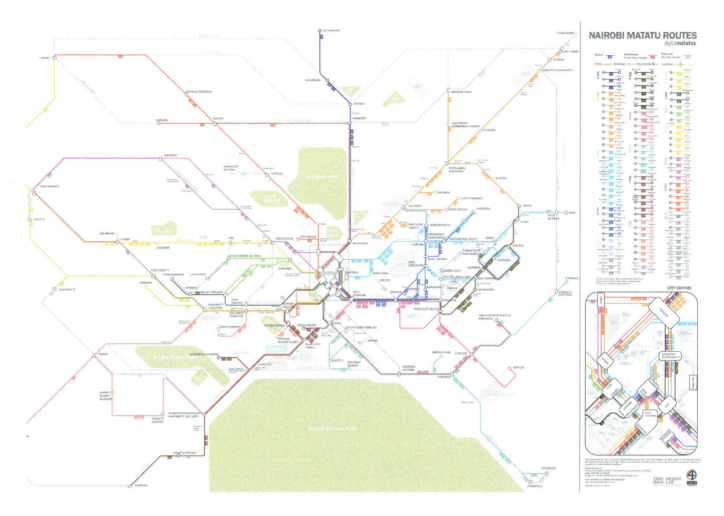

3 Nairobi's Informal Transit System as mapped by the Digital Matatus team. (Source: Digital Matatus)

collection, data sharing, and the development of visualizations and civic tools with that data.

Data visualizations are powerful vehicles for generating debate and evidence for planning strategies. The stylized transit maps developed by the project allowed the government to engage in conversations with the public. Nairobi's Matatu operators, who are currently the de facto planners of the systems, used the map to identify and develop new routes for the system. Most importantly, the citizens of Nairobi now have vital information for navigating their city.

Development and dissemination of data needs to be inclusive and open in order to allow multiple civic actors to trust the data for their research. By engaging the transit community and

opening the data up for anyone to use, the project was able to generate new products and tools for planning, including the development of mobile applications for citizens and the development of new transportation projects in the form of BRT lines.

This unprecedented growth of data has generated excitement about using it to reshape the way we live. However, "Big Data" will not change the world unless it can be acquired and transformed into visualizations and civic tools that can be operationalized by governments, designers, and other civic actors to advocate and develop urban change. The Digital Matatus project provides an example of how we can use big data to develop necessary changes to the urban environment.

DISCIPLINES + DISRUPTION

PEER REVIEWED PROJECTS

Fracture, Parallel States of the Abstract and the Physical

Chandler Ahrens
Washington University in St. Louis

John Carpenter
Oblong Industries & USC Media Arts + Practice

Aaron Sprecher
Technion Institute

1   Projected kinetic image on parallel translucent screens, viewer at mid-distance from the sensor (Chandler Ahrens, 2016, © OSA).

Fracture explores the parallel conditions of the real and mediated through technology. The way we perceive our built environment is intimately associated with the way we use information technologies to visualize torrents of information. The nature of the image in the field of architecture is in transition due to technology's capacity to gather, filter and embed information into the design process. For several years, the image has been transitioning away from a primarily representational mode towards the inclusion of operational procedures. Similar movements have been occurring beyond the periphery of the architectural discipline in the arts and sciences, creating tension in the way images are used. The scientific historian Peter Galison frames the dichotomy about the nature of scientific imagery in terms of attraction and opposition. The intricate relationship between knowledge and information is revealed in images, but these are also deceptive because they bypass the mathematics of pure science (Galison 2002, 301) The intuitive interpretation of images as representation versus the image as evidence of a computation-based process is similarly an issue in architecture.

Architectural theoretician Mark Linder discusses the transition of images in architecture as moving away from representations of something else toward a more literal and non-idealized result of a procedure. The image is literally the process of making visible the end result of an operation (Linder 2010, 37) Therefore, images are the evidence of the process by which they were generated or experienced, similar to Experiments in Art and Technology's 1970 Pepsi pavilion in Osaka. The

PRODUCTION NOTES

Interactive Design: John Carpenter

Architect: Open Source Architecture

Client: Murmuration Festival

Status: Completed

Site Area: 400 sq. ft.

Location: Cortext Innovation District, St. Louis, Missouri

Date: 2016

2 Black tensile fabric generates a dark interior day and night (Chandler Ahrens, 2016, © OSA).

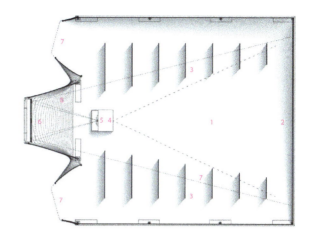

3 Floor plan: central interactive sensor space defined by the openings in the parallel translucent screens (© OSA)

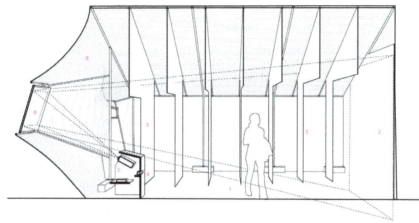

1. Interactive sensor area
2. Opaque projection screen
3. Translucent screens
4. Sensor
5. Projector
6. Mirror (short-throw projection)
7. Entry
8. Fabric skin

4 Section: Short-throw projection mirror allows the image to fill the entire end screen and the edges of the parallel translucent surfaces (© OSA)

pavilion generates its own "images [that] are real instead of being represented" (Rose 1972, 62), where images are not metaphorical or representational, but can be sensed from the pavilion's generation of light, sound, space, and air.

Image and experience are bound together through technology that enables the coexistence of parallel states between abstract and physical environments in the project Fracture. The abstract environment consists of real-time interactive media that senses the visitor's body movement, processes the information, and then responds through a digital projection in the physical space. A kinect sensor scans the environment for movement and translates real-world information into computer code, which is already an abstract system. The distance, direction and speed of a visitor's body provide the variables to affect the movement of a computationally generated form. The form occupies the center of the projection surface and is not homogenous, but rather fractured into a series of triangles. The fracturing creates a reading of a field of triangular elements that are flocking. The input of

the visitor's movement information is processed in real time in order to disrupt the geometric pattern, affecting scale, speed and direction of the triangles. The information of the fractured interpretation of the form is projected within the space, generating an abstract environment that is continuously augmented by the input from the sensor.

The abstract environment exists in parallel with the physical through digitally generated interactive media projected onto a physical fabric surface, creating an atmosphere constantly in flux and blurring the legibility of space versus image. Housed within a black mass that is both familiar and strange, the computationally generated image is multiplied when projected through a series of parallel translucent voile scrims, thickening and spatializing the kinetic image so that it can be simultaneously perceived and occupied. The looseness of the relations of the elements of projected image and physical surface diffuses the distinction between the parts, resulting in the generation of an illusionistic space. The juxtaposition challenges the nature of image and

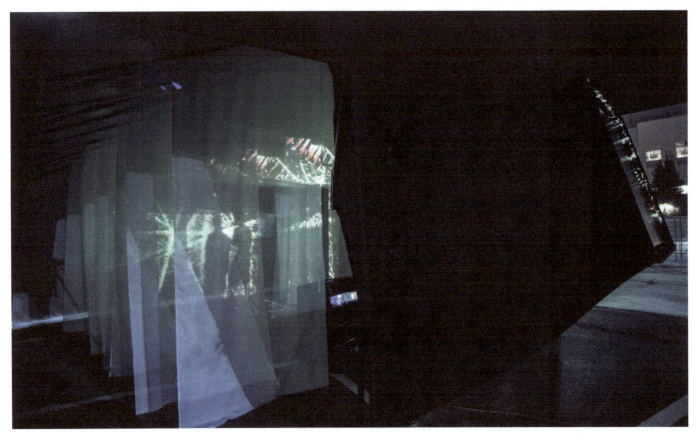

5 Translucent parallel screens, circulation on the side, and sensor/ projector podium in the central axis of the space (Chandler Ahrens, 2016, © OSA).

6 Scale of the form increases the greater the distance the viewer is from the sensor (Chandler Ahrens, 2016, © OSA)

7 Direction of movement affects the dispersion of the flocking of the triangles (Chandler Ahrens, 2016, © OSA)

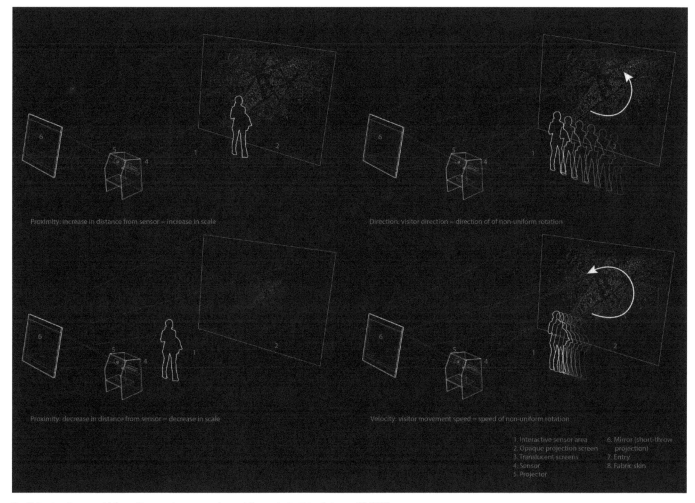

8 Behavior diagram of information sensing, processing and the projected kinetic image (© OSA)

object, generating a physical environment that is responsive and immersive while allowing them both to coexist simultaneously as composite image and object, abstract and real.

ACKNOWLEDGMENTS

The installation was part of the inaugural Murmuration Festival in the Cortex Innovation District, St. Louis in 2016. We would like to thank the organizers, Brian Cohen and Dennis Lower, President and CEO of Cortex, Inc. We would also like to thank the art coordinator Meridith McKinley.

REFERENCES

Galison, Peter. 2002. "Images Scatter Into Data, Data Gathers Into Images." In *Iconoclash*, edited by Bruno Latour and Peter Weibel, 300–323. Cambridge, MA: MIT Press.

Linder, Mark. 2010. "Drawing, Literally." In *Architecture as a Craft: Architecture, Drawings, Model and Position*, edited by Michiel Riedijk, 35–51. Amsterdam: Sun Architecture Publishers.

Rose, Barbara. 1972. "Art as Experience, Process, and Environment." In *Pavilion: Experiments in Art and Technology*, edited by Billy Kluver, Julie Martin, and Barbara Rose, 60–104. New York: E.P. Dutton & Co.

Chandler Ahrens is an Assistant Professor at Washington University in St. Louis as well as a co-founder of Open Source Architecture (OSA), which is an international transdisciplinary collaboration developing research and commissioned projects. His focus is on the intersection of material investigations, environmental phenomena, and computational design processes. His teaching focuses on digital fabrication studios and seminars that produce full-scale prototypes. His work with OSA is part of the collection at the Fonds Regional de Architecture (FRAC) in Orleans, France. He was a co-curator of the Gen(h)ome Project and co-exhibition chair of Evolutive Means, ACADIA 2010.

John Carpenter is a digital artist and designer whose work explores the use of gesture with complex data and spaces. Based in Los Angeles, he's a spatial interaction designer for Oblong Industries, and is a visiting professor at the University of Southern California's School of Cinematic

9   The black object is simultaneously familiar and strange (Chandler Ahrens, 2016, © OSA)

Arts, Media Arts + Practice. John earned his MFA from the department of Design Media Arts at UCLA with his thesis qualitative spaces
in interactive art + design (2009). He has recently exhibited works at
INHORGENTA MUNICH, the LA Arboretum, the Murmuration Festival,
Young Projects, ACME. Los Angeles, and the Academy Awards. http://
johnbcarpenter.com/

Aaron Sprecher is Associate Professor at the Technion Israel Institute of
Technology, Faculty of Architecture and Town Planning. He is co-founder
and partner of Open Source Architecture, a collaborative research group
that brings together international researchers in the fields of design,
engineering, media research, history, and theory. His research and design
work focuses on the synergy between information technologies, computational languages, and digital fabrication systems, examining the way in
which technology informs and generates innovative approaches to design
processes. Aaron Sprecher is co-editor of Architecture in Formation
(2013, London: Routledge), and the forthcoming book Instabilities and
Potentialities, Notes on the Nature of Knowledge in Digital Architecture
(2013, London: Routledge). He is a member of the Editorial Board of the
Journal of Architectural Education (JAE), and a member of the Board of
Directors of the Society for Arts and Technology (SAT, Montreal).

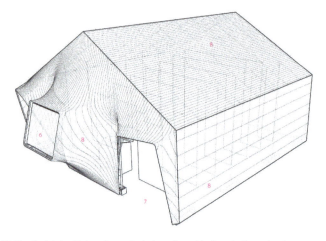

10   Tensile fabric skin topology adapts from the gable form to the entry doorways
and mirror for the projection system (© OSA)

11 Tensile exterior surface compared to the genlty billowing suspended interior translucent voile screens (Chandler Ahrens, 2016, © OSA)

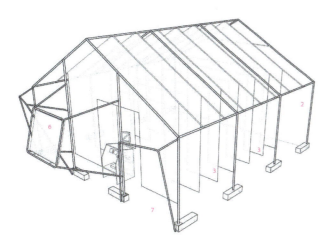

12 Steel tube framing system added to prefab canopy system to support interior parallel translucent surfaces, doorways, and short-throw projection mirror (© OSA)

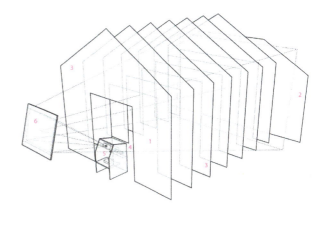

13 Interior parallel translucent surfaces, sensor/projector cabinet, and short-throw projection mirror (© OSA)

Hedracrete: Prefab, Funicular, Spatial Concrete

Masoud Akbarzadeh
Polyhedral Structures Laboratory,
School of Design, University of
Pennsylvania, Philadelphia, US

Mehrad Mahnia

Ramtin Taherian
TheAlliance, Tehran, Iran

Amir Hossein Tabrizi
AT Architects, Tehran, Iran

1 Front view of the built structure (Deed Studio ©).

Hedracrete structure is the result of a workshop on 3D graphic statics at the Contemporary Architecture Association of Iran, with 31 participants in collaboration with various material and fabrication service providers. It is a unique research project aiming to address three important topics in the field of digital design and fabrication. These topics include efficient structural form finding in three dimensions, fabrication of complex spatial systems, and the innovative use of conventional construction materials. Multiple aspects of the project will then be described with respect to these topics in the following paragraphs.

Structural Form Finding
The form of the structure is a funicular polyhedral frame, which is an efficient configuration of members with compression-only and tension-only axial forces (Figure 1). The maximum height of the structure is 3.33 m, spanning from three supports located 5.4 m from each other. The structure consists of 45 prefabricated joints, 54 compression-only and 30 tension-only members sitting on steel supports connected by steel rods. The structural concept has been developed using 3D graphic statics (3DGS), a state-of-the-art geometric structural design method demonstrating the static equilibrium of forces in three dimensions using polyhedral geometry (Akbarzadeh 2016). This method has recently been developed based on a 150-year-old proposition by Rankine (1864), and Hedracrete is the first built prototype designed using this method. Thus the structure is aimed at proving the theories of 3DGS in practice. What makes the form-finding process in 3DGS quite

PRODUCTION NOTES

Leads:	Masoud Akbarzadeh
	Mehrad Mahnia
	Ramtin Taherian
	Amir Hossein Tabrizi
Location:	Tehran, Iran
Material:	Glass Fiber Reinforced Concrete, Steel plates
Date:	2016–2017

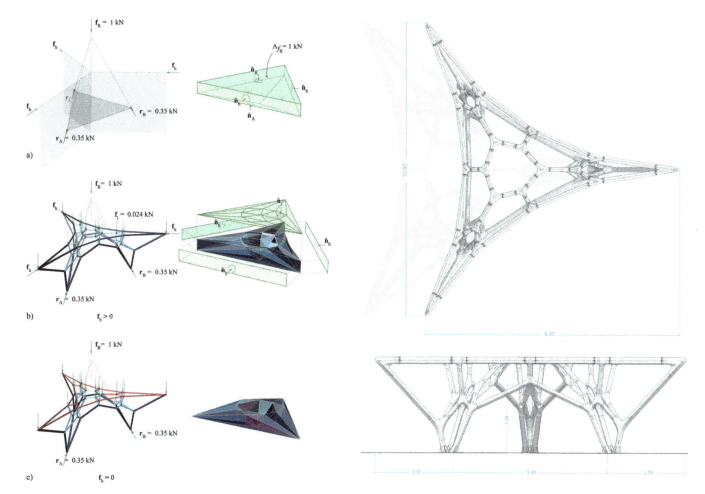

2   Structural form finding using 3DGS methods: (a) setting the support locations and the externally applied loads; (b) subdividing global equilibrium to drive the compression-only form; and (c) removing lateral forces to get a form with both compression and tension members.

3   Plan and elevation of the structure, the units are in meters.

unique and intuitive is that the designer has full control over the form of the structure and its internal and external equilibrium of forces. For instance, in this structure, by changing the magnitude of the horizontal forces f_h to zero in the 3DGS model, a designer can explicitly change the internal forces in the structure from compression-only forces to a system with both compression and tension forces (Figure 2).

Volumetric Design

Once the static equilibrium is achieved and the bar-node structural geometry was developed, it was then translated into a volumetric architectural model (Figure 3). The architectural model consists of discrete elements including spatial nodes connected by linear members. The most challenging task in designing the volume of the structure was to derive the geometry of the nodes where multiple members with various cross sections meet. Ranging from 15 to 25 cm, the diameter of the cross section for each member is unique and corresponds to the magnitude of its internal force derived from the 3DGS model. To find an

appropriate geometry for the node that can smoothly combine different member sizes, specific mathematical and geometrical definitions were developed based on the topology of the 3D convex hull for each node and its connected members.

Materialization

To extend the use of concrete in design and fabrication of discrete spatial systems as opposed to its conventional, mono-lithic use, glass fiber reinforced concrete (GFRC) in prefabricated elements was chosen as the material and the construction method for the project. To reduce the self-weight of the concrete, perlite, pumice aggregate, silica fume and chopped glass fibers were used as the main ingredients. Note that the form of the structure is in static equilibrium if it is subjected to the applied loads on its top chord. Since the finished structure would not have specific applied loads on its top chord, the tension members were also constructed out of concrete to act as the applied loads for the compression members. This keeps the structure in equilibrium and preserves the design consistency

4   Side view of the built structure (Deed Studio ©).

Hedracrete; Prefab, Funicular, Spatial Concrete Akbarzadeh, Mahnia, Taherian, Tabrizi

5   Coating foam molds and preparing them for concrete casting.

7   CNC bending the steel plates for the supports.

6   Treating the demolded nodes with water to reduce the cracking rate.

8   A completed support including bent steel plates welded to the base surface.

of the project. To improve the tensile capacity of the members, a single piece of steel rebar (d = 12 mm) was embedded in the cross section of the members of the top chord to carry tensile forces between the joints (Figure 4).

Fabrication

The main objective in the fabrication process was to develop a simple and inexpensive technique to produce the prefab parts of the system. The construction of the project was quite constrained by the total allocated budget ($8500), and the fabrication tools were limited to a 3-axis CNC machine and a CNC foam cutter. To reduce the construction time, and therefore the milling costs, the structure was designed with three planes of symmetry, so that fewer molds would be constructed. The molds were made out of styrofoam and each was used to cast three members (Figures 5 and 6). Therefore, it could cut the mold-making costs by a third.

The supports were made out of CNC-bent steel plates, bolted and welded, first together, then to a base plate at specific angles

to receive the members and transfer their axial forces precisely to the ground minimizing any potential moment in the supports (Figures 7 and 8).

Fabrication

Each compression member is dry-placed on a node without mortar. A simple male/female tube was embedded in each piece as a registration point in three-dimensional space to ease the assembly process. In contrast, the tension members were bolted to their adjacent nodes on the top chord. The assembly process of the project was accomplished by initially finishing the compression members and adding the tension members successively on the top (Figures 10 and 11). A simple scaffolding system was used to support the members during the assembly process.

ACKNOWLEDGMENTS

The authors of the paper would like to thank all the students who worked on the project, people whose hard work and endeavors played a signifi-cant role during both design and fabrication processes: Nematollah Safari,

9 View of the completed structure in Sa'adabad complex, Tehran, Iran (Deed studio ©).

Alireza Bayramvand, Parham Gholizadeh, Soroush Garivani, Fatemeh Salehi Amiri, Seyed Ali Mirzadeh, Nastaran Saeidi, Niloofar Imani, Pooria Gachpazan, Maryam Shahabi, Sobhan Sarabi, Armin Shayanpour, Yasamin Samaee, Kimiya Safakhah, Anahid Attaran, Banafsheh Tavassoli, Sepehr Farzaneh, Ayeh Fotovat, Maryam MollaAsadollah, Shahryar Abad, Neshat Mirhadizadi, Mohammad Hossein Karimi, Mohammad Ebrahimi, Pedram Karimi, Mobin Moussavi, Mehrzad Esmaeili Charkhab, Sahar Barzani, Atiyeh Sadat Fakhr Hosseini, NiloufarNamdar, Setareh Houshmand, Ehsan Heydarizadi. We are also thankful to Contemporary Architects Association for organizing the workshop and Sa'adabad Complex officials for hosting the final prototype.

The fabrication process was conducted in collaboration with the following companies: CODON Interactive Media: 3D printing; Horon Co.: CNC milling; ParsFoamCut: wire cutting of polystyrene foam blocks; Fateh Workshop: laser cutting and CNC bending services of metal sheets; and, Vandidad Sepehr Co.: lightweight concrete mixture and material of the project.

The project was partially funded by Cultural Heritage, Handicrafts and Tourism Organization of Iran, Kheiri Co, Omid Amini and Partners, and Sizan Co. In addition, the authors would like to express their gratitude towards Alireza Behzadi, Sina Ahmadi, Kristjan Plagborg Nielsen, Abbass Naseri, Nima Sadeghinejad, Davoud Mohammad Hassan, Amirali Zinati, Paniz Farrokhsiar, Mehdi MollaAsadollah, Ahmad and Gholam for their individual contribution to make this work possible.

REFERENCES

Akbarzadeh, Masoud, Mehrad Mahnia, Ramtin Taherian, and Amir Hossein Tabrizi. 2017. "Prefab, Concrete Polyhedral Frame: Materializing 3D Graphic Statics." In *Interfaces: Architecture. Engineering. Science, Proceedings of the IASS Annual Symposium 2017*, edited by A. Bögle and M. Grohmann. Hamburg, Germany: IASS.

Akbarzadeh, Masoud. 2016. "3D Graphic Statics Using Reciprocal Polyhedral Diagrams." PhD. diss., ETH Zürich,.

Rankine, W. J. M. 1864. "Principle of the Equilibrium of Polyhedral Frames." *Philosophical Magazine*, Series 4 27 (180): 92.

10 Prefabricated elements and nodes prepared for assembly.

11 Constraining the compressive members with the tensile members in assembly.

Masoud Akbarzadeh is an Assistant Professor of Architecture in Structures and Advanced Technologies and the Director of the Polyhedral Structures Laboratory (PSL) at the School of Design, University of Pennsylvania. He holds a PhD from the Institute of Technology in Architecture, ETH Zürich and two degrees from MIT: a Master of Science in Architecture Studies (Computation) and an MArch, the thesis for which earned him the renowned SOM award. He also has a degree in Earthquake Engineering and Dynamics of Structures from the Iran University of Science and Technology. His main research topic is Three-Dimensional Graphical Statics, which is a novel geometric method of structural design in three dimensions.

Mehrad Mahnia is an architect and designer and the founder of TheAlliance, a design-to-production studio, with the main concentration on computational design and advanced fabrication methods. He is very iterested in fusing digital production with local and conventional industries. He holds a B.Sc. from Azad University of Tehran, South Branch, and an unfinished MArch degree in Sustainable Design from Iran University of Science and Technology. He has the experience of teaching and organizing multilpe workshops including FaBrikation (2012), ComStruct (2015) and Hedracrete (2016).

Ramtin Taherian is an Iranian architect, designer and educator with a B.Sc. in Architectural Engineering from Tehran University of Arts, and a M.Sc. in Architectural Technology from University of Tehran. He has the experience of working with companies like Kamvari Architects and TheAlliance focusing on innovative approaches to architecture and design. He has taught in many educational workshops and fabrication courses including CRAFT 2014 and 2015, COMSTRUCT, and HEDRACRETE.

Amir Hossein Tabrizi is an Iranian architect, designer and educator and the founder of AT Architects. He holds B.Sc. and M.Sc. in Rehabilitation and Restoration of Monuments from Cultural Heritage University of Tehran, and Islamic Azad University of Tehran. He has the experience of working on some important world heritage sites such as Bistoon, Takht-e-Soleyman, and Perspolis and has won multiple national and international awards in the field of architecture and preservation.

Non-Modular Muqarnas

A Design Tool for Creating Non-Modular Muqarnas Using
Topological-Based Computation

Amin Bahrami
Helioripple Studio

Raana Dorneshan
Helioripple Studio

1   The exhibition of muqarnas prototypes at Pars University, Tehran

Muqarnas, A Traditional Ornament

Muqarnas, as an architectural element, has a deep history of design and fabrication, found in
various types in most Islamic historical cities, and its production has evolved through the eras.
However, the original design of muqarnas has remained unchanged, requiring a change in ways of
thinking about its creation. In this project, a fundamental metamorphosis has occurred mainly in
the design phase, implementing a series of algorithms assembled as a new design tool. In this new
attitude toward muqarnas in the field of computational design, only one method has been utilized
to unite all the existing and non-existing muqarnas styles and generate a wide new range of them.
In addition, it is able to redesign and regenerate the old ones. The following research projects,
collectively titled "Non-Modular Muqarnas," examine new possibilities for creating muqarnases in
today's architecture in the field of computational design.

Research

The project has been developed from a series of advanced research-based architectural design
courses, titled "Implementation of Digital Technology in Architecture" at Pars University under the
supervision of Helioripple Studio, and focused on the subject of ornament and craft through the
exploration of computationally generated patterns and digital fabrication processes. The main
aim was to create muqarnas as an ornamental element through a different approach. This process
established a probative approach to learning by allowing students to discover the precedents of

PRODUCTION NOTES

Supervisor: Amin Bahrami
Host: Pars University - Tehran
Team: Helioripple Studio
Date: Feb.2017

2   Individual outcome models of muqarnas. These prototypes were fabricated using FDM techniques for the presented stage.

muqarnases and speculate as to how the ancient and contemporary muqarnases had been designed and fabricated, contemplate the main idea behind them, and observe the limitations on their creation due to their design methods.

The Logic Behind the Design Tool

Parnassus-Design-Tool, represented as a Grasshopper-plug-in, acts as a machine to produce muqarnas out of almost every two-dimensional pattern. The idea behind this tool comes from a topological thinking towards the concept of muqarnas, in contrast to the privileged knowledge of design, and builds

muqarnas to have a composite-based view, depending on the intended style.

Irrespective of the type of the muqarnas, they all followed the same geometrical concept. A muqarnas consists of a number of layers, named "Level-lines," made up of a list of points with the same height. "Qouse," another parameter existing in all kinds of muqarnas, is implemented to control how the convex patches must be shaped. This parameter is defined in the plug-in as an independent object type to shape each non-horizontal edge of the muqarnas. In this approach, the muqarnas is defined by

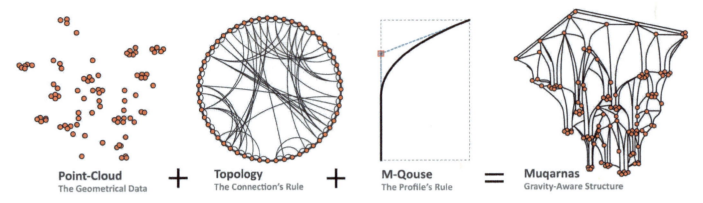

Point-Cloud
The Geometrical Data

+

Topology
The Connection's Rule

+

M-Qouse
The Profile's Rule

=

Muqarnas
Gravity-Aware Structure

3   Illustrating the components of a muqarnas based on the logic followed by this research.

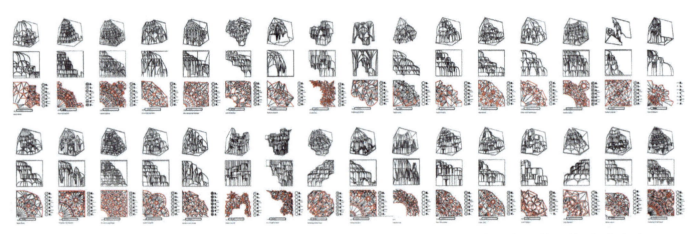

4   A part of the generated alternatives used for the next step. These models are created using the Muqarnas plug-in by the students of Pars University. During the procedure the plug-in was under development and contained errors, which the users faced, while the students were permitted to try any irregular map as the input base for the machine.

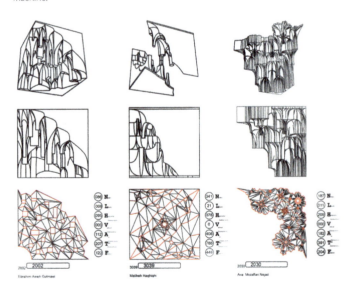

5   Three enlarged alternatives demonstrating the structure of muqarnas. the bottommost row represents the baselines separated into two colors. The red lines shows the levels (tires) of muqarnas and the black ones define the topology (the rule that tells how and by which vertexes these levees must be interconnected). At the right side of each model, the statistics of vertex, types of edges, patches and topology are showing.

nodes, topology (how these nodes connect too each other) and qouse, whereas a mesh is defined by just nodes and topology. So muqarnas is defined as a gravity-aware mesh, controlled by the qouse parameter.

The Result
Proceeding in the studio, students apply the tool to regenerate some existing muqarnases and subsequently create their own. The plug-in processes all data derived from the maps and creates the muqarnas components. All processes were done by topologically analyzing the two-dimensional arbitrary or geometrical maps in the last part. Although the tool was also able to generate unrolled patches for fabricating muqarnas out of the sheets, because of the different level of complexity of the final result models, they were better to build via FDM techniques at this stage.

Thinking widely, this plug-in under development is able to produce other kinds of objects based on topological viewpoints extended in the design phase. This is being developed to distinguish patches without user interference, that is, it will be

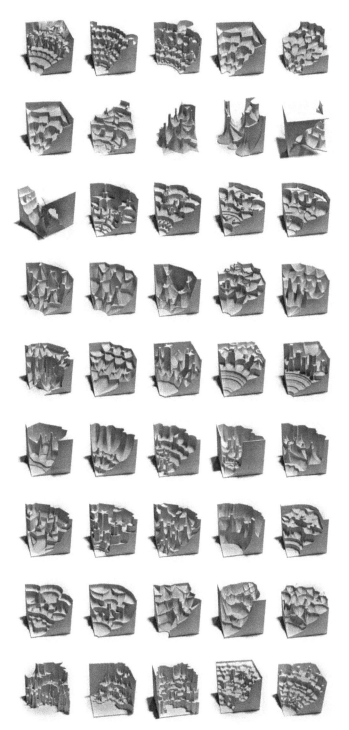

6   The catalog of the built alternatives

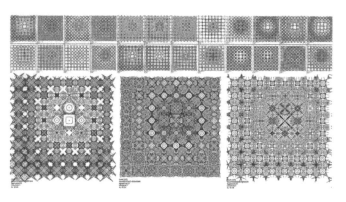

7   Computational Islamic patterns generated by the plug-in. This breeding is based on uncertainty, generating initial scribble lines; subsequently, it produces two different base patterns and the morphs them together. The plug-in, in the future, is assumed to extract the seemly topology in order to feed in to the muqarnas machine.

8   The presented models, classified in different parts by the team of juries

9   Representing different muqarnas styles designed by the Muqarnas Design Tool

a smarter topology modifier for finding regions in more accidental lines, and for breeding an infinite number of muqarnas species by mixing generated scribbles and random parameters. It's hoped that "Topological Attitude" will open up new gateways to embracing uncertainty through the process of design, which may pave the way for emerging perspectives toward architecture, suitable for the fuzzy future world.

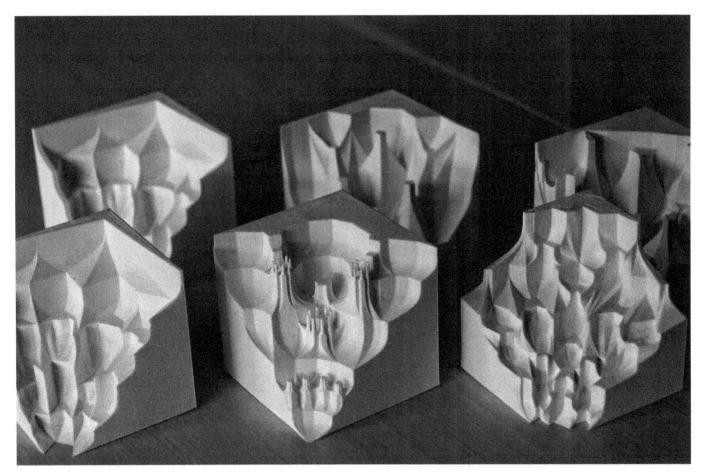

10   Examples of outcome models implemented in the Muqarnas plug-in.

ACKNOWLEDGMENTS

This research was supported by the team of Helioripple Studio. We are grateful for the support of FabLab.ir especially "Yahya Nourian," the team who provided expertise that assisted in fabricating the prototypes. We also appreciate the effort of students at Pars University who actively engaged in the learning process. We thank Sonay Servatkhah and Hoda Farazande, both from Helioripple Studio, for their assistance during the research, and express our gratitude to Prof. Mahmood Golabchi for comments that greatly improved the process. Lastly, we also thank the two "anonymous" reviewers of ACADIA for their comments, leading us to this point.

REFERENCES

Castera, Jean-Marc. 1999. "Zellijs, Muqarnas and Quasicrystals." In *Proceedings of the International Society of the Arts, Mathematics and Architecture*, edited by N. Freidman and J. Barrallo, 99–104. San Sebastian, Spain: ISAMA.

Dold-Samplonius, Yvonne. 1992. "Practical Arabic Mathematics: Measuring the Muqarnas by Al-Kshi." *Centaurus* 35: 193–242.

Grünbaum, Branko, and G. C. Shephard. 1993. "Interlace Patterns in Islamic and Moorish Art." In *The Visual Mind*, edited by Michele Emmer, 147–155. Cambridge, MA: MIT Press.

Kaplan, Craig S. 2005. "Islamic Star Patterns from Polygons in Contact." In *Proceedings of the Graphics Interface Conference*, 177–85. Victoria, BC: GI.

Syed Jan, Abas, and Salman Amer Shaker. 1995. *Symmetries Of Islamic Geometrical Patterns*. Singapore: World Scientific.

Yaghan, Mohammad, and Mitsui Hideki. 1995. "Muqarnas Typology: A tool for Definition and a Step in Creating a Computer Algorithm for Muqarnas Generation System." In *Proceedings of the 42nd Annual Conference of the Japanese Society for the Science of Design*, 156. Tokyo: JSSD.

Yaghan, Mohammad. 2001. "The Muqarnas Pre-Designed Erecting Units: Analysis, Definition of the Generic Set of Units, and a System of Unit-Creation as a New Evolutionary Step." *Architectural Science Review* 44 (3): 297–318.

–––. 2005. "Self-Supporting Genuine Muqarnas Units." *Architectural Science Review* 48 (3): 245–255.

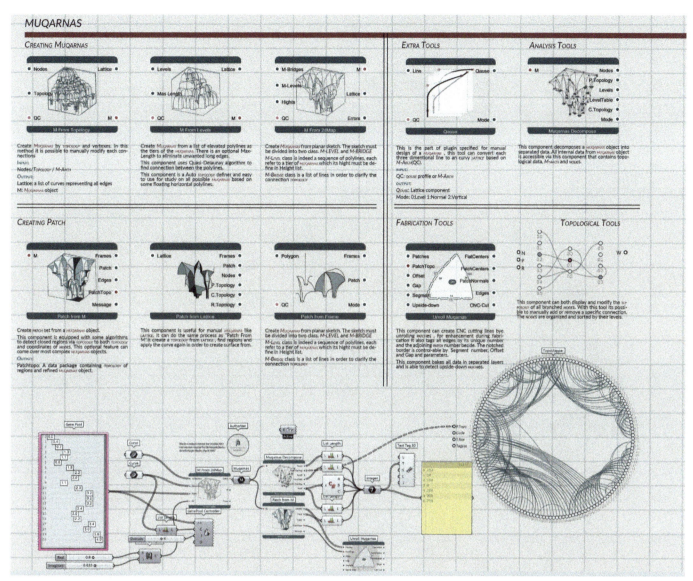

11   Explaining the Muqarnas Design Tool and the way that it works by adding sample definition from design to extracting pieces for fabrication, and representing various topological input and output data.

———. 2010. "The Evolution of Architectural Forms. Through Computer Visualisation: Muqarnas Example." In *Proceedings of the International Conference on Electronic Visualization and the Arts*, 113–20. London: EVA.

Yanxi Liu, Hagit Hel-Or, Craig S. Kaplan and Luce Van Cool. 2001. *Computational Symmetry in Computer Vision and Computer Graphics.* Hanover, MA: Now Publishers Inc.

Amin Bahrami is an architect and a musician experienced in computational design, having collaborated in various architecture projects as a supervisor, a design director or as lecturer in university. He taught Electronic Music and computational sound designing at the Tehran Music School. He has various research and practical experience in fields such as morphology, network topology, uncertainty-based processes, agent-based design, micro-interface design, etc. As the co-founder of Helioripple Studio, he is the winner of some architecture competitions and has created plug-ins for Grasshopper known as Heteroptera, Cicada, Instance Manager, and Heteroduino, implemented in many architecture firms and schools.

Raana Dorneshan is an architect active in Canada, focusing on integration of art and architecture to enhance public spaces. She is collaborating with Helioripple Studio's research program, and is interested in art and mathematics, where her aim is to apply those interests specifically in public installations. She has experience working with firms and teaching architecture and a new appreciation for spaces and urbanism, spaces and time, spaces and life. At the University of Manitoba, she also worked in FabLab, involved in fabrication using technology for design and architecture .

Ceiling Pressurized Ocular Diffusers (PODs)

Nathan Bishop
PARTISANS

Pooya Baktash
PARTISANS

Ivan Vasyliv
PARTISANS

1   Rendering of Union Station's new retail concourse with ceiling PODs (2017, © Norm Li).

The Ceiling PODs are the culmination of extensive research into the architectural potential of combining multiple building infrastructure systems into singular sculptural objects.

Off-the-shelf building systems products are economical, low-risk solutions to increasingly complex HVAC requirements—and their intractable practicality has become a significant, albeit de facto, element of architecture. As Rem Koolhaas lamented in his *Elements of Architecture* exhibition at the 2014 Venice Biennale of Architecture, "the ceiling has become a thick volume full of machinery of which the architect has very little to say" (Rem Koolhaas, quoted in Hobson 2014). The PODs disrupt this status quo and reinvent the possibilities of the ceiling by blurring the distinction between architecture and systems design.

The PODs were developed as part of a commission to design the interiors of a 200,000 ft^2 public retail concourse and food court at Toronto's Union Station (Figure 1). The PODs integrate an HVAC pressure vessel, light diffuser, speaker, and sprinkler head into a single rigorously performative architectural object (Figure 2). This custom, systems-oriented architectural language was a solution to the dual constraints of exceptionally low ceilings in the existing concourse, and substantial HVAC requirements. Combining systems into a single object had the additional downstream benefits of streamlined coordination, accelerated installation, and simplified layout changes.

PRODUCTION NOTES

Designer: PARTISANS
Client: Osmington
Status: Under-construction
Site Area: 200,000 sq. ft.
Location: Toronto, Canada
Date: 2015-18

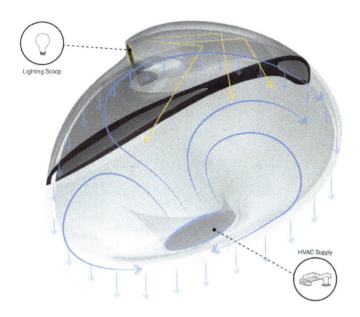

Lighting Scoop

HVAC Supply

2   Light + Diffuser + Sprinkler—initial concept diagram (2015 © PARTISANS).

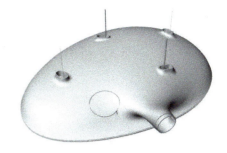

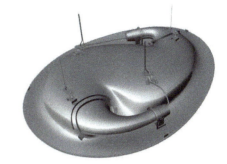

3   Rendering of the 8' diameter ceiling POD, including the outer shell (top), inner shell, view from above (middle), and inner shell, view from below (bottom) (2016, © PARTISANS).

The PODs consist of two shells that nest together to form a plenum (Figure 3). The outer shell forms the HVAC pressure vessel and duct inlet, conceals lighting equipment, and provides hardware for installation. The inner shell diffuses light and, when combined with a surface transducer, acts as a diaphragm for the speaker. The gap at the edges of the two shells serves as the diffuser; the sprinkler head is accommodated in a pocket at the apex. The geometry was developed collaboratively with various consultants, including aerodynamic, lighting, and mechanical engineers. Numerous digital simulations, including CFD analysis and illuminance studies, were conducted for both individual and aggregated PODs (Figures 4–6) to inform the geometry and demonstrate feasibility. Performance was later verified with extensive testing of full-scale mock-ups (Figures 7 and 8).

Diffuser

The PODs are pressure vessels that distribute cooling and fresh air. The pressurized cavity slows incoming air flow to eliminate jet effects. When combined with a uniform gap around the circumference of the two shells, non-directional airflow is ensured. The height of the gap is however eccentrically adjustable, allowing localized control of directionality, velocity, and pressure. The aggregation of individual PODs is governed by a series of guidelines that specify minimum and maximum limits for optimal effectiveness. These features make the diffusers adaptable to the unique HVAC requirements of the various spaces and conditions of the concourse (Figure 9).

Light

The PODs are designed to provide fully programmable and polychromatic ambient light to support spatial programming. The organic geometry of the inner shell was carefully calibrated using numerous digital simulations to produce diffuse light and to eliminate hot spots and light spillage.

Fabrication

The two shells that comprise the PODs are cast of lightweight, non-combustible, fibreglass-reinforced gypsum. The fabrication

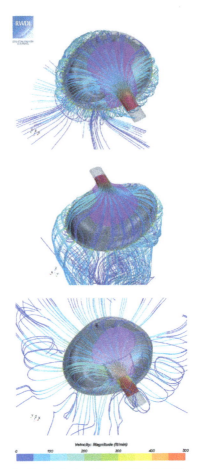

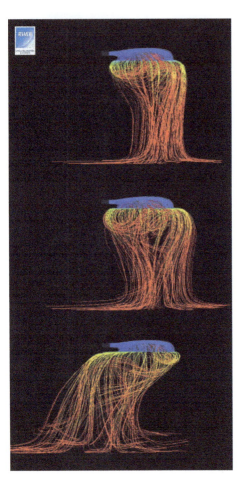

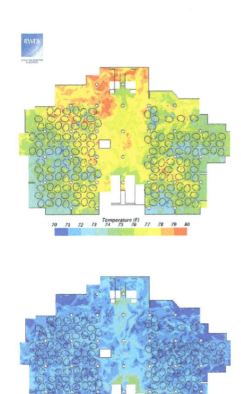

4   Air velocity simulations (2016, © RWDI)

5   Air temperature simulations (2016, © RWDI)

6   CFD simulation of temperature (top) and velocity (bottom) of the aggregated PODs in the food court by our airflow consultant (2016, © RWDI)

7   Airflow testing mock-up with rigid duct by RWDI (2016, © RWDI).

8   Airflow testing mock-up with flexible duct by RWDI (2016, © RWDI).

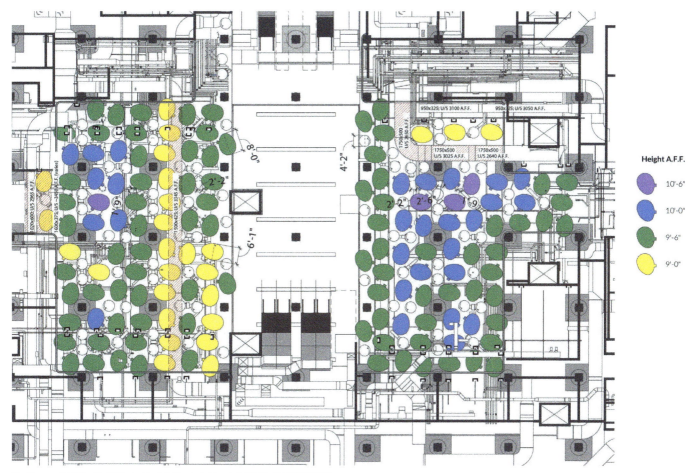

Height A.F.F.

- 10'-6"
- 10'-0"
- 9'-6"
- 9'-0"

9   Proposed RCP with PODs and installation height noted (2016, © PARTISANS).

process involves casting the gypsum mixture in a reusable mold made from a CNC-milled MDF form (Figures 10 and 11). After curing, the pieces are assembled (Figure 12) and given a finish coat (Figures 13 and 14). The completed shells are then joined to form a pod and are packaged for shipping (Figures 15 and 16). The casting process permits mass production at a reasonable cost and speed. On-site installation simply involves the wiring and installation of the PODS and connecting the ductwork.

Conclusion

The Ceiling PODs are an example of how architecture and infra-structure systems can be combined into mass producible, highly functional sculptural forms using advanced digital modeling and simulation to disrupt the segregation of AEC disciplines.

ACKNOWLEDGMENTS

Ceiling PODS was conceptualized and designed by PARTISANS in collab-oration with our aerodynamic consultant RWDI, mechanical consultant TMP, and lighting designer Light Emotion. The geometry was developed with Rhinoceros (www.rhino3d.com) using T-Splines (www.tsplines.com), and was later refined in CATIA for fabrication by Formglas. In addition to the authors, the PARTISANS project team includes co-founder Alex Josephson and project manager Michael Bootsma.

REFERENCES

Hobson, Ben. 2014. "Rem Koolhaas' Elements exhibition in Venice aims to 'modernise architectural thinking.'" *Dezeen*, June 6. Accessed April 17, 2017, https://www.dezeen.com/2014/06/06/rem-koolhaas-elements-of-architecture-exhibition-movie-ven-ice-biennale-2014/

10 Forming the wooden mold for the inner shell of the 8' diameter POD with a CNC router (2016, © Formglas).

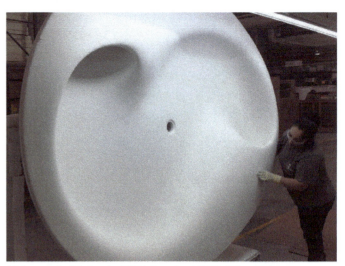

13 Inner shell of 8' diameter POD being primed (2017, © Formglas).

11 Reusable mold for the inner shell of 8' diameter POD (2017, © Formglas).

14 Outer shell of 8' diameter POD with final finish (2017, © Formglas).

12 Assembled inner shell of 8' diameter POD (2017, © Formglas).

15 PODs being prepared for shipment (2017, © Formglas).

Ceiling PODS Bishop, Baktash, Vasyliv

16 Completed 8' diameter POD being tested in the factory prior to shipment (2017, © Formglas).

Nathan Bishop completed his Master's of Architecture degree at the University of Toronto in 2014 where he was the recipient of numerous awards including the ARCC King Student Medal for excellence in Architectural and Environmental Research. Nathan has worked with PARTISANS since 2014, and previously worked with Ensamble Studio in 2013. Nathan also partook in an artist residency lead by Nat Chard and Perry Kulper at the Plug-In Institute of Contemporary Art in 2015.

Pooya Baktash studied architecture at the University of Azad in Tehran, Iran, where he also worked at renowned architecture firm EBA, recipient of the Aga Khan Award. In 2007, he came to Canada to pursue a Master's degree at the University of Waterloo School of Architecture. Pooya has a record of achievement on major civic projects, including Union Station. He co-founded PARTISANS in 2012 and has taught design studios at the University of Toronto's Daniels Faculty of Architecture since 2015.

Ivan Vasyliv joined PARTISANS in 2012 following completion of his Bachelor of Architectural Science degree at Ryerson University. He later completed an MBA from the Ted Rogers School of Management at Ryerson University in 2016, specializing in management of technology and innovation. Ivan's contributions in design, research, and fabrication at PARTISANS have received global recognition and numerous awards. He currently pursues projects with geometric and fabrication complexities.

Monolithic Earthen Shells and Robotic Fabrication

Stephanie Chaltiel
Institute of Advanced Architecture of Catalunya / UPC

Maite Bravo
Institute of Advanced Architecture of Catalunya / UPC

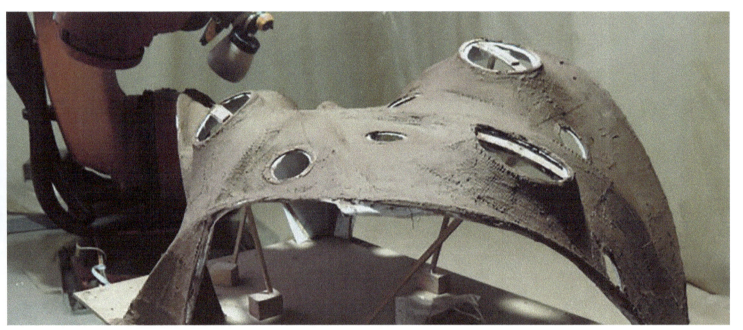

1   Perforated earthen shells. Third layer of clay mix being sprayed robotically. This additive manufacturing technique allows freeform structures. IAAC Seminar 2016.

This project explores the implementation of additive manufacturing for monolithic shells based on the deposition of different clay mixes through robotic spraying over a temporary fabric formwork. The framework sits at the intersection of ancient construction traditions, digital modelling techniques, and robotic control protocols.

Raw mud can be found in ancient construction traditions, from mud huts to wattle and daub techniques, to the recent appearance of 3d printed extrusions in several academic research projects. Thin shell vaulting has relevant precedents throughout the 20th century, incorporating a variety of formwork methods for spray concrete ranging from pneumatics to fabrics to the recent fabric removable formwork and metal mesh reinforcement for robotic spray concrete (Veenendaal and Block, 2014).

This highly sustainable project is actively implementing the principle of "resistance through form" (Eladio Dieste, 1996) at the design stage, by using geometries with curvatures that result in active surfaces that are optimized and tested in 3d modelling softwares (Rhino, Grasshopper and Karamba).

Robotic actions prove crucial to facilitate the laborious tasks associated with traditional craft techniques, providing control for the deposition of the correct thickness and homogeneity of the

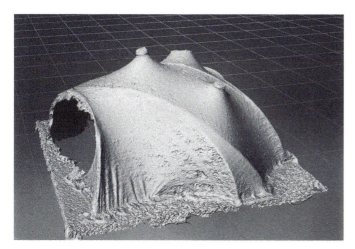

2   Seminar IAAC 2017. 3D scan performed through Agisoft and simplified in Rhino

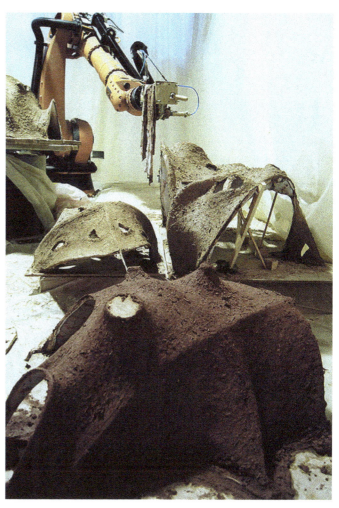

3   Fabric and branches formwork removal. Smart Geometry workshop 2016

4   Various robotically sprayed earthen shells of 1 x 1 x 70 m. IAAC Workshop 2016.

different clay mixes, allowing recalibrations according to matter changing properties (i.e. level of viscosity, humidity), permitting adjustments on the deformations and displacements experienced during depositions. The contribution of the earthen mono-lithic shell project lies in being the only robotically sprayed clay research on a temporary fabric formwork seeking a full-scale prototype.

Physical experiments have successfully resulted in the construc-tion of several 2 m high shell prototypes with 3cm thickness, implemented in workshops such as the Smart Geometry, AA visiting schools (Lyon 2012-2015), and IAAC seminars (2015-2017). During the experiments, a precise iterative protocol was implemented, consisting in sequential loops for placement, consolidation, and finishing. The placement stage starts with a stretched fabric supported by a series of bending arches, followed by fitting the robotic arm with a series of conventional construction paint sprayer nozzles that deposit different types of clay mixes. During several stages of the deposition, iterative 3D

scans are conducted to provide updated readings on the shell's evolution and to identify suitable thicknesses for each layer.

A digital mesh informs the continuous shell optimization by high-lighting tension, compression, and problematic areas. A constant recalibration of the robotic spray provides adjustments in the settings driving the robotic trajectories (KUKA prc) that control the path, pressure, speed, and deposition angle. The consolida-tion stage deposits clay mixes high in fibres to reach appropriate thickness while providing a lightweight reinforcement. The finish loop includes the removal by hand of the temporary formwork and concludes with the final robotic application of natural stabilizers.

5   Top: Detail of robotically poured natural resin embedded in earthen shells. Bottom: Parrot drone projecting mini balls on earthen shell in progress. IAAC Workshop 2017

Monolithic Earthen Shells & Robotic Fabrication Chaltiel, Bravo

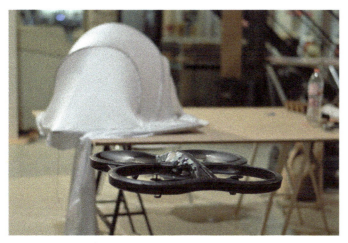

6   Parrot drone 3D scanning of the earthen shell in progress. IAAC 2017

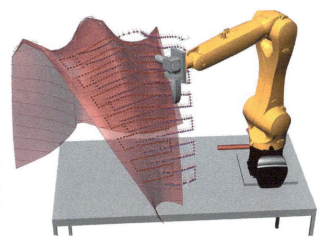

7   Continuous robotic spraying, KUKA prc simulation. Smart Geometry 2016.

8   Karamba/Rhino stress lines analysis for reinforcement.

evaluate deformations from previous scan

9   Earthen shell thickness variation according to tension or compression zones

This technique currently seeks further degrees of automation for architectural scale implementation. Active bending for the formwork frames could insert the support rods in the fabric and robotically scan and bend the arches. Reinforcement strips could be robotically placed in specific locations with variations according to stress lines and changing structural conditions during fabrication. Real time 3D scanning can expand with the use of drone flight control (on site or remote), facilitating a series of fast decision-making options during the fabrication process. Current work involves increasing the interactivity between the material deposition process and monitoring by working with agricultural drone companies to perform 3D scans (photogrammetric, thermal), at the same time evaluating the drone's load capacity to carry the clay mix and perform the spray. Augmented reality devices are also being explored to show the structure's distortion in real time linked to robotic actions, opening unique features for earthen monolithic shell fabrication.

ACKNOWLEDGMENTS

This research forms part of the Marie Skłodowska-Curie Actions, ITN Innochain, grant number #642877.

REFERENCES

Bravo, Maite. 2013. "Parametric Logics in the Architecture of the 20th Century: Some Referents and Principles." In *Cutting Edge in Architectural Science: Proceedings of the 47th International Conference of the Architectural Science Association*, edited by Marc A. Schnabel and J.-Y. Tsou, 147–56 . Hong Kong: ANZAScA.

Chaltiel, Stephanie, and Maite Bravo. 2017. "Paste Matter 3D Printing in Monolithic Shells Fabrication Methods." In *Proceedings of the International Conference of Kine[SIS]tem: From Nature to Architectural Matter*, edited by Maria João de Oliveira and Filipa Crespo Osório, 10–18. Lisbon, Portugal: Kine[SIS]tem.

10 Concrete hand sprayer as Agkus KUKA Robot end effector used to spray middle fibrous layers of the earthen shells. Smart Geometry 2016

Huijben, Frank, Frans Van Herwijnen, and Rob Nijsse. "Concrete Shell Structures Revisited: Introducing A New 'Low-Tech' Construction Method Using Vacuumatics Formwork." In *Structural Membranes: Proceedings of the 5th International Conference on Textile Composites and Inflatable Structures*, edited by E. Oñate, B. Kröplin and K.-U.Bletzinger, 409–420. Barcelona, Spain: CIMNE.

Veenendaal, Diederik, and Philippe Block. 2015. "Design Process of Prestressed Membrane Formworks for Thin-Shell Structures." In *Proceedings of the International Society Of Flexible Formwork Symposium*, Amsterdam, The Netherlands: ISOFF.

IMAGE CREDITS

Photos credits 1-12 by workshop´s participants

Stephanie Chaltiel Originally from France, Stephanie has over 10 years experience as an architect. Stephanie has worked for Bernard Tschumi in New York (Elliptic City- IFCA-2006), For OMA in Paris (Monaco Extension on the water- 2008), and for Zaha Hadid in London (Pierres Vives Construction – 2010). Stephanie also has valuable experience in countries such as Mexico, and French Guyana, applying sustainable materials and techniques for housing solutions. Stephanie has been teaching in France and in London, at SUTD in Singapore and currently at IAAC Barcelona. Stephanie has also been directing the AA (Architectural Association) Visiting School in Lyon which has investigated and explored the use of digital technologies in conjunction with earth construction. She is currently a Marie Curie researcher and PhD candidate investigating the potential of combining small robotics with earth architecture principles.

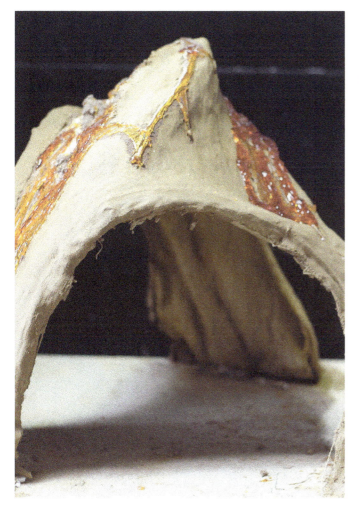

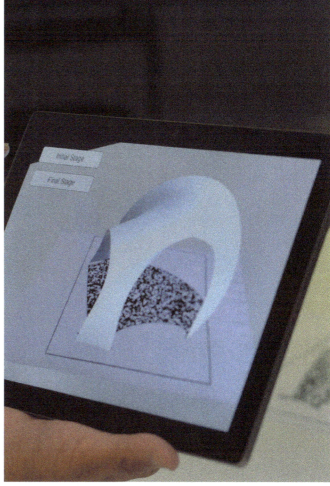

11 Resin robotically poured on wet earthen shell. IAAC 2017

12 Augmented reality experiment showing earthen shell deformations, IAAC 2017

Maite Bravo Architect from the University of Chile (FAU UCh), Master of Advanced Architecture (IAAC), and Master in Theory and Practice of Architectural Design (ETSAB-UPC). She obtained a PhD International Mention with a "Cum Laude" distinction at the UPC Architectural Design Department, studying concepts and design methodologies emerging from the use of parametric digital design and its immersion into the architectural praxis. Her academic experience includes the University of Chile (UCh), the British Columbia Institute of Technology (BCIT Canada), and IAAC since 2008. She has been a visiting professor at ETH Zürich, and a guest lecturer or jury member at several international universities. She is currently the academic coordinator of the IAAC-Urban Sciences Lab, the co-director of the IAAC Theory for Advanced Knowledge Group (TAK), and faculty for several courses at IAAC.

Taut: Tensioned Surface Morphologies in the Production of Textile Composites

David Costanza
Rice University, DC/S

1   Taut detail (DC/S, 2017).

Taut: Tensioned Surface Morphologies in the Production of Textile Composites

Taut is the culmination of extensive research exploring the potentials of tensile surface morphologies to define the geometry of a vacuum-assisted, resin-infused, textile-composite structure. The geometric language of the research emerged from early work by German architect and structural engineer Frei Otto, who developed a method using soap films to derive the shape and structure of tensile membranes. Otto produced an isotropic membrane by tying one end of a string into a loop and submerging it in a dish containing soap and water. As Otto pulled the other end of the string from the dish, he formed a "cable loop," also known as an "eye" due to its shape. The forms derived from the soap films were extremely efficient and lightweight, capitalizing on the potentials of structural form finding. Due to the surface tension of the soap solution, the formed surface minimized its area in relation to its given boundary conditions, forming a minimal surface operating in pure tension.

PRODUCTION NOTES

Architect: David Costanza

Status: In-process

Location: Houston, TX

Date: 2017

2   Taut strutural analysis of force vectors (DC/S, 2017).

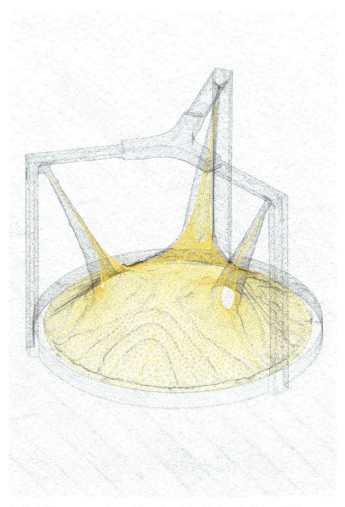

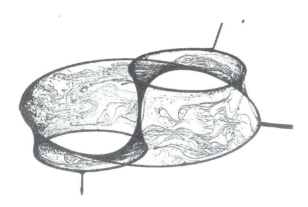

3   Frei Otto, single minimal surfaces (IL-Bach/Klenk 1987).

4   Taut 3D scan comparing prototype 2 and simulated mesh (DC/S, 2017).

Tensile membrane structures have evolved dramatically since their initial conception, but have consistently relied on elaborate systems of cables, tie-downs, and masts in order to maintain their structural integrity. The extent of fixturing required for membrane structures is distinctly evident in Gunther Behnisch and Frei Otto's stadium for the 1972 Munich Olympics. These fixture components must remain for the life of the structure, often projecting into and around a building, limiting possible applications of tensile structures. In addition, the fabric remains a malleable textile, always vulnerable to puncture and collapse.

Tensile structures are unparalleled in their ability to enclose vast spaces with minimal material. This is made possible through the close alignment of geometry, material, and structure. Double curvature in opposing directions, at any point on the surface, guarantees the stability of the membrane. Through the geometric and structural constraint of an anticlastic membrane, formal surface typologies emerge that are both complex and efficient.

Taut seeks to combine the research on tensile membrane structures with that of composite structures. Its geometry is defined through tensioning a single surface within a scaffolding frame, and it is made rigid with vacuum-assisted resin infusion. The most challenging aspect of composite manufacturing, as it relates to architecture, is the production of the mold. Large, custom molds are extremely expensive to construct and are only viable in an economy of scale. Instead, the tensioned surface would be constructed using a simple frame with cables, replacing the role of the mold in the production of a composite structure.

The scaffolding frame supports the edges of the textile surface while it is stretched taut and infused with epoxy resin. Early prototypes were constructed using multiple layers of burlap fabric on either side of a foam infusion core, facilitating the infusion of the textile through the use of a vacuum pump. The vacuum pulls the resin through the textile, wetting out the fibers while also compressing the composite assembly. After the infusion of the textile membrane, the scaffolding frame is

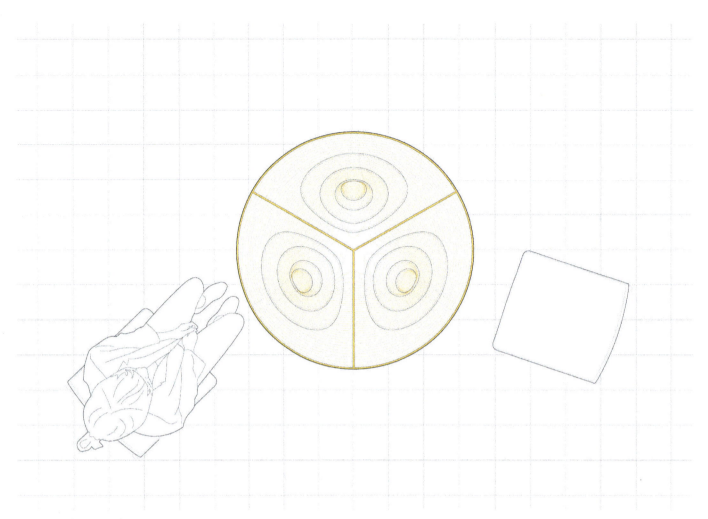

5   Taut plan (DC/S, 2017)

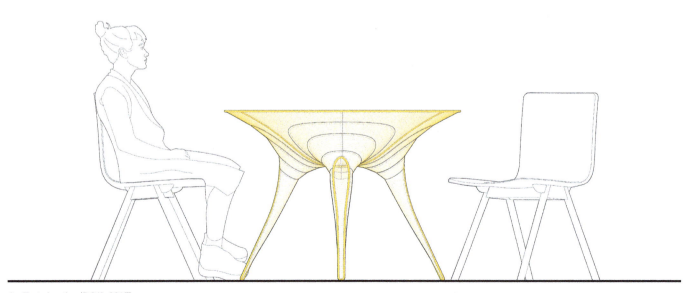

6   Taut elevation (DC/S, 2017).

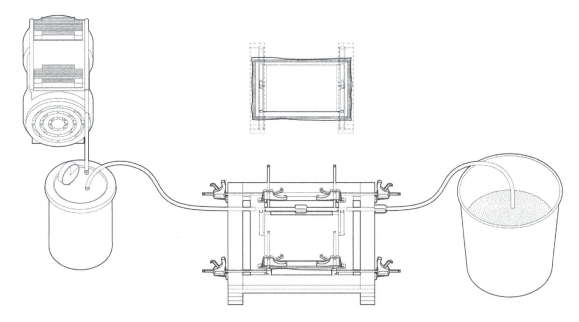

7   Taut infusion test drawing (DC/S, 2017).

8   Taut material and infusion research showing flex, tension, and the final, rigid composite (DC/S, 2017)

disassembled and removed, leaving behind a permanent, rigid, composite structure.

Taut: Design Development

Taut was designed and simulated using the Kangaroo physics engine plugin for Grasshopper and Rhino. The capacity to simulate the soap film studies in a digital environment with great accuracy made possible the design of the table. Rather than a single cable loop being pulled along a single vector, as was the case with the physical soap films, the table is designed as three radial cable loops, each with a unique trajectory. The resulting mesh is an anticlastic, purely tensioned surface.

The discretization of the mesh into flat cut patterns was a result of both the drapability of the textile and the strategy used for resin infusion. The fabric assembly was laminated, laser cut, and stitched into a textile preform. Though inherently flexible, when stretched taut, the preform takes the shape of the simulated mesh.

9   Taut infusion frame (DC/S, 2017).

10   Taut, bagged, tensioned, and under vaccuum (DC/S, 2017).

11   Taut resin infusion in process (DC/S, 2017)

12   Taut infusion complete (DC/S, 2017).

ACKNOWLEDGMENTS

I would like to acknowledge the Rice School of Architecture and Dean Sarah Whiting for the support and funding. The development of the project would not have been possible without the extensive effort of my research assistants Philip Niekamp, Ekin Erar, and Samantha Schuermann.

REFERENCES

Otto, Frei. 2005. *Frei Otto: Complete Works: Lightweight Construction, Natural Design.* Basel, Switzerland: Birkhäuser.

DC/S is a multi-disciplinary architecture and design studio located in Houston, which operates at a range of scales from furniture to landscape to building scale projects. David Costanza is the director and lead designer of DC/S as well as the Technology Fellow at Rice University School of Architecture. Through practice and teaching, his focus has been establishing a dialog between the computational tools used in design, digital tools used in manufacturing, and the emergence of advanced building materials. David Costanza is a graduate of the Massachusetts Institute of Technology where he received both a Masters of Architecture and a Masters of Science in Architecture.

13 Taut at home (DC/S, 2017).

Collaborative Parametric Design of a Theatroacoustic System

Scott Crawford
LMNts/LMN Architects

Stephen Van Dyck
LMN Architects

1   View looking up at Theatroacoustic System (Tim Griffith, 2017 ©).

Design collaboration within parametric modeling environments is in its infancy. Inefficiency and disconnection abound as multidisciplinary teams struggle to incorporate the work of a variety of areas of expertise and disparate design platforms. This project represents an attempt to leverage computation for closer collaboration and increased design performance.

Six consultants and their design inputs fed the architect's initial research and resulting design process. Their inputs of performance characteristics, design objectives, and systemic constraints helped define the ultimate outcome, but also their method of working and type of design deliverables informed the basis of the digital collaboration process. The resulting design process was crafted to accommodate all levels of computational 'comfort' as well as the evolving needs and discoveries made during design and simulation. This flexibility is critical on real world projects given that not all collaborators are themselves attempting to explore new potentials of technology.

The focus of this design process was the development of a Theatroacoustic System located within a 700 seat concert hall. Initial acoustic analysis indicated the need for an acoustically reflective element to be located above the stage to increase a sense of acoustic intimacy in the space. This element is traditionally a single element suspended over the stage. For cost-efficiency, the design team integrated structural trusses within the primary acoustic volume.

PRODUCTION NOTES

Architect:	LMN Architects
Client:	U. of Iowa School of Music
Status:	Complete
Site Area:	184,000 sq. ft.
Location:	Iowa City, IA
Date:	2016

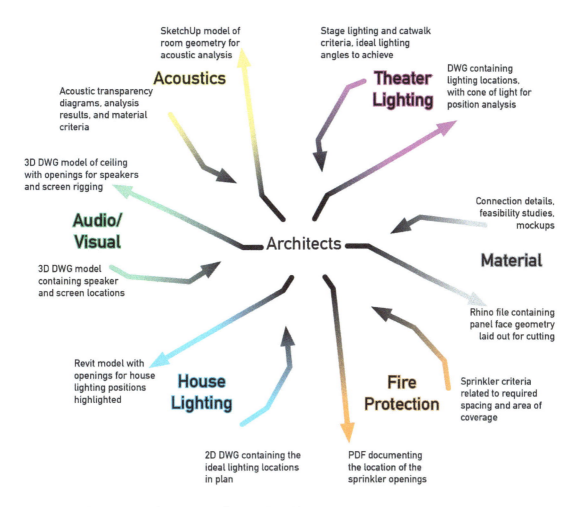

Acoustics

SketchUp model of room geometry for acoustic analysis

Acoustic transparency diagrams, analysis results, and material criteria

3D DWG model of ceiling with openings for speakers and screen rigging

Audio/ Visual

3D DWG model containing speaker and screen locations

Revit model with openings for house lighting positions highlighted

House Lighting

2D DWG containing the ideal lighting locations in plan

Architects

Theater Lighting

Stage lighting and catwalk criteria, ideal lighting angles to achieve

DWG containing lighting locations, with cone of light for position analysis

Material

Connection details, feasibility studies, mockups

Rhino file containing panel face geometry laid out for cutting

Fire Protection

PDF documenting the location of the sprinkler openings

Sprinkler criteria related to required spacing and area of coverage

2   Diagram of collaborative exchange of information into Architect's parametric model

To aesthetically unify this potentially disparate ceiling condition, the architects developed a single unifying surface to visually cover the exposed truss space while strategically creating openings to accommodate lights and A/V components while allowing acoustic transparency for the full volume of the room to operate as needed from an acoustical perspective. The challenge of the process became coordinating the location of these systems with the constantly evolving acoustically driven form of the Theatroacoustic System.

A central parametric model was developed to provide a single interface for all governing design requirements and performance objectives. The structure of this interface allowed each discipline an input category that was customized to its preferred file-format.

The parametric model would use each input as a basis for its initial logic, and gave the architects the ability to balance these inputs against each other in a consistent and evolving manner

to optimize the design. As each input is updated, a new design solution is generated based on the rebalancing of requirements defined within the parametric model. This interface evolved over the course of design to encompass the full pipeline of production, from conceptual sketches and base parameters to the ultimate final fabrication geometry. Design, simulation, and documentation all proceed in parallel with the ability to make changes at any level of detail and have all other information update to the current level of design understanding and refinement.

The resulting process establishes a new standard for digital collaboration, enabling almost instantaneous analysis, synthesis, and optimization of often conflicting requirements to produce a seamless methodology for design. Design actions and discussions moved away from the traditional process of comparing and contrasting various ideas and instead became an iterative process of defining and then refining the performance characteristics or 'behaviors' of the overall design approach.

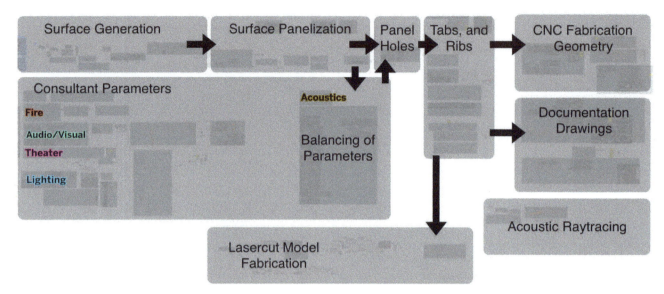

3   Structure of parametric definition

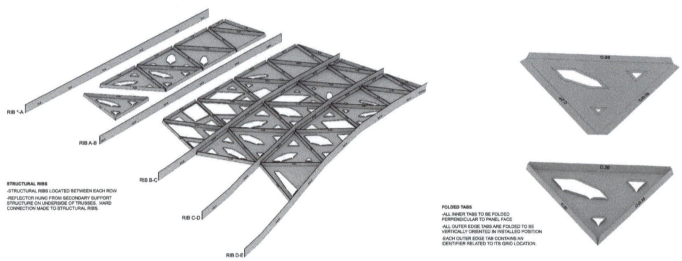

STRUCTURAL RIBS
-STRUCTURAL RIBS LOCATED BETWEEN EACH ROW
-REFLECTOR HUNG FROM SECONDARY SUPPORT STRUCTURE ON UNDERSIDE OF TRUSSES. HARD CONNECTION MADE TO STRUCTURAL RIBS.

FOLDED TABS
-ALL INNER TABS TO BE FOLDED PERPENDICULAR TO PANEL FACE
-ALL OUTER EDGE TABS ARE FOLDED TO BE VERTICALLY ORIENTED IN INSTALLED POSITION
-EACH OUTER EDGE TAB CONTAINS AN IDENTIFIER RELATED TO ITS GRID LOCATION.

4   Example Detail from Construction Documents

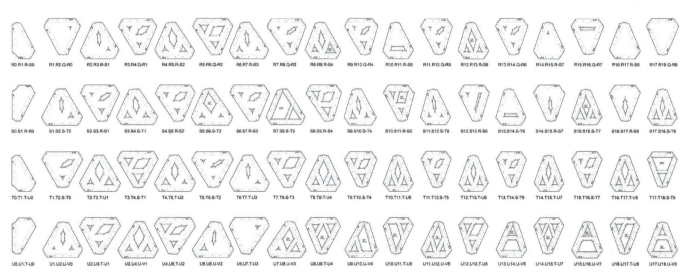

5   All panels were individually documented in drawing set as well as provided to the fabricator as a 3D file

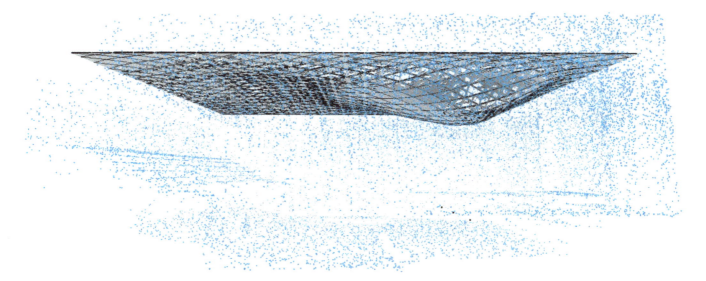

6   Custom analysis tools were developed which produced a point cloud of the room by reflecting thousands of source points from the stage off the reflector

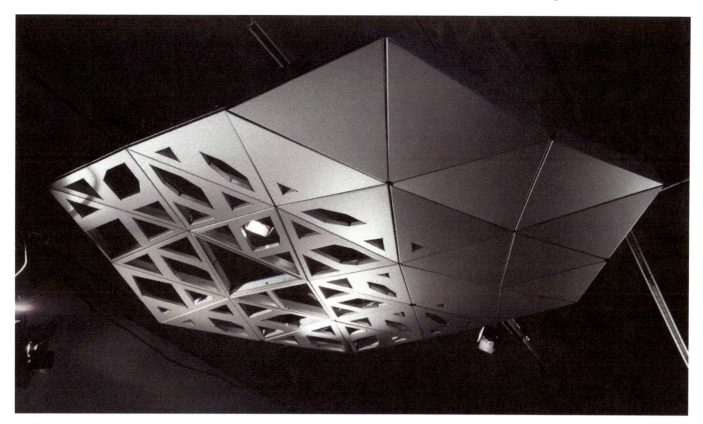

7   **Early on,** the Architects fabricated their own mockup of the ceiling system in an effort to prove the viability of the system to collaborators

Scott Crawford has a key role in LMN's design process as a Design Technologist. Scott is part of the LMN Tech Studio, the interdisciplinary R&D and applied technology group at LMN, and also works as a designer on LMN projects. He utilizes computational design tools to more easily explore and analyze large numbers of design iterations bringing efficiency to the design of better buildings.

Stephen Van Dyck is a partner at LMN Architects and has earned a reputation for innovation, design technology and collaborative leadership. He is widely recognized as an industry authority in the adoption of emerging technologies. His project experience encompasses a wide range of public assembly, performing arts, higher education and mixed-use projects.

8 Theatroacoustic System installed in the 700 seat performance hall at the University of Iowa School of Music (Adam Hunter, 2016 ©)

9   View from catwalks

Migratory Landforms

Dana Cupkova
Carnegie Mellon School of
Architecture

Colleen Clifford
Carnegie Mellon School of
Architecture

Thomas Sterling
Carnegie Mellon School of
Architecture

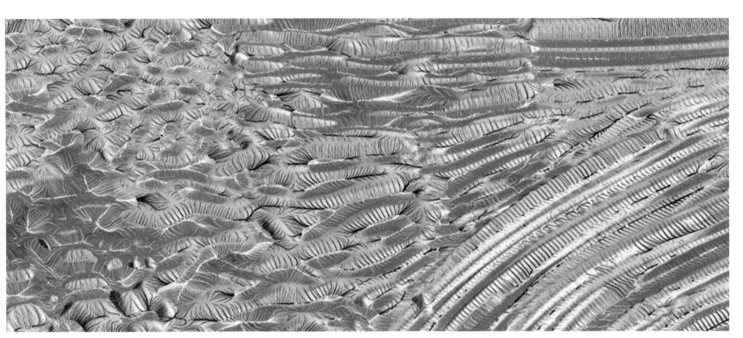

1   Terraformed landscape geomtries, simulation close up detail.

Migratory Landforms is a project that explores land-building urbanization strategies inspired by
natural sedimentation processes. Expanding on the protective phenomena of barrier islands formed
at the cusp of the Mississippi River, Lake Pontchartrain and Black Bay, we propose a large-scale
landscape expansion procedure for a changing planet. As climate change precipitates the loss of
habitable ground, ground building and terraforming is becoming central to the design discipline.
The urgency to urbanize and protect vulnerable coastal areas accentuates the need to interweave
natural and industrial processes in order to robustly support urban and ecological environments.

Our proposal couples a simulation flow strategy that negotiates sediment deposition with the
industrial practice of building oil rigs in the ocean in order to produce new migratory landforms.
These landforms are semi-stabilized by pier-based infrastructures that support further sediment
accumulation, expanding new contingent territories. The accumulative conglomeration of elevated
urban islands will trigger secondary human connectivity while simultaneously protecting the
shore from extreme weather events and allowing for shifting sedimentary landscapes to grow into
new bio-mass, encouraging the growth of new ecologies, natural habitats and water fluctuation
processes.

Using computational flow simulation (Cupkova et al. 2015) that is based on mesh subdivision and

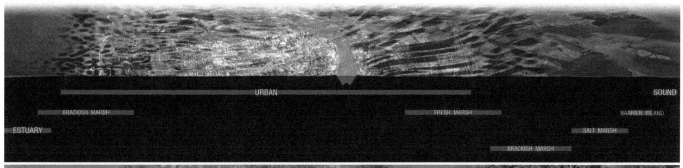

2　First degree sediment flow and accumulation along the river basin

recursive downhill flow interpolation, this project attempts to understand the potential of a land formation combined with large-scale industrial rigging structures to perpetuate a controlled sedimentation process that can help to expand the land territory and protect the shore from extreme weather events. The simulation helps to identify the flow paths and drainage basins based on specific mesh topology. The identified drainage areas receive sediment accumulation. The computational basin subdivision routine allows for better understanding of large-scale formation trends relative to water flow. The recursive logic of the flow visualization illustrates how water effects the potential land morphologies and vice versa. This is a speculative project that focuses on visualization of landmass-flow morphology.

Migratory Landforms is rooted in a discursive framework that negotiates the autonomous character of physical artifacts and the relational setup of socio-ecological systems. In the context of Morton's (2013) writing on "hyperobjects," our work supports the physical autonomy within the framework of global relationality, hence shifting the focus of design away from the contextual truth of information into the constraints of bio-synthetic logic.

Design Process

Three simulations illustrate the temporal progression of Migratory Landforms: terraforming, sedimentation, and transportation networks. The terraform series begins with a simluation of emergent flow and drainage patterns from the existing landscape of urban transportation networks. Hard, inflexible and engineered systems such as New Orleans' network of levees and locks produce highly volatile disaster conditions.

The second stage uses natural flow patterns to generate a terraformed landscape, facilitated by the removal of levees and locks, as well as strategic dredging operations. The imposition of a soft landscape increases ecological resiliency and systemic redundancy.

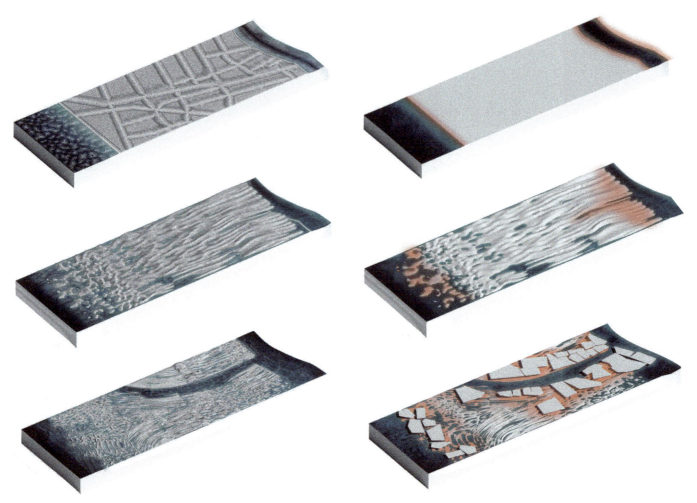

3   Phase 1: Terraforming simulations

4   Phase 2: Sedimentation simulations

The third stage of landscape terraforming emerges from continued natural sedimentation and erosion caused by tidal flows and large storm events. The absence of hard boundaries between land and water produces an ever-shifting network of brackish ponds, rivers, and streams.

The first sedimentation stage requires constant dredging to maintain navigability and ensure the operability of storm-mitigation infrastructure. Catastrophic failure occurs when the combined pressure of water and sediment exceeds levee capacity. The second stage allows the landscape to shift in response to natural sediment deposition patterns, increasing the systemic resilience of the landscape in large storm events while allowing for the creation of new urban territory. The third stage optimizes urban resilience by using floating neighborhoods to capture additional sediment around the barges. The localized accumulation of sediment ensures greater urban and ecological resilience.

The first stage of transportation networks facilitates contraflow during storm events. The second stage of networks uses existing infrastructural patterns to link floating neighborhoods together, and the third stage reflects the shifting landscape beneath the floating city. As neighborhoods move up and down the coast in response to large storm events and shifting waterways, transportation networks are re-optimized and reconfigured.

ACKNOWLEDGMENTS

Migratory Landform project received an honorable mention in the D3 Naturals Systems Competition. Thank you to Maratntha Dawkins for her editing and writing contribution.

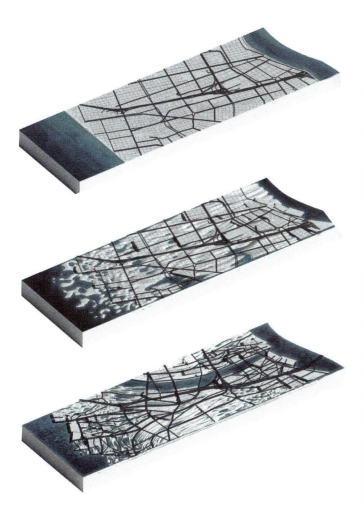

5   Phase 3: Transportation network overalay

6   Relationship of rigged platforms within the sedimented landform

REFERENCES

Cupkova, Dana, Nicolas Azel, and Christine Mondor. 2015. "EPIFLOW: Adaptive Analytical Design Framework for Resilient Urban Water Systems." In *Modelling Behavior: Design Modelling Symposium 2015*, edited by Mette Ramsgaard Thomsen, Martin Tamke, Christoph Gengnagel, Billie Faircloth, and Fabian Scheurer, 419–431. Cham, Switzerland: Springer.

Morton, Timorthy. 2013. *Hyperobjects: Philosophy and Ecology after the End of the World*. Minneapolis: University of Minnesota Press.

Dana Cupkova is an Assistant Professor at the Carnegie Mellon School of Architecture and is a principal of *EPIPHYTE Lab*, an architectural design and research collaborative. Her design work engages the built environment at the intersection of ecology, computationally driven processes, and systems analysis.

Colleen Clifford is a recent graduate of Carnegie Mellon School of Architecture. Her interest lies in soft architecture, parametric design, and sustainable design. A proponent for tactile experimentation, Colleen is currently focused on refining the process between digital and physical geometries. A unique experience in fashion design influences the tools, materials, and techniques she uses for architectural thinking.

Thomas Sterling is a graduate of the Carnegie Mellon School of Architecture and a designer at studioTechne in Cleveland, Ohio. His research investigates the resilience of hybrid ecological systems relative to the emergent conditions of the anthropocene.

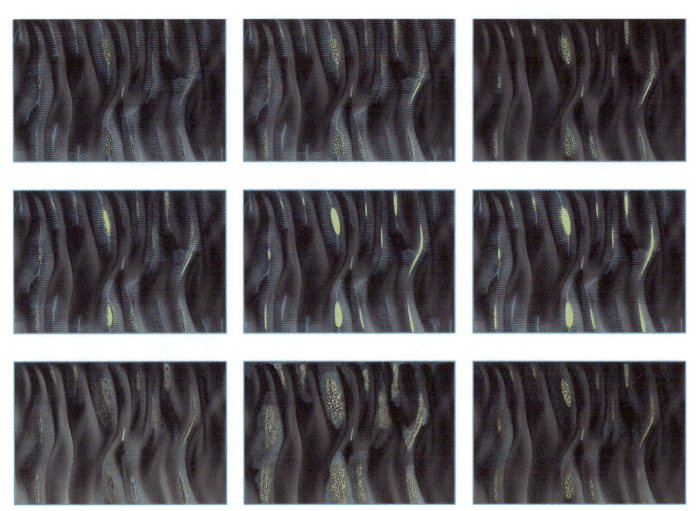

7   Sample topographical simulation of pattern flow and density

8   Concept rendering

Migratory Landforms Cupkova, Clifford, Sterling

9   Floating island networks: Landform projection visualization

Smallest Parts

How a Design of Great Complexity Can be Completed with Great Simplicity

Ricky del Monte
A. Zahner Company

Jo Kamm
A. Zahner Company

1   The Chrysalis at Merriweather Park in Symphony Woods. Columbia; Maryland. Photo © Jeffrey Totaro.

Digital fabrication has promised a world of unlimited complexity. It has promoted this idea that anything is now possible—from designs with a million unique parts to infinitely precise components that combine to form an exquisitely intricate whole. However, while it has never been easier to design with complexity, the construction industry is still constrained by current realities of fabrication, engineering codes, and installation requirements. In order to realize ambitious projects of increasing complexity, it is necessary to balance conceptual design with the messy reality of the built world. This narrative of compromise disrupts the promise of unlimited complexity, but it also points to a way forward by developing increasingly sophisticated methods for limiting variation with built-in tolerance for handling what variation remains.

This way forward is exemplified by The Chrysalis Amphitheater in Columbia, Maryland. The design by Marc Fornes/THEVERYMANY brings forth a dual-curving skin surface made of ridges that wrap around the stage to form 9 legs. The shell is covered with over 8,000 painted aluminum skins that define a gradient of green shades from dark to light.

PRODUCTION NOTES

Designer:	Marc Fornes THEVERYMANY
Client:	Inner Arbor Trust
Contractor:	Whiting Turner
Architect:	Living Design Studio
Landscape:	Mahan Rykiel
Engineer:	Arup
Steel:	Walters Group
Fabrication:	A. Zahner Company
Status:	Completed
Site Area:	6000 SF
Location:	Columbia, Maryland
Date:	April, 2017

2   Fabricators at the Zahner manufacture Chrysalis parts. Photo © Zahner.

3   Zahner installers hang ZEPPS assemblies for The Chrysalis. Photo © Zahner.

4   A single ZEPPS assembly is lifted into place. Photo © Zahner.

The three biggest challenges in this project were: (1) the use of a tube steel structure to support the ridged shell, (2) the definition of the shell using aluminum contour fins, and (3) the rationalization of the skin pattern.

The structure posed a significant complication. The initial design by Marc Fornes featured a self-supporting skin structure. Due to load requirements for equipment, wind, and snow, the design was adapted to include steel members. These were rolled and rotated about their centerlines using splices to form the curves as the main structural member. Despite careful description of the steel for fabrication, Zahner recognized the need for flexibility and adjustment between the steel and adjacent aluminum panels. Custom clips aligned along the tube steel created a flexible tolerance for adjustment between the steel and aluminum contour panels.

Defining the ridged form of the shell presented another engineering hurdle, because the initial design outlined 900 uniquely contoured fins. In order to simplify and control this aspect of the

project, Zahner adapted the form into ZEPPS assemblies (Zahner Engineered Profile Panel Systems). Each assembly grouped a number of adjacent fins into a single megapanel that was shipped and lifted into place. This strategy increased precision by locating and verifying positions of fins in smaller groups, and reducing the number of parts to assemble in the field. The 900 fins were reduced to 88 panels, greatly reducing the complexity while maintaining the aesthetics of the design intent.

The skin pattern on Chrysalis presented significant challenges to both fabrication and installation. Initial designs called for 8,000 unique skins, and while this is a small concern digitally, the physical management of 8,000 unique parts led Zahner to seek alternative solutions. Due to the sequential nature of skin placement, the damage or loss of a single skin could hold up installation for the whole project, not to mention the concerns of following individual parts through fabrication processes. The pattern was ultimately rationalized to 44 types across 4 colors, with a small number of custom panels fabricated on-site to bridge irregular conditions.

5   The Chrysalis at Merriweather Park in Symphony Woods. Columbia; Maryland. Photo © Jeffrey Totaro.

Smallest Parts del Monte, Kamm

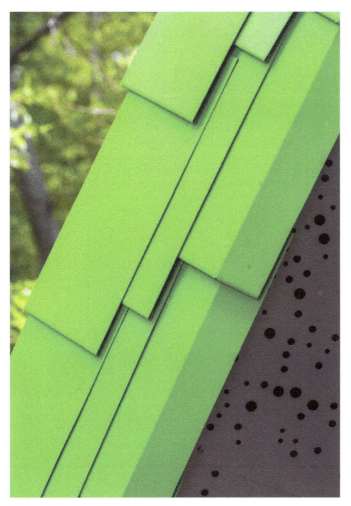

6   Detail of the skin system used on The Chrysalis. Photo © Zahner.

7   Steel clips connect the ZEPPS assemblies to steel structure. Photo © Zahner.

8   Interior structure of The Chrysalis. Photo © Jeffrey Totaro.

The most difficult aspect of installation was locating the skins. In a less complex construction project, the gridlines and elevation drawings would communicate the locations of parts. For this project, these aids did not prove useful because the building curves continuously and provides very few defined reference points. To resolve this, Zahner engineers provided runs of skins along ridge lines that were defined by color and type. This allowed the installation team to identify the skins and meet the requirements of the design without forcing installers to find the exact location for each of the 8,000 skins.

Digital modeling tools are making complexity increasingly achievable, but realizing these designs requires innovation in the construction industry. Increased understanding and development of the fabrication and installation processes will allow architecture to continue to push forward with more ambitious, more complex designs, and its the job of engineers and manufacturers to rise and make these challenging designs possible.

ACKNOWLEDGMENTS

The Chrysalis was made possible by a coordinated effort of specialists. This included designers, engineers, consultants, contractors, and manufacturers. At its center was Michael McCall of Strategic Leisure, who worked at the local, city, and state level to bring about this contemporary work of art.

Ricky del Monte served as the Engineering Lead for the production phase of The Chrysalis. He has a degree in Mechanical Engineering from the University of Kansas and has been with Zahner for three years, working on complex projects that include the Petersen Automotive Museum, United Methodist Church of the Resurrection, and Rogers Place Edmonton Downtown Area.

Jo Kamm provides algorithmic design and process automation for Zahner. His work on complex projects such as The Chrysalis has resulted in increased efficiency without sacrificing aesthetics or design intent. As a graduate of the Kansas City Art Institute, Kamm maintains a studio art and design practice, exploring generative patterns through sculpture and drawings.

DATAField

Marcella Del Signore
New York Institute of Technology
Cordula Roser Gray
Tulane University

1   View from Broad Street at Lafitte Corridor

Founded on soft ground and situated mostly below sea level, New Orleans has found itself in constant battle with the physical conditions of its chosen location. New Orleans' unfathomable proximity to water and natural systems, as well as vulnerable man-made water management infrastructure, reminds us of the many threats and opportunities that lie within this negotiated existence. Its topography, much unnoticed until Hurricane Katrina, has provoked both ingenuity and hazardous decision making, leading to the implementation of successful protective measures as well as strategies for resilience.

Building on the rich history of the city's water management infrastructure, DATAField draws its inspiration from the desire to establish a connection between the city's subtle yet life-defining topography and its intricate system of pumping stations, essential to the continued existence of the city within its current footprint. Using parametric modeling software as a means of generating the geometry, a network of macro and micro points is established based on the relationships between pumping stations and their respective capacities. Linking these points to a sectional representation of the topography establishes a visible network of nodes visualizing the underlying water management system and creating a three-dimensional map of the city.

PRODUCTION NOTES

Architect:	Marcella Del Signore Cordula Roser Gray
Client:	Sewerage and Water Board of New Orleans; Arts Council New Orleans
Status:	under construction
Location:	New Orleans
Date:	2017

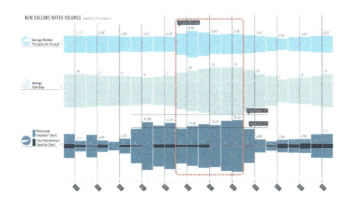

2 New Orleans water volumes

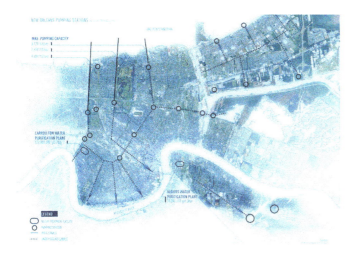

3 New Orleans pumping stations

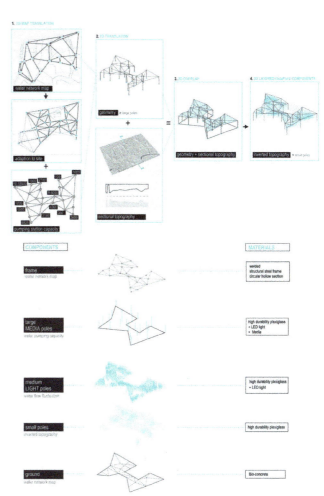

4 Generative process (3D water network map): Spatial components/materials

Design Strategy

DATAField consists of a dense field of data poles overlaid over an abstracted map of the New Orleans drainage network. Two different categories of poles are placed to index varying data streams in relation to water management activities. The larger macro poles, steel poles clad in translucent plastic, are placed in direct conjunction with pumping station locations, providing general user and systems capacity information. In support a field of medium poles record frequency and intensity of pumping activity at several New Orleans pumping stations referencing real-life data. The experience is completed by densifying the field through the addition of translucent tubes, alluding to the configuration of the water network and framing the pedestrian pathway leading through the space.

Media/Responsive Strategy

The large macro poles respond to real-time data (water pumped from pumping stations) and real-time messages sent from apps (to raise awareness about water conservation, management and quality) displayed through fluid vertical LED text strips. In addition, the medium poles consist of vertical linear LED fixtures programmed through custom software connected to a light system manager, thus registering the overall water fluctuation in the city and translating it through light intensity; as soon as the water flow at a pumping station changes, an immediate response is displayed through a change in color in the LED poles.

The urban intervention becomes a real-time map of the dynamic water conditions of the city, always experienced differently according to the input received. Citizens become the primary actors in the construction of the collective/public experience of space.

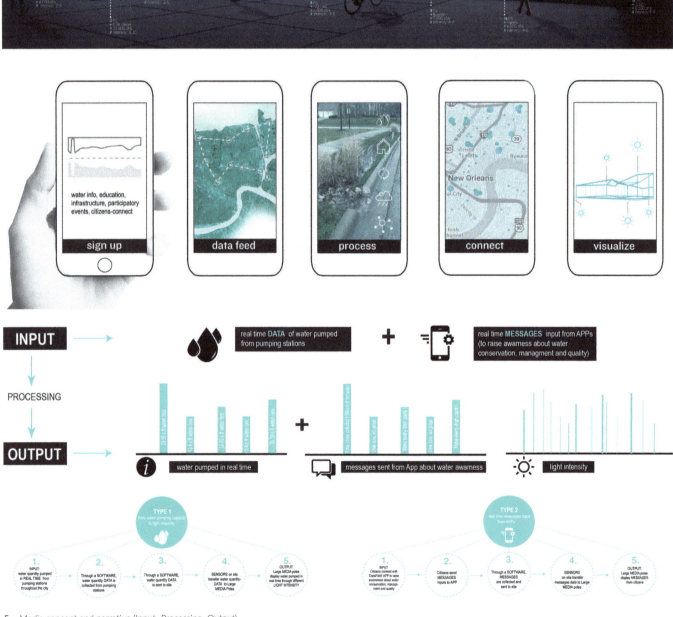

5 Media concept and narrative (Input–Processing–Output)

6　View from the Lafitte Corridor

7　View through the Lafitte Corridor towards Broad Street

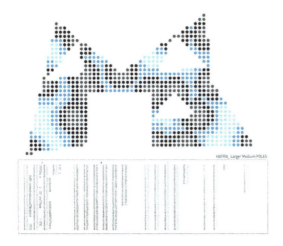

8　Components: Poles/gradient map

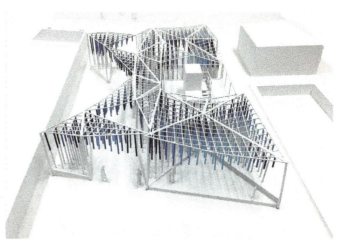

9　Arial view: Model photo

DATAField is designed to raise awareness of the water network of the city of New Orleans, making it visible to draw the general community towards water-related issues. The intervention aims to establish a platform for citizens to share and communicate the challenges and opportunities that New Orleans faces in living with water.

ACKNOWLEDGMENTS

Design Team: Marcella Del Signore, Cordula Roser Gray, Christian Ardeneaux.

Support and Sponsorship: Sewerage and Water Board of New Orleans; Arts Council New Orleans.

Marcella Del Signore is an Associate Professor at the New York Institute of Technology (NYIT), School of Architecture and Design. She is the principal of X-Topia, a design-research practice that explores the intersection of architecture and urbanism with digital processes. She holds a Master in Architecture from University La Sapienza in Rome and a Master of Science in Advanced Architectural Design from Columbia University in New York.

Her work concentrates on the relationship between architecture and urbanism by leveraging emerging technologies to imagine scenarios for future environments and cities. The notion of urban-digital prototyping has been at the core of her research. She currently serves on the Board of Directors of ACADIA (Association for Computer Aided Design in Architecture).

She taught and collaborated with academic institutions in Europe and USA including Tulane University, Barnard College at Columbia University, the Architectural Association, IaaC (Institute of Advanced Architecture of Catalonia), University of Waterloo, LSU School of Architecture, IN/ARCH- National Italian Institute of Architecture and University of Trento.

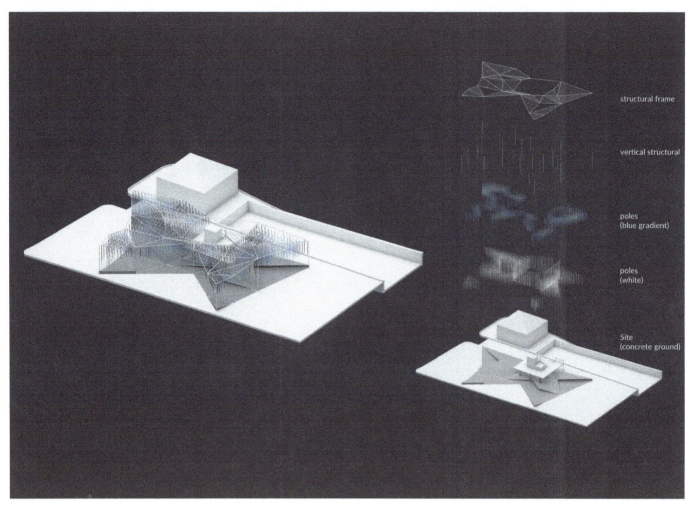

structural frame

vertical structural

poles
(blue gradient)

poles
(white)

Site
(concrete ground)

10 Exploded Axon: Layering of the spatial components

At Tulane University, she was the Director of the Study Abroad Program in Rome and in 2016 she was appointed as the Kylene and Brad Beers SE Professor at the Taylor Center for Social Innovation and Design Thinking. She has received several awards and lectured, published and exhibited widely.

Cordula Roser Gray is the principal of crgarchitecture, a multidisciplinary design firm based in New Orleans. With previous experiences abroad and in New York, the firm focuses on the development of proposals that address economic, ecological and cultural aspects at the community scale, from the single family residential to urban community and regional master planning scale.

Crgarchitecture, in conjunction with other local practitioners and organizations, investigates multi-scalar responses to immediate contextual conditions, merging urban analysis, planning and academic research with the challenges of identifying and connecting local and extended communal opportunities.

Ms. Roser Gray is an appointed Professor of Practice at the Tulane School of Architecture and a frequent team member of the Small Center for Collaborative Design.

11 1:1 full-scale prototype of 3D spatial module

12 Zoom-in: 1:1 full-scale prototype of 3D spatial module

IM_RU

Shelby Elizabeth Doyle
Iowa State University

Erin Linsey Hunt
Iowa State University

1   IM_RU completed in the ISU Computation & Construction Lab.

Pavilions simultaneously create tools for transformative action and develop visions of new social realities. Festivals as sites, and pavilions as fragments of possible architectural futures, serve as a method for advancing and expanding the possibilities of public engagement, critique, and speculation. The IM_RU pavilion is presented as evidence of this claim. By blurring light, color, and a cloud of fragmented reflections, the pavilion created a space to confront the identity politics and activist undercurrents of the Flyover Fashion Festival in Iowa City, Iowa,

IM_RU was designed and built by fifteen students majoring in architecture, landscape architecture, and interior design as part of an interdisciplinary undergraduate studio at Iowa State University. Constructed from low-cost 3D-printed joints, mirrored acrylic, wires, and LEDs, the pavilion was designed using computational methods to be structurally flexible, simple to assemble, and lightweight for transport. The project was constructed in the ISU studios, deconstructed, and then transported 130 miles (210 km) and reassembled at the festival. IM_RU was a project of the ISU Computation & Construction Lab (CCL), a research group established to connect developments in computation to the challenges of construction and to leverage these tools for public engagement with non-profits and cities.

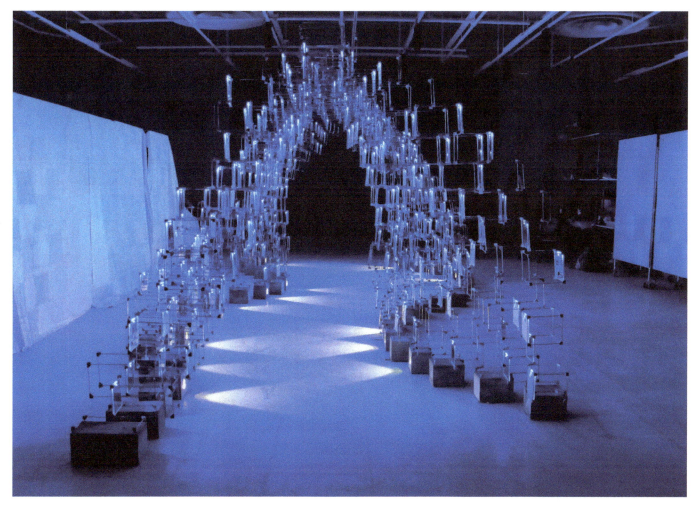

2   IM_RU completed in the ISU Computation & Construction Lab.

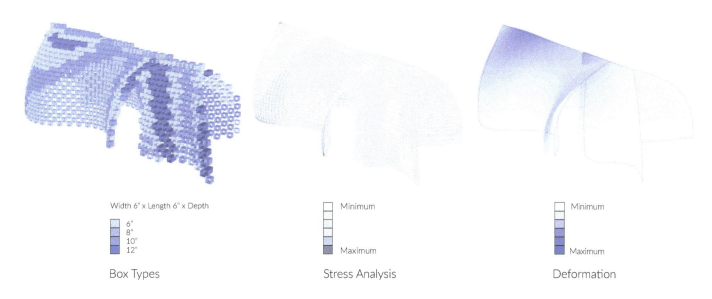

Width 6" x Length 6" x Depth

☐ 6"
☐ 8"
☐ 10"
☐ 12"

Box Types

☐ Minimum
☐
☐
☐
☐ Maximum

Stress Analysis

☐ Minimum
☐
☐
☐
☐ Maximum

Deformation

3   The project model was constructed in Rhino using Grasshopper and analyzed with Karamba. The analysis results were then applied to the design and used to identify areas where deeper boxes were required to resist stress and reduce deformation. The resulting structure was materially flexible enough that deformations were not structurally problematic. Consequently, the final assembly did not directly reproduce the digital model.

4   IM_RU at the Flyover Fashion Festival, a fashion, music and ideas festival in downtown Iowa City. The programming consisted of a unique mix of runway events, in-depth conversations with fashion entrepreneurs and innovators, artist exhibitions, and musical performances. The festival is dedicated to showcasing Iowa fashion and creative talent by connecting Iowa's emerging fashion community to the world.

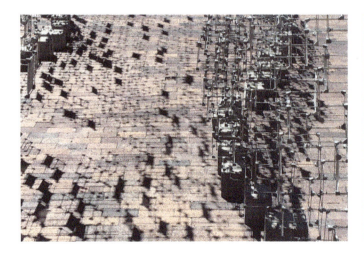

5   IM_RU mid-installation at the Flyover Fashion Festival. Events included clothing made from recycled materials and a panel discussion about the plus-size revolution in women's fashion.

6   The festival aimed to make design and fashion approachable and inclusive. Speakers included journalist Noor Tagouri, the first woman to wear a hijab in Playboy Magazine, who discussed how politics plays a role in modern fashion.

7   IM_RU at the Flyover Fashion Festival. Flyover is typically a term used pejoratively or defensively, however, the festival claims this space as an asset. Flyover refers to the interior regions of the country passed over during transcontinental flights, particularly flights between the nation's two most populous urban agglomerations, the Northeastern Megalopolis and Southern California. Iowa is often considered a "flyover state," referring to the part of the country that some Americans only view by air and never actually see in person at ground level.

Through transparency, form, and light, IM_RU challenges users with reflections of their incomplete selves and considers the role of the individual in the summation of societal identity. The project, sited at the Flyover Fashion Festival in Iowa City, is an inhabited passageway of 500 mirrored surfaces arranged in a dissolving, voxel grid. The IM_RU Pavilion's name is short-hand for the dialogue users unconsciously encounter between their perception of reality and others' reality: "I am... are you?" An individual's reality is inescapably subjective, and is there-fore embedded with "I am" statements. In this way, we utilize ourselves as reference points. In our increasingly digital world, humans perceive and engage with the environment through a selectively fabricated lens. Our perceptions of ourselves, and our perceptions of the world, although perhaps convinc-ingly accurate, are subjective, and therefore certainly include counterfeit realities. Ultimately, the IM_RU Pavilion presents architecture and public space where an individual is simultane-ously confronted with a multiplicity of individual and collective

perceptions. By exploding and scattering what is seen, IM_RU prevents passersby from using themselves as reference points. All reflections become deconstructed units of the collective, and each fragment becomes lost in the nonhierarchical sea of other fragments. In a seamless mirror's reflection, one perceives one's self as the foreground and the key reference point by which everything else in the reflection is understood. With IM_RU, indi-vidual perceptions of reality are realized amongst one another as amalgamated and equally subjective fragments of the collective.

A student team proposed the design and manufactured the tools to enable its construction. The project relied upon a para-metric model that allowed the interdisciplinary group of fifteen students to collaboratively design and then fabricate and build the project directly from the digital model, without producing allographic drawings. Manufacturing relied almost entirely upon 3,200 low cost ($0.18 each) 3D-printed PLA joints fabricated with four Dremel 3D20 Printers ($800). By focusing on low-cost

8   The IM_RU Pavilion presents architecture and public space, where an individual is simultaneously confronted with a multiplicity of individual and collective perceptions.

9   IM_RU at the ISU Computation & Construction Lab.

10 The project relied upon low-cost PLA joints fabricated quickly on four low-cost ($800) Dremel 3D printers: 18 cents per joint and 14.25 minutes to print. All materials for the project totaled $4,200. In doing so, this project also challenges the expected costs of built computational projects, a parameter that often keeps these technologies cloistered in specific institutions and communities.

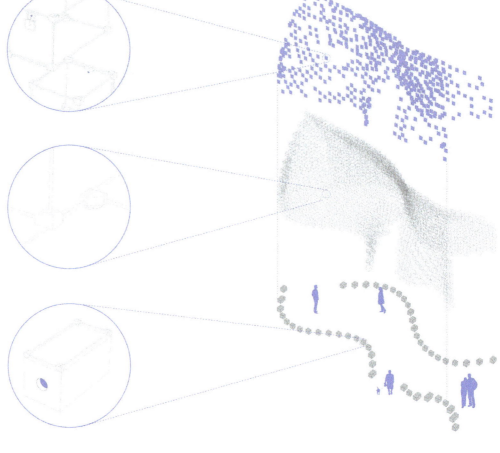

11 The final joint design was a truncated triangular joint designed to reduce material use and printing time. The PLA was most brittle at the connection point to the wire; therefore, material was added to the side of the clip to strengthen the assembly detail. .

Final ← ——————————————————————————————————————— → First

12 The project under construction at the ISU Computation & Construction Lab. IM_RU was a project of the ISU Computation & Construction Lab (CCL), a research group established to connect developments in computation to the challenges of construction and to leverage these tools for public engagement with non-profits and small towns. (Paul Gates Photography, 2017 ©).

technologies, the design team was able to introduce to a public audience a fabrication method (3D-printed plastic) that is often relegated to representational models rather than full-scale construction. In doing so, this project also challenges the expected costs of built computational projects, a parameter that often keeps these technologies cloistered in specific institutions and communities.

Online

Videos and additional information can be found at: *ccl.design.iastate.edu*

Students

[*Architecture*] Joshua Cobler, Austin Demers, Erin Hunt, Jaehee Hwang, Lingchen Liao, Kale Paulsen

[*Interior Design*] Alexa Barr, Cassie Cook, Brooklyn Fenchel, Jenna Strasser, Joelle Swanson

[*Landscape Architecture*] Nick Dentamaro, Maria Novacek, Jake Oswald, Billy Pausback

ACKNOWLEDGMENTS

Primary funding for the studio was provided the Stan G. Thurston Professorship in Design Build. Additional support provided by the Iowa State University College of Design, the Iowa State University Department of Architecture, ISU Office of the Vice Provost for Research, and the Flyover Fashion Festival.

Shelby Elizabeth Doyle, AIA is an Assistant Professor of Architecture and Daniel J. Huberty Faculty Fellow at the Iowa State University College of Design. Her scholarship is broadly focused on the intersection of computation and construction and specifically on the role of digital craft as both a social and political project. Doyle was hired under the ISU President's High Impact Hires Initiative to combine digital fabrication and design/build at ISU. This led to the founding of the ISU Computation & Construction Lab with Nick Senske and Leslie Forehand. She holds a Master of Architecture degree from the Harvard Graduate School of Design and a Bachelor of Science in Architecture from the University of Virginia.

Ownership/Authorship In Three-Dimensional Photographic Reproductions

Wendy W Fok
Parsons SDS/ WE-DESIGNS

Michael Koehle
Autodesk Pier 9

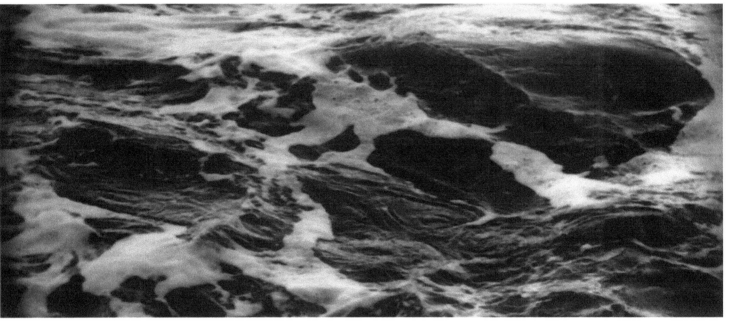

1   Detail of Wave CT scan of the relief from figure 2. (Scanned by Michael Koehle, 2016, © Michael Koehle).

Photopolymerization Additive Manufacturing

With the advent of digital technologies proliferating in the additive manufacturing industry, our research-based exploration offers rigor to questions about the ability to generate creative inquiry into its processes, and innovate alternative design methodologies that challenge the traditional means of reproduction. In our case, we look to challenge and compare traditional photographic reproduction inquiry through the use of modernized tooling.

As an interdisciplinary applied research project, our collaborative (architectural and design engineering) approach to the project questions the use of photopolymerization as a tool of digital and physical discovery. We look to generate a dialogue that brings out the integral playfulness in digital craft and the embedded material agency of resin-based additive manufacturing. Through both single and multi-material additive printing explorations and visual forming processes, we questioning the novelty of intellectual property and creative license in the reproduction of digital goods.

Within the next phase of research development, we are interested in the socially and culturally beneficial aspects of merging the abilities of digital production with artful reproduction. We would like to ask whether the technology and methods of producing through additive printing adds value to the art world, and seek to increase the tactile function of art exploration to communities that are visually impaired and blind.

PRODUCTION NOTES

Researchers: Wendy W Fok & Michael Koehle

Machines: Object Connex (Stratasys, MN)

Status: Work in Progress

Production Facility: Autodesk Pier 9

Location: San Francisco, CA, USA

Date: 2016

2   3D-printed height map relief developed from a photograph. (Photo by Michael Koehle, 2016, © Michael Koehle).

3   3D-printed relief from figure 2 printed in grayscale. (Photo by Michael Koehle, 2016, © Michael Koehle).

4   Simulated view of a relief with .25 inch depth (above) / 10 feet depth (below) (Render by Michael Koehle, 2016, © Michael Koehle).

The exploration of material agency in photopolymerization that treats public domain imagery occurs on newly found territory that raises intellectual property rights issues surrounding photographic works. Legally, photography tends to be protected by the law through copyright and moral rights. In copyright law, photographers and creators retain the rights and ownership of photographic works. The attribution of moral rights applies both to anonymous and pseudonymous creations. These are solely the permissible rights of creators in their copyrighted works, generally recognized in civil law jurisdictions and, to a lesser extent, in some common law jurisdictions. Therefore, the experimentation enabled through our research challenges the circumstances that adjudicate systematic processes of design and law, humans and machines, and physical and digital fabrication processes. Through the transference of material and the collaboration of human and machine digital fabrication methods, we investigate photopolymerization, using both single and multi-material agencies to look into composite forming processes that inherently absorb embedded responsiveness, both in visual and material effects.

This new form of additive manufacturing through the production of photographic works lends a questionable hand to leading research that questions the legality of digital reproduction—and also ownership and authorship rights—through largely creative exploration and research that extends beyond the originality of the photographic piece, lending to access within the public domain. We look into the craft of digital fabrication processes that also hold to reproduction as much as to exploration.

Processes of Research

A seldom explored application of additive manufacturing is in the reproduction of two-dimensional images. The resolution of some technologies, like photopolymerization, is comparable to 2D printers, making it possible to recreate images with similar fidelity. However, these technologies typically lack the capacity to mix shades or colors. Or, if this capability exists, it is limited and difficult to apply. But by taking advantage of the third axis, these images can still be reproduced.

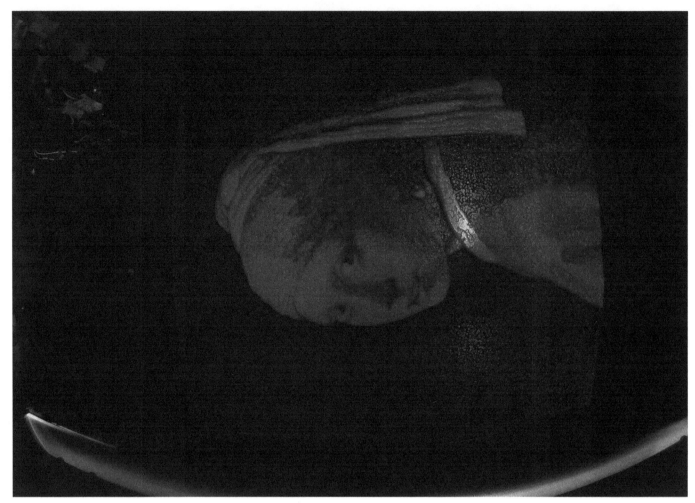

5   Video time lapse of the printing of Girl with a Pearl Earring. (Video Screenshot by Michael Koehle, 2016, © Michael Koehle).

Following are descriptions of two techniques that take advantage of the third dimension to reproduce two-dimensional images.

Images can be reproduced in three-dimensions by translating the image into a relief whose top surface is a height map of the image. The height of the relief scales with the intensity of the image (Figure 2). The grayscale information is now present in the object, but is not immediately visually accessible.

In a second technique, the grayscale is printed into the image relief using multi-material photopolymerization. The relief's digital model is sliced horizontally into layers, where each layer is assigned a mixture of black and white materials. The models shown in Figures 3 and 6 were created by using 8 mixtures of TangoBlackPlus and VeroWhite.

Future of 3D Reproductive Ownership
With the renaissance in technological explorations of the machine and the possibilities of the next phases of use for this

project, we are looking to further the creative techniques for reproducing photographs as three-dimensional reliefs, using additive manufacturing processes. Although photographic images are the source of these reliefs, these reproductions change the way the content is viewed. Because the image now has physical depth, the apprehension of the image becomes conditional and changes as one moves around the work.

Additionally, new ways of decoding the image are possible, including touch and medical imaging technologies like x-rays. These changes and additions to the perception of the image raise interesting questions about the ownership and authorship of the content.

ACKNOWLEDGMENTS
This body of research and collaboration between Wendy W Fok and Michael Koehle would not have been made possible without the generous support of Autodesk and Pier 9, in making available facilities,

6 3D-printed grayscale height map of the Mona Lisa (Photo by Michael Koehle, 2016, © Michael Koehle).

machines, and the gracious support staff and administrators, such as Carl Bass, Vanessa Sigurdson, and Noah Weinstein. Additional research and theoretical mentorship is provided by Prof. Antoine Picon and Prof. Martin Bechthold of the Harvard Graduate School of Design, and Prof. William "Terry" Fisher of the Harvard Law School and Berkman Center. Wendy W Fok would also like to thank the Library of Congress John W. Kluge Center.

ANNEX

(Figure 1) Accessing the visual content or the reliefs requires a process that senses depth. X-rays can transverse materials opaque to light. Their penetration attenuates with depth. By taking an x-ray or CT scan, the image can be decoded from the solid model (Figure 2). The image can also be decoded by touch. Using a CMM device (a coordinate measuring machine), the spatial information of the relief could be obtained and translated back to a grayscale image.

(Figure 5) Video time lapse of the printing of Girl with a Pearl Earring. Video Link: https://vimeo.com/166255734 (Michael Koehle and Wendy W Fok, 2016)

Wendy W Fok, trained as an architect, is the creative director/founder of WE-DESIGNS, LLC (Architecture/Creative Strategy), and an Assistant Professor of Integrated Design at Parsons School of Design. She is featured as Autodesk Remake's list of 25 Women in Reality Computing (2017), Young CAADRIA Award (2015), Digital Kluge Fellowship awarded by the Library of Congress (2014/15), et al. Fok is completing her Doctor of Design at Harvard's GSD. She has a Master of Architecture and Certification of Urban Policy/Planning from Princeton University, and a Bachelor of Arts in Architecture with a Concentration in Economics (Statistics) from Barnard College, Columbia University.

Michael Koehle received his BA in Art Practice at UC Berkeley, his MS in Biomedical Engineering at UC Davis, and his MFA in studio art from Mills College. He has received the Headlands Center for the Arts Graduate Fellowship, the Murphy Cadogan Fellowship, and most recently was an artist in residence at Autodesk's Pier 9. Koehle lives and works in Oakland.

Architecture Challenge 2016 "Robotic Contouring"

Andrei Gheorghe
University of Applied Arts Vienna, IoA

Robert Vierlinger
Bollinger + Grohmann Engineers

Philipp Hornung
University of Applied Arts, RWC Lab

Manora Auersperg
Die Angewandte, Textiles Gestalten

Sigurd Reiss
Clever Contour GMBH

1   Robotic Contouring, final structure, upward view

This project investigates the development of three-dimensional profile folding without the use of expensive formwork. A robotic workflow is employed to achieve the production of a highly intricate spatial installation in a fast and efficient fashion. Parametric computation was applied to design the overall configuration towards the detailing and fabrication setup.

The "Robotic Contouring" project was conducted as part of the Architecture Challenge 2016 summer school at the University of Applied Arts in Vienna, in collaboration with Clever Contour GMBH and Bollinger + Grohmann Engineers. The workshop was intended for students interested in exploring digital design and fabrication while simultaneously designing a full-scale built project following an integrated, multidisciplinary process. The workshop was enriched with robotic design strategies combining Grasshopper plugins such as the KUKA|prc and Karamba platforms.

Formally, the project introduces an idea of spatial frames with a high degree of freedom, bending and twisting in space. Applying finite element analysis, a bundling system is used to develop a vertical structure made of light plastic profiles. Textile surfaces were produced with the support of the Department of Textiles Gestalten out of linear elements, creating different spatial and surface effects.

The bundling system is able to produce a continuous structural behavior from two-meter-long 3 x

PRODUCTION NOTES

Status: Design/Build
Site Area: 3 x 3 x 5.5 m
Location: Vienna, Austria
Date: 2016

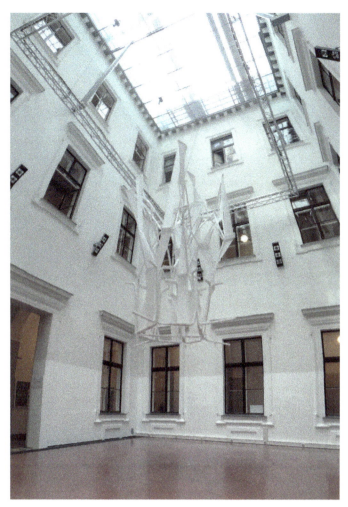

3 Final structure with textile surfaces

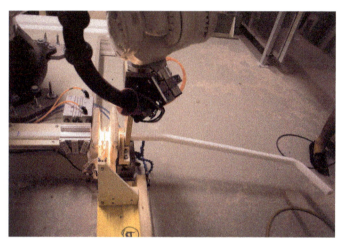

2 Final lightweight structure, suspended

4 Heating process with IR heater ring

3 cm polyethylene plastic profiles. With connections in multiple directions, the structure achieves a height of approximately 5.5 meters. The organization of material and orientation of components were defined with the constant and real-time feedback of the Grasshopper/Karamba structural analysis. Experts from Bollinger + Grohmann Engineers supported the structural optimization process. Design options were tested and improved involving the multi-criteria design optimization tool Octopus, until a maximum displacement of 40 mm (under gravity load) and a material utilization of 40% was achieved.

Rationalization of the overall form fed the fabrication system, creating a seamless flow from design to materialization. The geometry was translated into robotic production through KUKA|prc with the help of specialists from the RWC Lab at die Angewandte, allowing the simulation and pre-visualization of each component. The construction setup was developed and optimized using a continuous digital design chain towards full-scale production. The robot setup is based on a new fabrication

method developed and patented by Clever Contour GMBH in Vienna for earlier research, conducted with the support of the Austrian Research Promotion Agency. All pieces were fabricated using an automatic production pipeline involving a KUKA robot arm with an IR heater ring to soften the material before bending and an air cooling system to harden the material after the bending process. The process involves the following steps: (1) robot end effectors grab the plastic profile; (2) the profile is pulled by the robot to the exact position for the first bend; (3) the ground grippers nos. 1+2 fix the profile; (4) the IR ring heats up for about 3 minutes; (5) ground gripper no. 2 releases; (6) the robot bends the softened material three dimensionally; and (7) holds it in space until the air cooling solidifies the material and the whole process is repeated for the next bend.

An intense testing phase was required to define the optimal heating time to sufficiently soften the plastic material so that the end effectors of the robot can first apply the bending movement, and then solidify the material by air blasting to achieve enough

5   Final structure

Robotic Contouring Gheorghe, Vierlinger, Hornung, Auersperg, Reiss

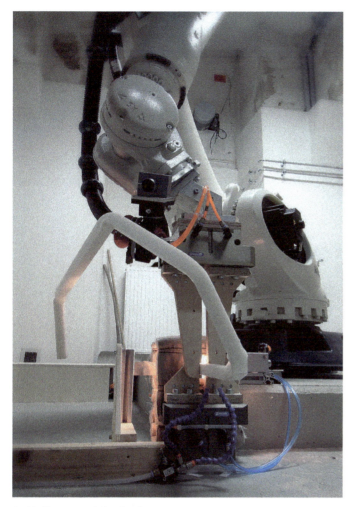

6   Heating process before bending

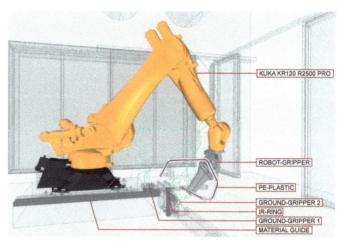

7   Robot setup

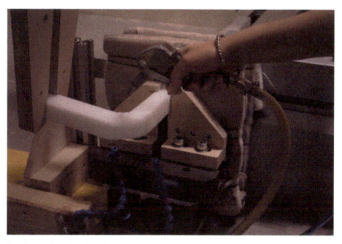

8   Air cooling after bending

stiffness for the subsequent pulling process. These parameters had to be calibrated according to material constraints, as a thicker/thinner member or a different type of plastic would require time adjustments. The whole process, including pulling, heating, and cooling, requires about 8 minutes per bend, therefore each structural member with 3 bends could be produced in about 30 minutes.

Future research attempts to incorporate hole drilling for element-to-element connection in the fully automated setup. This would remove the need for human-applied clamps for fixation; instead, the pieces could be directly attached and screwed to each other.

Aligned with the aim of the conference, this project envisions novel design methods by developing a new workflow for the production of plastic members, and hereby introducing a new, innovative way of creating freeform geometries. This entirely digital construction process attempts to create a direct link between virtual freeform design and physical full-scale geometrical creation.

www.2016.architecturechallenge.org

ACKNOWLEDGMENTS

Clever Contour GMBH, Bollinger + Grohmann Engineers, University of Applied Arts "die Angewandte" Vienna, Institute of Architecture, RWC Lab, Textiles Gestalten

Instructors

Andrei Gheorghe (Universität für Angewandte Kunst Wien, IoA), Manora Auersperg (Universität für Angewandte Kunst, Textiles Gestalten), Robert Vierlinger (Bollinger + Grohmann Ingenieure), Philipp Hornung (Universität für Angewandte Kunst, RWC Lab), Sigurd Reiss (Clever Contour GMBH)

Students

Zvonko Vugreshek, Hristina Kamenova, Jan Kováříček, Cristina Costea,

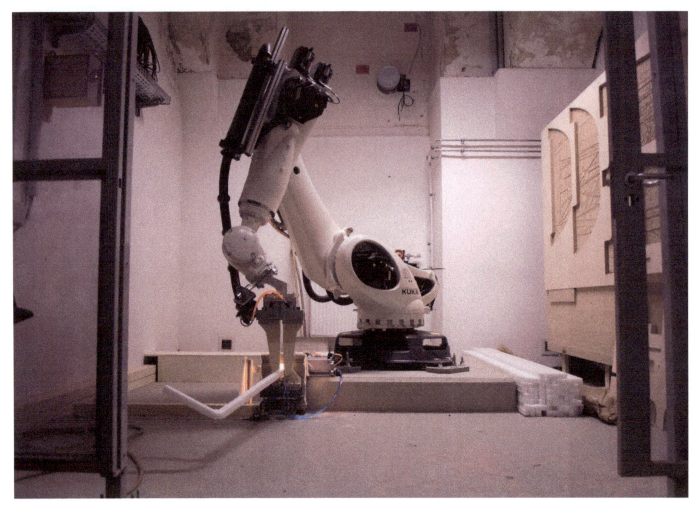

9   Robot setup

Ondřej Pokoj, Nicolas Stephan, Judyta Cichocka, Krzysztof Nazar, Victor Sardenberg, Alec Singh , Reem Alkaisy, Tony Guedes, Ioana Mladin, Carmen Mladin, Izabela Kowalska, Jonathan Paljor

REFERENCES

Steiner, F., F. Bleicher, and R. Vierlinger. 2016. "Software and Design Concept For a Thermoplastic Bending Process in the Application Architecture." In *Proceedings of THE 33rd Danubia-Adria Symposium on Advances in Experimental Mechanics*. Portoroz, Slovenia: DANUBIA.

IMAGE CREDITS

Angewandte Architecture Challenge 2016

Andrei Gheorghe is currently teaching as an Assistant Professor at the Institute of Architecture / University of Applied Arts in Vienna. Previously he was Assistant Professor at Portland State University, USA, where he developed pedagogy and research in digital media and fabrication. He studied at the Academy of Fine Arts Vienna, and after being awarded the Fulbright Scholarship at Harvard University, he graduated with distinction and received the Harvard GSD Digital Design Prize. Andrei has taught at various institutions such as Academy of Fine Arts Vienna, SCI-ARC Los Angeles and Harvard Graduate School of Design (Career Discovery Program). Previously, he worked as an architect for international offices such as Jakob + MacFarlane, dEcoi Paris and Foreign Office Architects (FOA) London.

Robert Vierlinger is a researching engineer and interdisciplinary consultant. Working on his PhD at the University of Applied Arts Vienna, he investigates digital representations and evolutionary design strategies. Robert develops the plug-ins Octopus and Octopus.e for Grasshopper, and is also involved in the development of Karamba. Parametric engineering and optimizations for international competitions and construction projects are the basis of his consultancy at Bollinger-Grohmann engineers. He studied structural design at TU Delft and TU Vienna, studied at Studio Hani Rashid Vienna, led workshops in Germany, England, Denmark, Hongkong and Austria, and teaches at Studio Zaha Hadid Vienna.

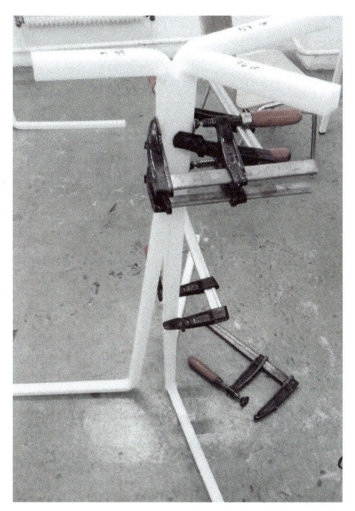

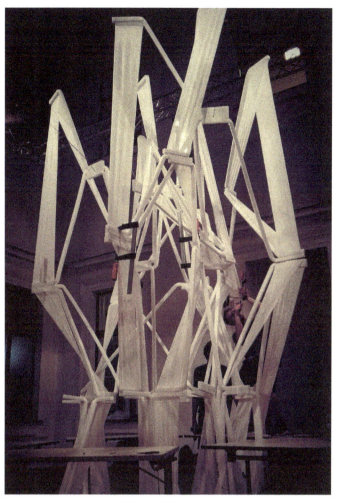

10 Assembly process of modules

11 Assembly process and textile fixation

Philipp Hornung studied architecture at the Georg-Simon-Ohm University in Nuremberg and the University of Applied Arts in Vienna at the master class of Zaha Hadid, Greg Lynn and Wolf Prix, where he received his degree with distinction. He gained experience at numerous internationally renowned architectural design offices such as Graft Architects and Coop Himmelb(l)au. Since 2014 he has been a research assistant at the "Robotic Woodcraft" research project at the University of Applied Arts in Vienna. His expertise is in the fields of parametric design and robotic fabrication.

Manora Auersperg is an artist and lecturer at the Department of Textiles – Free, Applied and Experimental Artistic Design, at the Institute of Art Sciences and Art Education, University of Applied Arts Vienna, since 2004. She studied Textile and Art Education in Vienna and Stage Costume Design in Berlin. With a thesis on the directed gaze—the relation between object, media and subject, she received her Master's degree. Her profession as Lecturer and her own artistic work are closely entwined. Interconnecting theory and practice, her artistic seminar

„Fläche/ Körper/ Raum" refers to the subject of the human body in relation to the spatial and social context.

Sigurd Reiss studied mechatronics/robotics before joining Clever Contour, where he became CTO and project manager. Clever Contour GmbH is a research and development company in the third and last year of grant-aided R&D. The outcome of these developments is a novel manufacturing technology to create freeform elements out of individual bent semifinished plastic products without mold/formwork construction. The core of this technology is a patented bending system for the thermoplastic deformation of plastic strands in all degrees of freedom to realize freeform construction at a large scale. This technology, in combination with a specific developed software plugin for Rhino/Grasshopper, closes the process chain between design, manufacturing and end product. The manufacturing technology enables Clever Contour to realize individual freeforms in full scale up to two-thirds cheaper than using common manufacturing methods.

CONCRETE LATTICE
Unitized Architecture of Assembly

Ryan Goold
University of Michigan

Daniel Fougere
University of Michigan

Tsz Yan Ng
University of Michigan

Wes McGee
University of Michigan

1   Final installation of Concrete Lattice structure at Taubman College Liberty Annex.

ABSTRACT

Concrete Lattice, produced for the graduate thesis studio Concrete Labor seeks to transform our understanding of this building typology by developing a system of prefabricated units using glass fiber reinforced concrete (GFRC). Lattice systems are porous, lightweight, and deployable; terms not typically associated with concrete structures, despite the material's economic advantages. This project alters that paradigm with a design of parametric units, rather than linear components (typical of lattice systems), and highlights issues of assembly in precast building systems.

Informed by a computational model that also dealt with the unit's aggregation into a system, the design evolved through a feedback loop between the computational design environment, fabrication tools, and physical prototypes. Our goal was to address the gap between design and production by exploring the development of complex lattice systems and by using digital design tools to streamline the production of units to be deployed on site. By utilizing the computational model as a live output and feedback loop for fabrication, this project attempts to integrate these techniques as part of the process for construction, not as an isolated moment divorced from the logistics of building.

PRODUCTION NOTES

Status: Completed
Site Area: 100 sq. ft.
Location: Ann Arbor, MI
Date: 2016

2 Casting units for the final construct: a schedule was determined through the code that allowed for both optimal output and economic use of jig parts.

3 Fabrication techniques included 3- and 5-axis CNC routing of wooden parts, CNC flat cutting of PETG, and 7-axis robotic bending of rebar to fit in the mold.

4 Inspiration from a precedent for concrete lattice structures: *Crease, Fold, Pour* (Kaczynski 2013)

5 3D-printed model of component parts to test tolerance, self-weight, and order of assembly at 1:6 scale.

Stemming from the work of Maciej Kaczynski, et al., in their project "Crease, Fold, Pour" (2013)—which used thin sheet plastics of polyethylene terephthalate glycol-modified (PETG) for formwork—this project utilized folding techniques at full scale to highlight both the formal aesthetics and structural performance of origami patterns. Our work moves away from Kaczynski's cast-in-place construct to working with a set of self-similar precast units as a comprehensive building system, capable of aggregating at various scales.

Many iterations of prototyping helped identify issues of material behavior in both PETG formwork and GFRC casts. An external adjustable jig was designed to both support the PETG during the casting process and ensure accuracy and precision across all unit types at joints.

The reconfigurable jig accounts for the various parameters of both the unit types and the overall lattice design. During assembly, the system was stacked in layers and the process made efficient by both post-tensioning in situ and vertical struts for leveling and support.

This project also takes cues from research in masonry compression-only systems explored by Philippe Block (Block and Ochsendorf 2008) and from variable-volume systems such as La Voûte de LaFevre by Matter Design (Clifford and McGee 2014). As precedents, these projects provided the framework to explore computational design processes where form is integrated with performance and optimized with material and structural considerations.

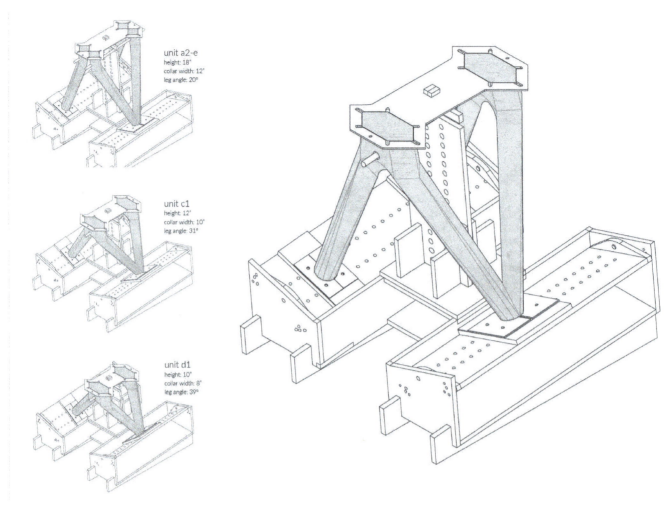

unit a2-e
height: 18"
collar width: 12"
leg angle: 20°

unit c1
height: 12"
collar width: 10"
leg angle: 31°

unit d1
height: 10"
collar width: 8"
leg angle: 39°

6   Axonometric of the PETG formwork design in the reconfigurable jig system.

7   In-progress installation view showing post-tensioning and vertical struts for leveling. Together, use of scaffolding was eliminated.

8   View displaying the adjustable jig and formwork set up for casting, under the lattice structure.

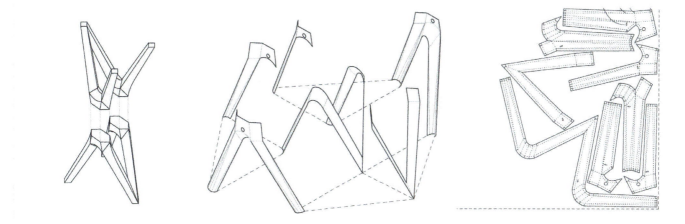

9 Lattice units split for casting, PETG parts assembled as the mold, and a cutsheet diagram for one unit: output from the computational model.

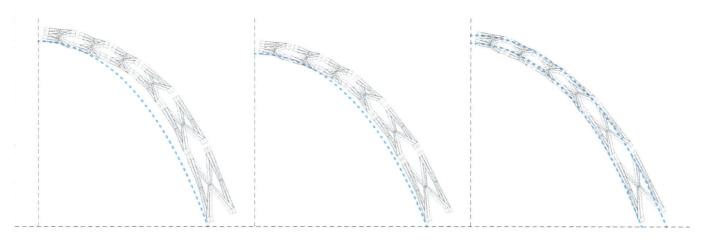

10 Structural studies of catenary curves, using Kangaroo to optimize the formal shape given the myriad parameters of the unit during iterations.

The geometric design of our lattice system explores part to whole assemblies derived from a diamond cellular structure. Catenary logic using Kangaroo, a physics-based plug-in for Grasshopper, informed the structural performance through interactive simulation and optimization of the variable units. Once tolerances and components were accounted for, the simulations revealed flaws in the overall form as the units were aggregated into place. Therefore, the various parameters were adjusted slightly and the computational model was optimized structurally before the final output of parts.

By implementing complexity and intelligence, this project advocates for computational design in both informing design decisions and managing the myriad contingencies involved in the production of a novel architecture. Concrete Lattice makes the role of digital technology explicit in the integration of design, engineering, and building, and challenges our normative association with the use of concrete as a building material.

Through the integration of R+D, crafting, and construction as a discursive process for experimentation, the outcome not only highlights the value of full-scale making for design studio learning, but also demonstrates that the academic setting can promote innovation to disrupt disciplinary conventions in material forming, building systems, and processes for construction.

ACKNOWLEDGMENTS
Concrete Labor was taught by Assistant Professor Tsn Yan Ng during the academic year 2015-2016. This thesis section was linked with the course Advanced Digital Fabrication taught by Assistant Professor Wes McGee. We want to acknowledge the aupport and guidance from their joint teaching. We also want to thank Taubman College of Architecture + Urban Planning, for the opportunity to realize this project, especially the support of the program chair, Sharon Haar. We also appreciate the fabrication support from Dustin Brugmann and Asa Peller at the FabLab.

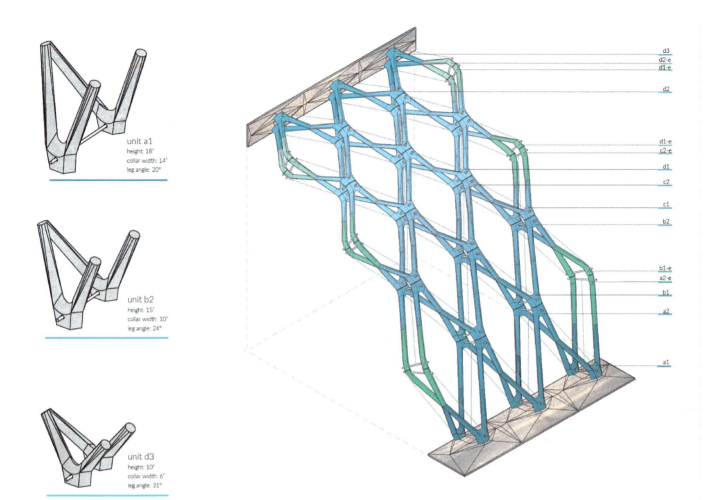

unit a1
height: 18"
collar width: 14"
leg angle: 20°

unit b2
height: 15"
collar width: 10"
leg angle: 24°

unit d3
height: 10"
collar width: 6"
leg angle: 31°

d3
d2-e
d1-e
d2
d1-e
c2-e
d1
c2
c1
b2
b1-e
a2-e
b1
a2
a1

11 Axonometric view of the Concrete Lattice organized by unit type with examples of variations.

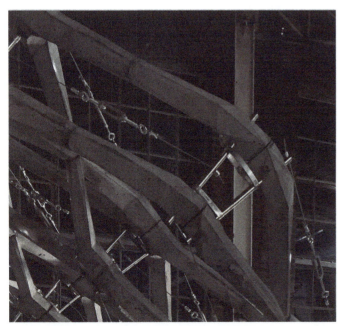

12 Side view showing the integral pipe, compressive node, and cable structure.

13 Detail view of the integrated post-tensioning connection.

Concrete Lattice Goold, Fougere, Ng, McGee

14 View under vault looking up at the lattice structure showing the compression- only connection at the wall and the network of post-tensioning cables.

15 Axonometric diagrams of the lattice system assembled as a full vault highlighting components, from post-tensioning to flexible skin.

REFERENCES

Block, Philippe, and John Ochsendorf. 2008. "Lower-Bound Analysis of Unreinforced Masonry Vaults." In *Proceedings of the VI International Conference on Structural Analysis of Historic Construction*, edited by Dina d'Ayala and Enrico Fodde, 593–600. Bath, UK: SAHC.

Kaczynski, Maciej P. 2013. "Crease, Fold, Pour: Rethinking Flexible Formwork with Digital Fabrication and Origami Folding." In *Adaptive Architecture: Proceedings of the 33rd Annual Conference of the Association for Computer Aided Design in Architecture*, edited by Philip Beesley, Omar Khan, and Michael Stacey, 419–20. Cambridge, ON: ACADIA.

Ryan Goold recently finished his Master's of Architecture degree at Taubman College and has several years of experience in professional practice. His background in construction also contributes to his interests in the intersection between design and production and in working hands-on with materials and parametric software.

Daniel Fougere is currently a designer at W.PA in Portland, Oregon and recently completed his Master's of Architecture degree at Taubman College. With his interests in research and digital fabrication, he strives to advance the way we design and produce the built environment.

Tsz Yan Ng is an Assistant Professor in Architecture at Taubman College. She was the Walter B. Sanders Fellow at the University of Michigan (2007-08) and the Reyner Banham Fellow at the University of Buffalo (2001-02). Ng's practice includes architectural designs and installations in visual art. Common to both practices are projects that deal with questions of labor in its various manifestations, with special focus on techniques in clothing manufacturing and concrete forming. Her design work has been exhibited in both solo and group exhibitions in Detroit, Los Angeles, Ann Arbor, Montréal, Ithaca, and Buffalo.

Wes McGee is an Assistant Professor and the Director of the FABLab at the University of MichiganTaubman College of Architecture and Urban Planning. His work revolves around the interrogation of the means and methods of material production in the digital era, through research focused on developing new connections between design, engineering, materials, and manufacturing processes as they relate to the built environment.

String Section

John Granzow
University of Michigan

Catie Newell
University of Michigan

Kim Harty
College for Creative Studies

1   Suspended speakers hold piano wire in tension forming a positive feedback loop (Catie Newell, © 2017).

FEEDBACK SYSTEM

String Section is an installation of long wires deployed as both a means of acoustic excitation and the simplest analog measure of an architectural distance. The work consists of an array of speakers suspended from resonant wires that span the vertical dimension of their enclosing room. These speakers (Figure 1) both excite and amplify the strings from which they are suspended, generating recirculating feedback signals. The system also amplifies and unfolds vibrations in the materials of the building. The result is a positive feedback loop whose behavior is influenced by the dimensions of the space, ambient vibrations in the materials of the edifice, gauge and tension of the string, as well as the division of the string via custom-made bridges (Figure 5). These bridges deform under the tension of the string and house the surface microphones that are fed back into the speakers (Figure 8).

This feedback system accumulates material vibrations and draws our attention to architectural sounds that are often considered symptomatic of poor design or entropy. Diachronic creaks and groans from the architectural site are recirculated and grow into synchronic masses of noise. Prolonging and accumulating these sounds brings them into our field of attention, awakening them from what Christoph Cox (2009) calls the "sonic unconscious."

PRODUCTION NOTES

Status: ongoing
Location: varies
Date: 2017

2   Custom automated pluckers (Catie Newell, © 2017).

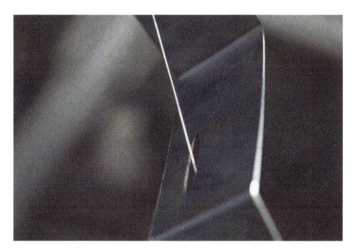

3   Wire passes through custom bridges (Catie Newell, © 2017).

4   Spatial array of 8 speakers. (Catie Newell, © 2017).

Audio feedback is an established method in sound-based installation work to foreground the spatial dimension of sound (Saladin 2017). Our engagement with architectural features to influence this system is redolent of Alvin Lucier's use of room modes to transform his voice, or Agostino Di Scipio's work, which uses such resonances to condition his interactive compositions (Anderson 2005). String Section presents a similar engagement with architectural sounds as inputs to a feedback system. However, rather than using the air modes of the room, structural vibrations in the building are amplified and added to the input. These sound sources are already present in the materials of the building or they may arise from the wider environment (rain or passing train).

Positive feedback systems exhibit exponentially growing amplitudes that can cause damage to both speakers and ears. This feedback or Larsen effect typically arises from a microphone amplified through a loudspeaker and captured again by the same microphone, causing a screeching sound that grows to harmful levels. To both draw the listener in as well as to protect the ear

from this default state, digital signal processing is used to allow the sounds to grow and diminish in prolonged undulations. String Section uses the ChucK audio programming language for this feedback control.

Developed by Ge Wang and Perry Cook, ChucK allows for time-synchronous manipulations of digital audio and was conceived for musical performances through live coding (Wang 2008). For our purpose the language facilitates real-time processing of live microphones with relatively low I/O latency. Specifically, a unit generator in ChucK called Dyno is used to implement compressors, noise gates, duckers, and limiters, established processing methods used to shape audio feedback. The variables of Dyno are set to retain the core behavior of the system, amplifying and circulating structural vibrations through the string. The processing is deployed not as a transforming effect but a transparent control module that still allows the system to evoke the process of feedback and the transduction of the site's structural sounds.

5 Custom bridges intentionally deflect with the tension of the string (Catie Newell, © 2017).

String Section Granzow, Newell, Harty

6   Live performance with bows (Catie Newell, © 2017).

7   Live performance with electronic DJ (Catie Newell, © 2017).

8   Surface microphone (Catie Newell, © 2017).

String Section is a feedback system that gives rise to a continuous experience of otherwise disparate room sounds often attributed to negative processes like entropy. These sounds now constitute a recirculating stream. They are brought into the fold of a perceptual contour like the voice or music of the building itself. The work may even provoke imaginaries of the edifice as a protracted sonic envelope with a vast constructive attack, settling decay, enduring sustain and an eventual dilapidated release.

ACKNOWLEDGMENTS

This research has been supported by the Taubman College of Architecture and Urban Planning at the University of Michigan as well as the University of Michigan School of Music, Theater & Dance and the College for Creative Studies, Detroit, Michigan.

The project was funded by a Taubman College Research Through Making Grant.

Principal Investigators: Catie Newell (University of Michigan), John Granzow (University of Michigan) and Kim Harty. (College for Creative Studies).

Project team: Kelly Gregory, Isabelle Leysens, Drishti Haria, Austin Mitchell, Leith Campbell, Rebecca Fisher, Spencer Haney.

Live performers: Sile O'Modhrain, Chris Burns, Mary Francis, John Granzow, Kim Harty

Live DJ: Wes McGee

REFERENCES

Anderson, Christine. 2005. "Dynamic Networks of Sonic Interactions: An Interview with Agostino Di Scipio." *Computer Music Journal* 29 (3): 11–28.

Cox, Christoph. 2009. "Sound Art and the Sonic Unconscious." *Organized Sound* 14 (1): 19–26.

Saladin, Matthieu. 2017. "Electroacoustic Feedback and the Emergence of Sound Installation: Remarks on a Line of Flight in the Live Electronic

9   Speaker array suspended from resonant wires (Catie Newell, © 2017).

Music by Alvin Lucier and Max Neuhaus." *Organized Sound* 22 (2): 268–275.

Wang, Ge. 2008. "The ChucK Audio Programming Language: A Strongly-timed and On-the-fly Environ/Mentality." Ph.D. diss., Princeton University.

John Granzow is Assistant Professor of Music at the University of Michigan's School of Music, Theatre & Dance. Granzow applies the latest manufacturing methods to both scientific and musical instrument design. After completing a masters of science in psychoacoustics, he attended Stanford University for his PhD in computer-based music theory and acoustics. Granzow started and instructed the 3D Printing for Acoustics workshop at the Centre for Computer Research in Music and Acoustics. His research focuses on computer-aided design, analysis, and fabrication for new musical interfaces with embedded electronics. He also leverages these tools to investigate acoustics and music perception.

Catie Newell is the Director of the Digital and Material Technologies Master of Science in Architectural Design and Research program and Associate Professor of Architecture at the University of Michigan's Taubman College of Architecture and Urban Planning. She is the founding principal of the art and architecture practice *Alibi Studio. Newell's work and research captures spaces and material effects, focusing on the development of atmospheres through the exploration of textures, volumes, and the effects of light or lack thereof. Her creative practice has been widely recognized for exploring design construction and materiality in relationship to location, geography, and cultural contingencies.

Kim Harty is the Section Head of Glass and Assistant Professor at the College for Creative Studies. Her work investigates the connection between craft and technology through sculpture, installation, video, and performance. She is heavily informed by her training as a glass blower, and draws on her personal history as a craftsperson to explore how kinetic knowledge can be tracked, embodied, and performed.

10 Section lines of existing building (Catie Newell, © 2017).

House 4178
A Robotic Pavilion

Nicholas Hoban
Jay Chenault
Alessandro DellEndice
Matthias Helmreich
Jesus Medina Ibanez
Pietro Odaglia
Federico Salvalaio
Stavroula Tsafou
ETH Zurich

Philipp Eversmann
ETH Zurich

Fabio Gramazio
ETH Zurich

Matthias Kohler
ETH Zurich

1   House 4178, designed and fabricated with two industrial robots (Gramazio Kohler Research, ETH Zurich).

House 4178 investigates the use of large scale robotic fabrication of a timber double story minimal living shelter through spatial assembly. The construction of a computationally designed and robotically fabricated minimal living shelter is an engineering and technical challenge, one that forces the development of innovative solutions and a set of novel robotic processes. House 4178 derived from a developed set of amalgamated computational design tools, integrating geometry generation, structural analysis and fabrication data production.

The principal factor within the geometry generation is preserving the planarity of the interfacing geometries. In plan view, the doubly curved structure can be radially split into co-planar subdivisions without affecting the interfacing planarity. This planarity exists by deriving the structural lines from the outer surface where the vertical beams define the slab, rather than defining the structure with the slab as a primary generator. The primary vertical beams are discretized into nodes and consequent triangulation of the faces through the development of a custom meshing algorithm. The meshing creates interior, exterior and bracing diagonals all contained within the exterior surface to allow for the direct fastening of the surface shingles on the exterior façade.

The structure is composed of 4178 wooden beams with 4 cross section sizes. To compute the structural capacity, an FEM model was developed in Karamba for Grasshopper. The FEM component inputs the points, lines and surfaces generated within the geometry generation algorithm.

PRODUCTION NOTES

Architect: Students of the Master
   of Advanced Studies ETH in
   Architecture and Digital Fabrication,
   Gramazio Kohler Research, ETH
   Zurich

Status: Completed

Site Area: 1,000 sq. ft.

Location: ETH Zurich Honggerberg

Date: 2016

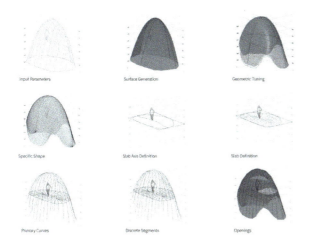

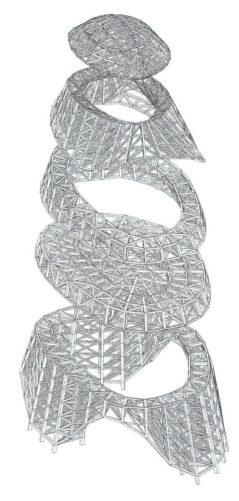

2 Geometry generation process, discretizing the surface into segments.

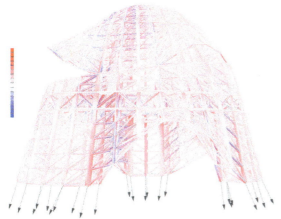

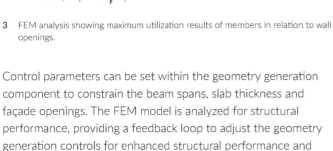

3 FEM analysis showing maximum utilization results of members in relation to wall openings.

4 Structural geometry in a vertical sequential order, demonstrating the assembly logic organized by rings.

Control parameters can be set within the geometry generation component to constrain the beam spans, slab thickness and façade openings. The FEM model is analyzed for structural performance, providing a feedback loop to adjust the geometry generation controls for enhanced structural performance and optimization.

The development and implementation of a computational workflow for the downstream fabrication data is vital to the robotic fabrication. The computational tools developed within the geometry generation, imbedded within each beam, contain the data array necessary to program the routines for robotic fabrication. The robotic fabrication cell consists of two ABB 4700 robots along a 6 m linear axis. Robot 1 is equipped with a custom shingling end effector for envelope construction; Robot 2 is equipped with a dual gripper working with a 3-axis CNC saw for structural fabrication. The structural fabrication with Robot 2 was developed through custom simulation plugins in Grasshopper with Python and C#. The custom components

generate the ABB code allowing the robotic routines to update in correlation to fabrication constraints. The simulation tools provide the opportunity to preview and change the robotic path simulation with direct writing of the robotic code. The envelope fabrication with Robot 1 operated in tandem with a scanning sensor, resulting in real-time updates to the placement position of the shingles based upon their variable width. The generated code was directly loaded into the ABB controller through Robot Studio for fabrication

House 4178 was fabricated in components in the robotic fabrication cell and transported to the site for final assembly. On site, foundational screw posts were installed allowing the primary ground ring components to be lifted into place. Once the primary ring was completed, the assembly sequence progressed to the next ring. In total 5 rings were created for the horizontal axis, split in a variable number of radial divisions. Finally, the roof was generated into two components and craned into place, reducing the complexity of the closing segments.

5   House 4178, upper interior space, view from stair access (Gramazio Kohler Research, ETH Zurich).

House 4178 Hoban, Chenault, DellEndice, Helmreich, Ibanex, Odaglia, Salcalaio, Tsafou, et al.

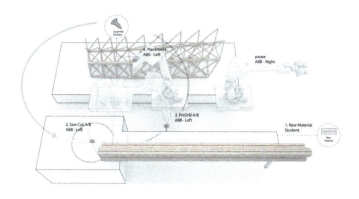

6   Structure fabrication loop, timber elements are cut and placed by Robot 2.

7   Robot 2 positioning a horizontal member in place (Gramazio Kohler Research, ETH Zurich).

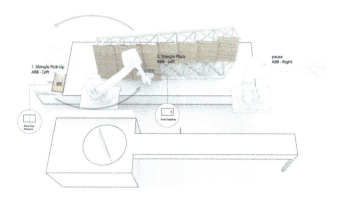

8   Shingle fabrication loop, shingles are scanned and placed by Robot 1.

9   Robot 1 moving to shingle scanning platform (Gramazio Kohler Research, ETH Zurich).

It is the first two-story robotically constructed house. The level of coordination and integration within the group members along with the digital workflow permitted the project to be constructed within a limited timeframe of 6 weeks.

10   Robot 2 working in conjunction with Schmidler CNC saw (Gramazio Kohler Research, ETH Zurich).

11   House 4178 ground entrance (Gramazio Kohler Research, ETH Zurich`).

ACKNOWLEDGMENTS

House 4178 was realized during the academic year 2015-16 of the Master of Advanced Studies (MAS) ETH in Architecture and Digital Fabrication at ETH Zürich. Run by Gramazio Kohler Research and tutored by Philipp Eversmann and Luka Piskorec, the pavilion was conceived and constructed by the students Jay Chenault, Alessandro DellEndice, Matthias Helmreich, Nicholas Hoban, Jesus Medina, Pietro Odaglia, Federico Salvalaio, Stavroula Tsafou as well as Shiu Lun Cheung, Jorge Christie, Remy-Maillet, José De Carvalho Paixao, Larisa Gabor, Katrin Hochschuh, Jesús Medina Ibanez, Ioannis Mirtsopoulos, Fabio Scotto, Wei Yu Hsiao, Anastasia Zaytseva. The MAS programme is supported by the National Centre for Competence in Research (NCCR) Digital Fabrication, funded by the Swiss National Science Foundation (SNSF). House 4178 partly uses results from the National Research Programme 66 of the SNSF project, a collaboration, a collaboration between Gramazio Kohler Research, ETH Zurich and Bern University of Applied Sciences Architecture, Wood and Civil Engineering. We would like to thank the companies Schilliger Holz AG, Rothoblaas, Krinner Ag, ABB and BAWO Befestigungstechnik AG for their generous support and Philippe Fleischmann and Michael Lyrenmann for their advice and continuous efforts for the robotic setup.

The Master of Advanced Studies ETH in Architecture and Digital Fabrication is a one-year full time educational program positioned within a vibrant multidisciplinary research environment. Jointly organised by the Chair for Digital Building Technologies and Gramazio Kohler Research, it enjoys strong links with the Institute of Technology in Architecture (ITA) and the Architecture Department (D-ARCH) of ETH Zurich. Furthermore, the MAS is the educational program of the National Centre for Competence in Research (NCCR) Digital Fabrication, one of the biggest

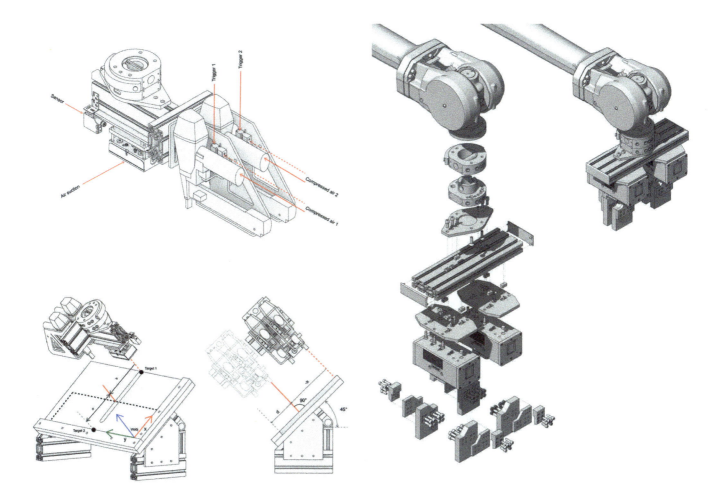

12 Robot 1 Shingle Tool End Effector, the shingle platform allows for sensor scanning to determine shingle width.

13 Robot 2 dual electronic SCHUNK grippers mounted on adjustable linear axis, allowing the gripper to adjust for beam width and length.

and world leading interdisciplinary research clusters on digital fabrication and robotics in architecture. The MAS ETH in Architecture and Digital Fabrication teaches advanced methods and technologies at the forefront of digital design and fabrication and their implementation in architecture and construction. With a focus on computational design, robotic fabrication and 3D printing, projects and assignments enable students to develop strong design concepts and realize large-scale prototypes using the unique robotic construction facilities and 3D printing laboratories at ETH Zurich. Courses are designed not only to teach a thorough understanding of computation and digital fabrication in architecture but also to foster students' understanding of how new technologies, materials and processes contribute to an advanced and sustainable construction culture.

www.masdfab.com

Data Moiré: Optical Patterns as Data-Driven Design Narratives

Alvin Huang, AIA
University of Southern California/
Synthesis Design + Architecture

Anna M. Chaney
IBM Watson Advanced Cognitive
Technology & Solutions

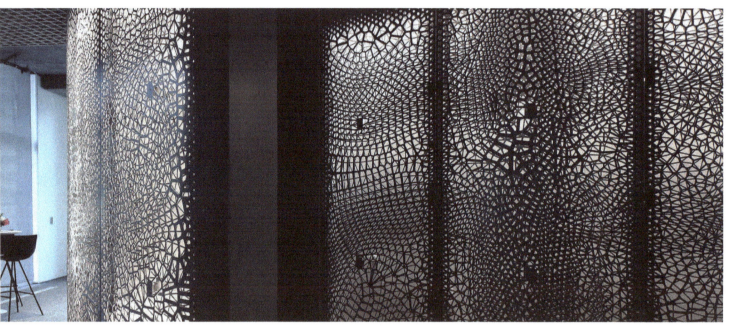

1   Entrance to the Immersion Room at the IBM Watson Experience Center, San Francisco.

Recent conversations in architectural discourse have theorized on the emergence of data-driven design as a paradigm shift that leverages computation in using the expansiveness of big data to conceive of an architecture that is understood as the registration of "reality as it appears at any chosen scale, without having to convert it into simplified and scalable mathematical notations or laws." (Carpo 2014) The term data spatialization has emerged to describe novel architectural materializations that utilize computational design processes to generate novel architectural expressions and spatial opportunities informed by big data (Marcus 2014).

In parallel, the media world has witnessed the emergence of a new form of storytelling as "data narrative," whereby stories are crafted through the collection and analysis of new or existing sets of big data. These data stories utilize data visualizations embedded with narrative components to produce a form of narrative visualization that tells a story through the analysis of data (Segel and Heer 2010).

Data Moiré is a large-scale data-driven feature wall that merges the territories of data spatialization and data narrative by using the cognitive computing capabilities of IBM to inform a data-driven generative design process that articulates a vast quantity of data as a spatial experience and marketing narrative for the IBM Experience Center in San Francisco, California. The result is a digitally fabricated physical installation that illustrates monthly spending cycles by mapping the growing

PRODUCTION NOTES

Architect: Synthesis Design +
              Architecture

Client: IBM Watson

Status: Built

Site Area: 30,000 sq. ft.

Location: San Francisco, USA

Date: 2016

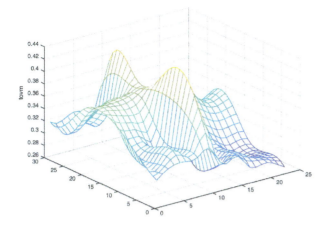

2 Last 10 weeks of data after cubic spline interpolation.

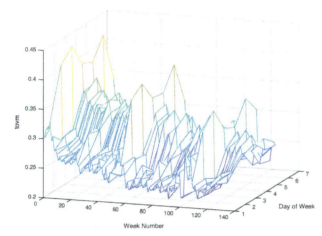

3 Surface of tovm values.

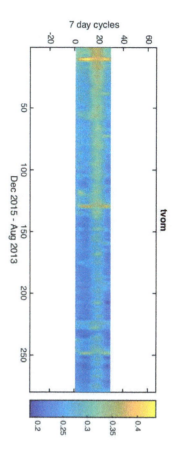

4 The final data set used to inspire the skin design.

influence of mobile devices on all digital sales from 2013 to 2015.

The data is materialized as a CNC-milled, double-layered aluminum, backlit screen wall that produces a moiré-like effect through abstract visual interference patterns produced by the overlaying of two mappings of the same dataset as the cladding of the Watson immersion room.

The resultant project provides a dynamic architectural feature that provides identity and enhances the visual and spatial experience of visitors to the Watson Experience Center, while simultaneously providing a uniquely spatial marketing narrative that highlights Watson's ability to analyze large quantities of unstructured data.

While the project is driven by data, the legibility of that data is abstract rather than literal. Rather than provide a statistical or analytical reading of the data, the project instead provides a

spatial and atmospheric reading that enhances the experience of visitors to the center, and encourages them to engage spatially. It is only through the guided tour of a docent where the legibility of this data is conceded through a verbal narrative. That oral explanation activates the skin to act as narrative visualization more than narrative visualization. It is not only able to illustrate the findings of the data that produced it (the chronological metrics of e-commerce affected by mobile sales), but it also serves to highlight the technology that produced it (the cognitive computing of IBM).

"The data visualisation focuses on beauty, seen as a kind of aesthetic engagement with big data, a form of knowledge encounter that turns on the complexity and aura of an unimaginable object." (McCosker and Wilken 2014)

Data Moiré capitalizes on two computational paradigms: the capacity of cognitive computing and machine learning to analyze and provide insights into massive amounts of unstructured data,

5 Photograph of the completed installation.

Data Moire Huang, Chaney

DATA SURFACE
THE GROWING INFLUENCE OF MOBILE ON DIGITAL SALES

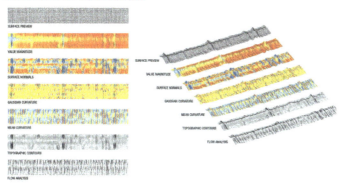

DESIGN SKETCHES
CONTOURS AND HATCHES

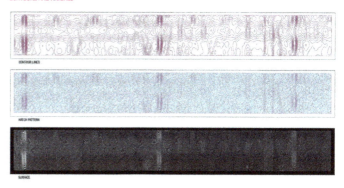

6 Processing raw given data into producing the patterned networks.

7 Contoured data utilizing the z-depth as a basis for generating cellular voids.

VORNOI- DELAUNAY PATTERN
MOIRE EFFECT

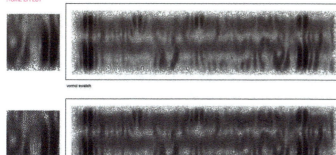

PATTERN UPDATE
AVOIDING CONFLICTS

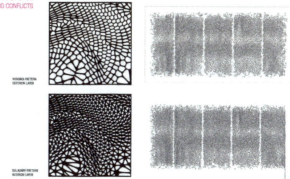

8 Voronoi and Delaunay pattern shown independently.

9 Network inherently avoids misalignments and conflicts.

including the ability of generative design processes to drive geometries that are informed by data. However, it is not the analysis nor the geometries themselves that are the impactful products of this project; rather it is the combined capacity of the analysis and the geometry to communicate.

ACKNOWLEDGMENTS

Design Team: Alvin Huang, Mo Harmon, Farnoosh Rafaie

Collaborators: IBM Watson Analytics (data analysis)

    Arktura LLC, Los Angeles (fabrication)

    Gensler, San Francisco (interiors)

REFERENCES

Andersen, Paul, and David Salomon. 2010. "The Pattern That Connects." In *LIFE in:formation, On Responsive Information and Variations in Architecture: Proceedings of the 30th Annual Conference of the Association for Computer Aided Design in Architecture*, edited by Aaron Sprecher, Shai Yeshayahu, and Pablo Lorenzo-Eiroa, 125–132. New York: ACADIA.

Carpo, Mario. 2014. "Breaking the Curve: Big Data and Design." *ArtForum International* 52 (6): 168–173.

Marcus, Adam. 2014. "Centennial Chromograph: Data Spatialization and Computational Craft." In *ACADIA 14: Design Agency, Proceedings of the 34th Annual Conference of the Association for Computer Aided Design in Architecture*, edited by David Gerber, Alvin Huang, and Jose Sanchez, 167–176. Los Angeles: ACADIA.

Segel, Edward, and Jeffrey Heer. 2010. "Narrative Visualization: Telling Stories with Data." *IEEE Transactions on Visualization and Computer Graphics* 16 (6): 1139–1148.

Schneider, Ann Marie. 2015 "Experiencing Information." *Kerb: Journal of Landscape Architecture* 23: 56–59.

Wade, Nicholas. 2016. "Moiré and Motion." In *Art and Illusionists*, 311–334. Cham, Switzerland: Springer.

10 Photograph of the completed installation.

Zanker, Johannes M. 2004. "Looking at Op Art From a Computational Viewpoint." *Spatial Vision* 17 (1): 75–94.

McCosker, Anthony, and Rowan Wilken. 2014. "Rethinking 'Big Data' as Visual Knowledge: The Sublime and the Diagrammatic in Data Visualisation." *Visual Studies* 29 (2): 155–164.

IMAGE CREDITS

All drawings and images by the authors.

***

Alvin Huang, AIA is the Founder and Design Principal of Synthesis Design + Architecture and an Associate Professor at the USC School of Architecture. He is an award-winning architect, designer, and educator specializing in the integrated application of material performance, emergent design technologies and digital fabrication in contemporary architectural practice. His work spans all scales ranging from hi-rise towers and mixed-use developments to temporary pavilions and bespoke furnishings.

His work has been published and exhibited widely and has gained international recognition with over 30 distinctions at local, national, and international levels including being honored as the Young Architect of the Year by the American Institute of Architects California Council in 2016, being selected of as one of 50 global innovators under the age of 50 by Images Publishing in 2015, being featured as a "Next Progressive" by Architect Magazine in 2014, and being named one of Time Magazine's 20 Best Inventors of 2013. He has been an invited critic, guest lecturer, and keynote speaker at various institutions in the US, Canada, Mexico, Chile, UK, Germany, Italy, Spain, Sweden, Switzerland, Israel, India, Thailand, Japan and China.

Alvin received a Master of Architecture and Urbanism from the Architectural Association Design Research Laboratory (2004) in London and a Bachelor of Architecture from the University of Southern California (1998) in Los Angeles.

11 Detail views of CNC-milled & powder-coated exterior skin vs. laser-cut and PVD-coated inner skin.

Anna M. Chaney With a BS in Applied Mathematics, and an MS in computer science, Anna launched her career in engineering in 2002 working on the Thirty Meter Telescope project. Over the next 12 years, she specialized in remote sensing algorithms, culminating as the principle investigator in an Office of Naval Research contract on the classification of signals. In 2014 she took her breadth of knowledge in applied research to the IBM Watson group. Within IBM Watson she has defined and measured key cognitive metrics necessary to track the improvement and value of the machine learning training cycle, and continues to be passionate about quantifying and improving systems that can improve people's lives.

Platform Sandbox
A Pedagogical Design Software

Damjan Jovanovic
Städelschule Architecture Class
Frankfurt am Main, Germany

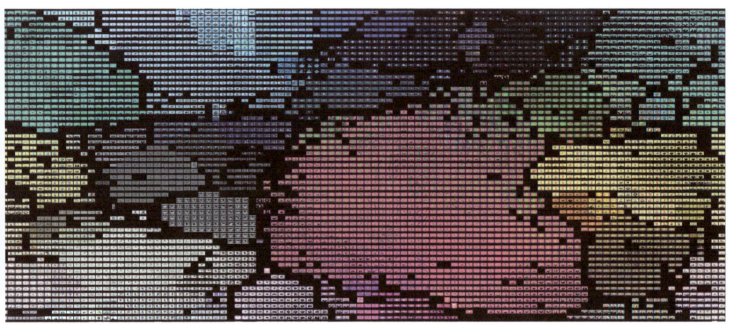

1   The 5800 screenshots, considered to be finished drawings in their own right, were submitted by 30 students after a two-week workshop in April 2017.

Software flattens the field of visual effects and enables messy encounters between drawing, painting, video and games. As a direct descendant of traditional design mediums, design software prescribes a very specific role to the user: that of a disinterested, disembodied subject that has full access to any projection space, and that operates on a spectrum of full visibility and full scalability. This approach continues and vastly expands a specific subjectivity of an architect operating in the "god-mode" of the traditional discipline.

Unlike other software, computer games tend to problematize the notion of subjective agency, either through exposing and putting into question the ability of a player, or by disturbing the notion of a goal. Because of their full-spectrum deployment of interactivity, games could be thought of as the most "medium-specific" type of software. The notions of agency and authorship are thus perceived in a different manner, which loosens the idea of control. It is precisely the notion of loose control that can be postulated as a possible new authorial model, pitted against the totalizing normativity of current computational design methods (Jovanovic 2016).

The Platform Sandbox software is based on these ideas and used as a pedagogical tool for design in a first-year studio at the Stadelschule Architecture Class in Frankfurt am Main, Germany. It is envisioned as "disciplinary-aware" design software, with the purpose of exposing the established conventions and defaults of software by making students aware of the underlying implications of

2   Cantilever structure by Shuruq Tramontini.

3   Dolmen structure by Shuruq Tramontini.

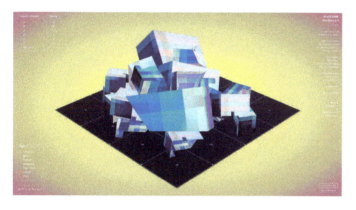

4   Mat structure by Young Kang.

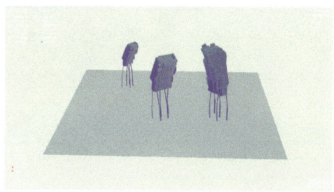

5   Character-like structures by Roberto Barbosa.

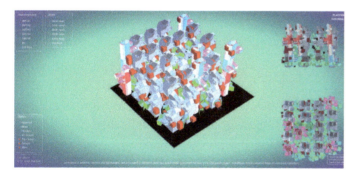

6   Box-like mass structure by Natalia Voinova.

7   Totem-like structure by Anna Arlyapova.

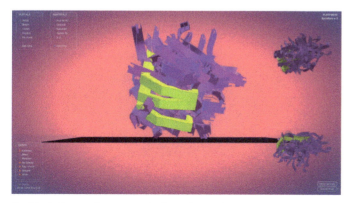

8   Spherical aggregation structure by Jose Luis Arias Reynoso.

9   Box constrained aggregation structure by Zi Yi Chua.

10 Platform Sandbox, customized by the student Darshan Rajendra. An example of a Polar aggregate ("Katamari") made of 40 objects with a design time of 14:54 seconds. The form is made from the parts of Le Corbusier's Chandigarh Assembly Hall.

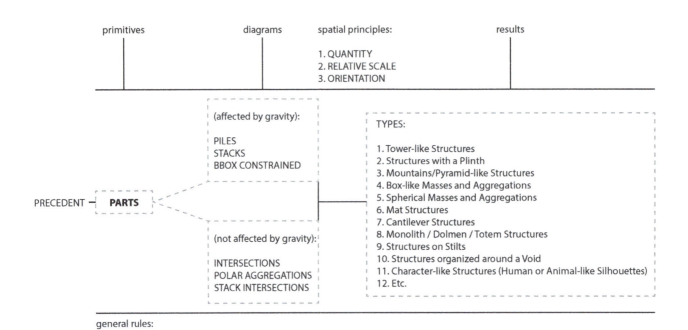

primitives   diagrams   spatial principles: results

1. QUANTITY
2. RELATIVE SCALE
3. ORIENTATION

(affected by gravity):

PILES
STACKS
BBOX CONSTRAINED

PRECEDENT — **PARTS**

(not affected by gravity):

INTERSECTIONS
POLAR AGGREGATIONS
STACK INTERSECTIONS

TYPES:

1. Tower-like Structures
2. Structures with a Plinth
3. Mountains/Pyramid-like Structures
4. Box-like Masses and Aggregations
5. Spherical Masses and Aggregations
6. Mat Structures
7. Cantilever Structures
8. Monolith / Dolmen / Totem Structures
9. Structures on Stilts
10. Structures organized around a Void
11. Character-like Structures (Human or Animal-like Silhouettes)
12. Etc.

general rules:

PHYSICS-BASED INTERACTIONS
EXCHANGEABILITY OF THE ORIGINAL MEANING OF THE PART
DESIGN CONSTRAINED TO 20 MINUTES
SCALE IS BASED ON THE NUMBER OF OBJECTS IN THE SCENE
RANDOM / CHANCE EVENTS

11 The Platform Sandbox workflow. The work starts with a library of parts and ends with an exported model.

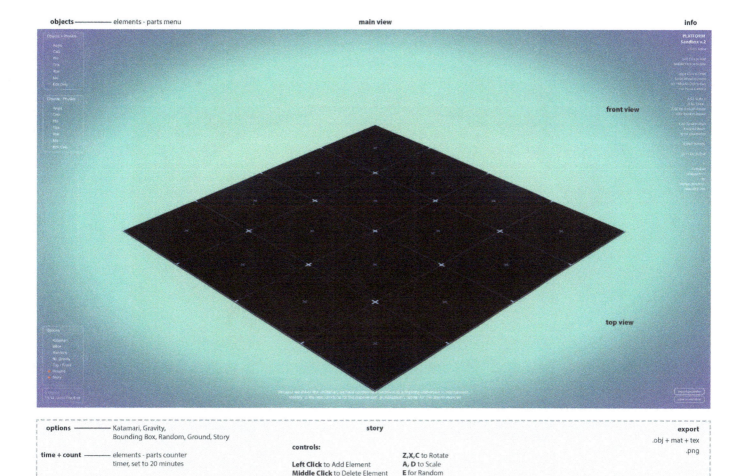

front view

top view

options ————	Katamari, Gravity,	story	export
	Bounding Box, Random, Ground, Story		.obj + mat + tex
		controls:	.png
time + count ————	elements - parts counter		
	timer, set to 20 minutes	**Left Click** to Add Element **A, D** to Scale	
		Middle Click to Delete Element **E** for Random	

Z,X,C to Rotate

12   The default version of the Platform Sandbox user interface features two object menus, an options menu as well as export buttons. Objects are imported and sorted into the menu structure based on whether or not they are affected by gravity. Separately, in the options, gravity can be turned on or off.

design tools. It was designed to resemble a standard, default way in which design software operates, and especially how it looks, but it works more like a game.

The methodology starts by asking a student to choose a building precedent, model it fully in 3D in a "traditional" program and then choose 5–7 "characteristic" parts (linear, flat and volumetric) from the precedent. These parts are imported into Platform Sandbox to serve as "primitives" with which a student works. A primitive can have a physics component attached to it, which means that it will respond to gravity.

The software produces six spatial diagram principles: piles, stacks, constrained piles, intersections, polar aggregates ("Katamari") and stack intersections. The formation depends on the initial setup of the design space world and the time-based interactions of the user. These diagrams produce further types of composition, based on the spatial principles and rules employed (Figure 11). The rules of the game set up the infinite remixability of the

parts in relation to their original meaning and position in the precedent.

To reinforce the importance of the volumetric diagram as a primary means of operation, interaction is only possible in the main perspective view, thus preventing any design from being done in either plan or section. Each design session is constrained to 20 minutes, after which everything is deleted and the software returns to default. The process of design is thus more imprecise, messy, and significantly faster, as chance interactions between primitives occur. In a defined time range, primitives randomly appear and are incorporated into the design. The "goal" of the game is to create compositions on the platform, in four scales, defined by the number of primitives in the scene. This configuration enables the creation of a massive amount of models in a relatively short time span, and this speed and quantity enable the emergence of genres of compositions within the studio.

13 Software outcome used as a base design. Project for a Cinema by Eda Tekirli.

14 Project for a Comic Book Club by Kishan Kumar.

15 Project for a Culture Lab by Darshan Rajendra.

16 Project for a Games Club by Jose Luis Arias Reynoso.

The results can be exported as geometry with textures to be further developed (Figure 17). The question then becomes: under what conditions do these objects (re)enter architecture, and how can we further develop these "found" objects, made out of fragments of other architecture?

The agenda of the studio is to understand software as the design medium, and this is why the user interface design, and some parts of the operation were customized by each student.

ACKNOWLEDGMENTS

The author would like to thank all the students of the 2016-17 first year group of the Städelschule Architecture Class, as well as Professors Johan Bettum and Peter Trummer for their support.

REFERENCES

Jovanovic, Damjan. 2016. "Fictions: A Speculative Acount of Design Mediums" In *Drawing Futures: Speculations in Contemporary Drawing for Art and Architecture*, edited by Laura Allen, Luke Caspar Pearson, 28–33. London: UCL Press.

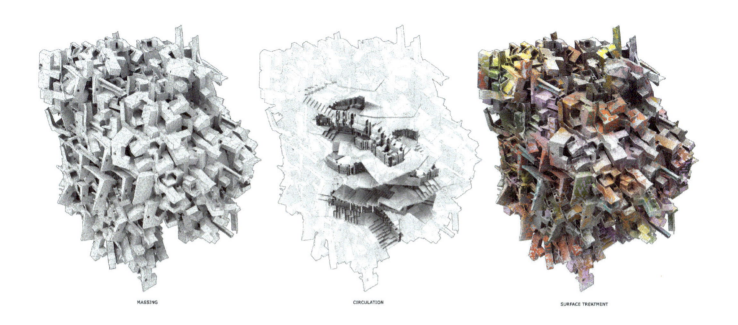

MASSING   CIRCULATION   SURFACE TREATMENT

17 The standard post-processing workflow. The exported model is further developed through the introduction of architectural conventions of representation. Texture and color is rentroduced and further specified. Project for a Computer Games Club, by Zi Yi Chua.

Damjan Jovanovic is a tutor and research associate at Städelschule Architecture Class. He finished the post-graduate Master of Arts in Architecture degree at the Städelschule with a thesis that won the AIV Master Thesis Prize in 2014. His interests lie in investigating the cultural effects of software in architectural design through the development of non-standard design tools as a means of questioning the prevalent design defaults. Recent projects include VR/AR works centered on rein-terpretation of the work by Marcel Duchamp and pedagogical software positioned between gaming and architectural design culture.

THE PRODUCTION OF THINNESS:
A Fabricated Concrete Pavilion

Julie Larsen
Syracuse University

Roger Hubeli
Syracuse University

1   Constructed Pavilion (CEMEX, April 18, 2017).

Abstract

Like much of today's culture, architecture is driven by a fascination for the "thin." Contemporary buildings reflect this most clearly in the design and construction of facades that are often reduced to high tech veneers that enclose mundane steel or concrete structures. "Thinness" is situated within this tension by hybridizing veneer and structure to create a new approach to being "thin." With the use of computational design combined with thin, high-performance, lightweight concrete, this project generates a new understanding of typology, structure, and surface quality. This project describes the collaboration between architecture professors, CEMEX Global R&D, and their material scientists to develop a lightweight modular concrete pavilion, and subsequently a new concrete mix for the project.

PRODUCTION NOTES

Architect: APTUM
Partner: CEMEX Global R&D
Status: Built
Site Area: 100 sq. ft.
Location: Brügg, Switzerland
Date: 2017

Objectives

By challenging the formal typology of a cross-vault, the aim was to achieve a complex geometry with "veil-like" walls that merges structure and skin through a new concrete material (Figure 1). The design and fabrication of the 10' x 10' x 10' pavilion consists of 16 mobile elements. The goals were to use surface optimization to rethink the aesthetics of modern concrete as a thin form. The fiber-reinforced concrete mixture had the ability to make very thin elements, made with only half-inch-thick walls (Figure 2). The cut down the center of the vaults, the pavilion's modularity, as well as the voids in the walls, reveal the concrete's flexural strength (Figure 8).

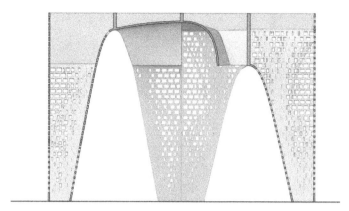

2   Section of pavilion cutting through 4 elements (APTUM, 2015).

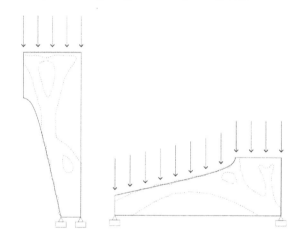

3   **Structural** diagram of elements in horizontal and vertical position (APTUM, 2015).

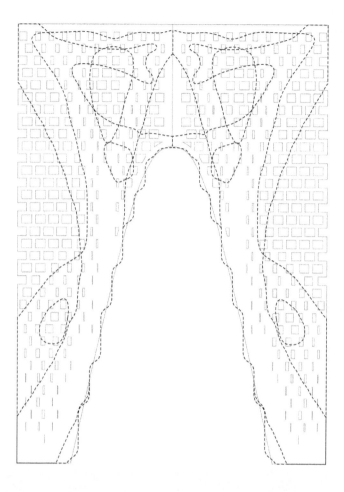

4   Bending moment diagram informing digital pattern on surface (APTUM, 2015).

Crafting the Digital

The pattern on the facade was generated from a "diffusion limited aggregation" technique in Grasshopper. The pattern responds to the overlapped stress and load patterns for the horizontal and vertical position of the element. Since the 16 elements are made mobile to accentuate their lightness, the structural analysis was to test where the highest stresses are located on individual pieces as they are carried from an upright to a horizontal position (Figure 3). To determine the ideal location to eliminate voids in the surface, the "diffusion limited aggregation" was altered with the structural diagram (Figure 4). The matrix of the mix, the additives, and the fiber reinforcement were continuously adapted to the form and the computational input for the pattern (Figure 9). The final scale of the voids were not ideal for the concrete mix because the mix required 17 mm long steel fibers, yet the mass between voids in the surface were only 15 mm wide. This resulted in CEMEX reducing the steel fibers to 15 mm in length and altering the flow of the mix in order for fibers to move through the formwork. Reduction of the fibers to

15 mm had not been attempted by CEMEX prior to the project.

Fabrication of Pavilion

The axonometric of the construction outlines the layers of formwork needed to fabricate the elements (Figure 11). The formwork is a combination of digital fabrication techniques, with waterjet-cut welded steel forms and waterjet-cut silicone inlays (Figure 6). These were used alongside the prehistoric technique of "lost wax molds." The columns of wax were poured and then the silicon was peeled away to reveal the wax columns (Figure 7). The wax inverse columns were self-supporting before adding the steel formwork back to encapsulate the wax molds (Figure 12). Once the steel exterior was back in position, each column of wax was melted away with long tube heaters running the length of the columns. The steel formwork was removed with only the concrete column remaining. The transparency of the elements provide a sense of lightness, a profound departure from preconceived notions of what concrete typically represents.

5   Rendering of Pavilion (APTUM, October, 2015).

The Production of Thinness: A Fabricated Concrete Pavilion Larsen, Hubeli

6   Silicon infill attached to steel formwork (APTUM, 2015).

7   Lost wax formwork (APTUM, 2015).

8   Interior vaults of pavilion where elements come together (CEMEX, 2016).

9   Final facade of pavilion articulating structural stresses in surface (CEMEX, 2017).

10 Prototype 3 of pavilion in Biel, Switzerland (CEMEX, April 2017).

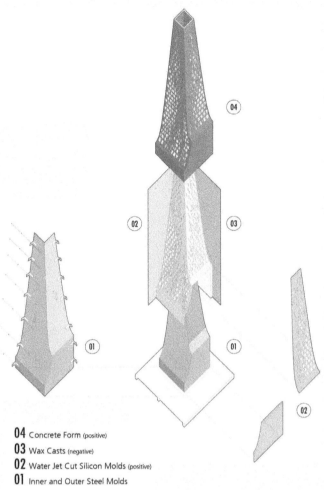

04 Concrete Form (positive)
03 Wax Casts (negative)
02 Water Jet Cut Silicon Molds (positive)
01 Inner and Outer Steel Molds

11 Axonometric of fabrication process (APTUM, October, 2015).

12 Lost wax formwork of column element (APTUM, October, 2015).

ACKNOWLEDGMENTS

This project would not be possible without the support of Davide Zampini, the Director of the CEMEX Global R&D, and his team, who were our collaborators on the project and constructed multiple prototypes of the elements. We would like to thank Dean Michael Speaks at the School of Architecture at Syracuse University for initially funding the project with a faculty research grant. And lastly, we appreciate the hard work and dedication of many Syracuse University students who contributed to the project, most notably Sean Morgan, our Research Assistant for two years.

Julie Larsen is an assistant professor at the School of Architecture at Syracuse University and co-founder of APTUM. She received her professional degree from Columbia University in 2002. Her expertise is in the role of digital fabrication as it applies to multiple scales; from material technology to ecological and infrastructural applications. In 2015, she co-hosted the ACSA Regional Fall Conference, "Between the Autonomous & Contingent Object," at Syracuse University. She received the MacDowell fellowship and the Rotch Traveling Studio Award in 2011. The firm is collaborating with CEMEX Global R&D in Switzerland on design applications for high-performance concrete and they recently received an AIA NY Project Merit Award in 2017 for Rhizolith Island a mangrove restoration project.

Roger Hubeli is an assistant professor at the School of Architecture at Syracuse University and co-founder of APTUM. He received his professional degree from ETH in Zürich, Switzerland and is a member of the Swiss Architecture and Engineering Association (SIA). His expertise is in emergent systems between tectonics, structure, and ecologies. In 2011, he was a fellow at MacDowell Colony in New Hampshire. And in 2015, he co-hosted the ACSA Regional Fall Conference, "Between the Autonomous & Contingent Object," at Syracuse University. The firm is collaborating with CEMEX Global R&D in Switzerland on design applications for high-performance concrete and they recently received an AIA NY Project Merit Award in 2017 for Rhizolith Island a mangrove restoration project.

Textile Hybrid

Dr. Julian Lienhard
HCU Hamburg, str.ucture GmbH

Dr. Christian Bergmann
Hadi Teherani Architects

Dr. Riccardo La Magna
KET, UdK Berlin, str.ucture GmbH

Jonas Runberger PhD
Chalmers Department of
Architecture and Civil
Engineering, White architecter

1   The Textile Hybrid at HCU Hamburg

Collaborative Modelling

In 2016 and 2017 a master class was held at HCU Hamburg which focused on collaborative design and engineering methods using textile hybrid structures as a case study. After an initial design competition where individual student groups explored design and modelling techniques, the winning design was chosen as a case study to build to scale. The challenge was to then set up a parametric workflow that allowed a large number of students, divided into expert groups, to work on one single design model. The expert groups covered the fields of design, form-finding, structural analysis, material testing, detailing, manufacturing and project management. A collaborative workflow template was set up, which equally addressed complex analysis as well as the need for continuous geometric adjustment to achieve a model that interactively functioned on design, structural and material levels.

The design framework included principles on how to integrate Flux (http://flux.io) as a cloud-based data exchange platform. Flux provided important links between several Grasshopper definitions, as well as additional links to Excel (used for the bill of quantities and material order sheets) and imports and exports from and to SOFiSTiK, the finite element software employed for the form finding, analysis and patterning of the structure. Flux currently requires the preliminary establishment of specific data keys external to Grasshopper, and this required a particular setup to handle versioning through the iterative process. With this setup it was possible to work on the detail

PRODUCTION NOTES

Master Class by Visiting Professor Dr.
   Julian Lienhard

Designed and built by Students from
   Architecture and Civil Engineering

Location: HCU HAMBUG
Date: 2016-2017

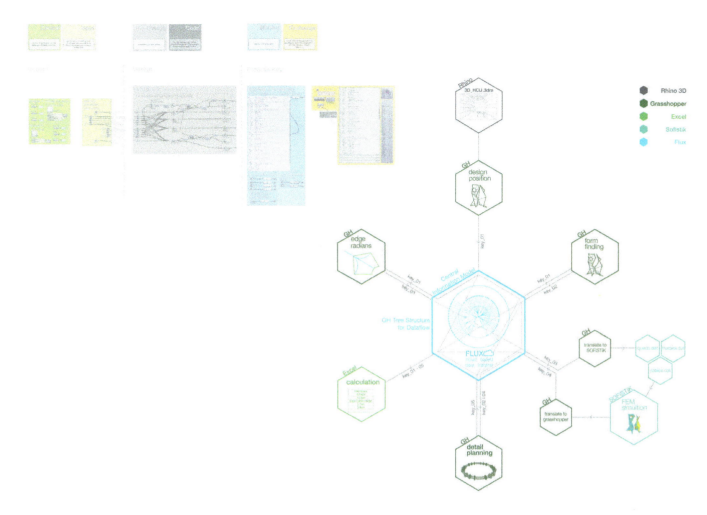

2   Digital workflow model with central information model stored in a cloud using Flux

design based on the form-finding result of an earlier version key while this form finding was optimized and updated for a current version key. This setup proved to be very powerful as the design was continuously optimized and underwent some major changes at a very late point in the process. Despite the large number of people working with and manipulating the same model, the versioning system provided by Flux eliminated the risk of clashes and multiple model duplicates by consistently downstreaming changes to all the working parties' models.

FEM as a Central Part of the Design System
Finite element analysis still remains the most reliable tool for structural analysis, offering the complete picture of the situation and the most accurate mechanical description of the analysed system. However, until recently, available finite element programs did not serve particularly well as design environments. It was notoriously complex to organize a complete simulation setup for quick design explorations with almost any FE program. The necessity and advantage of finite element analysis in the

development of Textile Hybrids lies in the possibility of a thorough and complete mechanical description of the system. Provided that form-finding solvers are included in the software, the possibility of freely combining shell, beam, cable, coupling and spring elements enables FEM to simulate the exact physical properties of the system in an uninterrupted mechanical description. These include: mechanical material properties, asymmetrical and varying cross-sections, eccentricities coupling and interaction of individual components, nonlinear stress-stiffening effects, nonlinear simulation of stresses and deflections under external loads, patterning and compensation.

Outlook
When bridging the gap between teaching and research we inevitably move into unknown territory, where a project's success is not only dependent on people's commitment but also on the results and findings coming from that very research. The two critical moments in the Textile Hybrid workshop were found to be in the digital communication and the physics-based modelling.

3   Impression of the Textile Hybrid installation in the foyer of HCU Hamburg

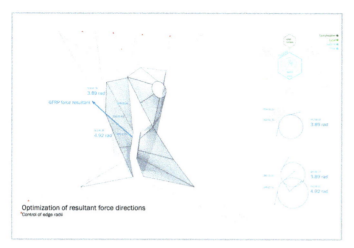

Optimization of resultant force directions
*Control of edge radii

4   Pre-processing and edge radius optimization

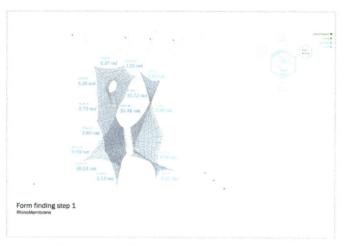

Form finding step 1
RhinoMembrane

5   Form finding step 1 with stiff rod elements

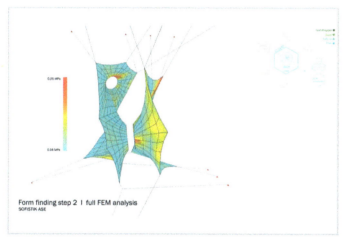

Form finding step 2 I full FEM analysis
SOFISTIK ASE

6   FEM form finding step 2: bending-active rods and analysis of the system

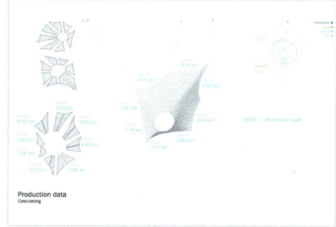

Production data
Calculating

7   Production data streamed from FEM back into the central information model

First of all, the project required the setting up of a digital communication platform that allowed independent expert parties to work on a single and interdependent information model. Second, the engineered hybrid equilibrium system had to work at full scale with little possibility of adjustment after its erection. In the case of the Textile Hybrid workshop, several teams achieved very advanced results: they not only carried through workflow-related conventions, but also contributed to new findings. Even so, the process faced critical conditions at several points in time.

At a late stage an initially included mirroring surface had to be removed since no appropriate product could be found. Here, the design system and the established frameworks allowed for design adjustments and the generation of a new equilibrium for the detailing and production data in the timespan of one week, thus proving the power of the comprehensive parametric digital system.

Several issues, such as fire and smoke, led to the use of a non-coated glass-fibre fabric with a compensation of less than

0.2%, something that posed a major challenge to the team while cutting and sewing the membrane that became visible in the final outcome in terms of wrinkling. As an additional challenge, the GFRP rods the team had planned and calculated could not be delivered on time, so an alternative, much stiffer rod had to be used. This led to additional challenges while pre-stressing the membrane. As such, it can be concluded that the challenges in focus, concerning digital communication and achieving a full-scale equilibrium system, were successfully managed. In detail, however, the accumulation of seemingly less important factors led to challenges in pre-stressing the membrane perfectly.

The challenges concerning digital communication methods and those of a physical nature are similar to those observed in the entire planning and building industry—especially when it comes to the shift from pure theoretical design and planning to manufacturing and building to scale. They are still some of the major burdens for innovation and sustainability and heuristically can only be overcome with a systemic cultural approach on a strategic level.

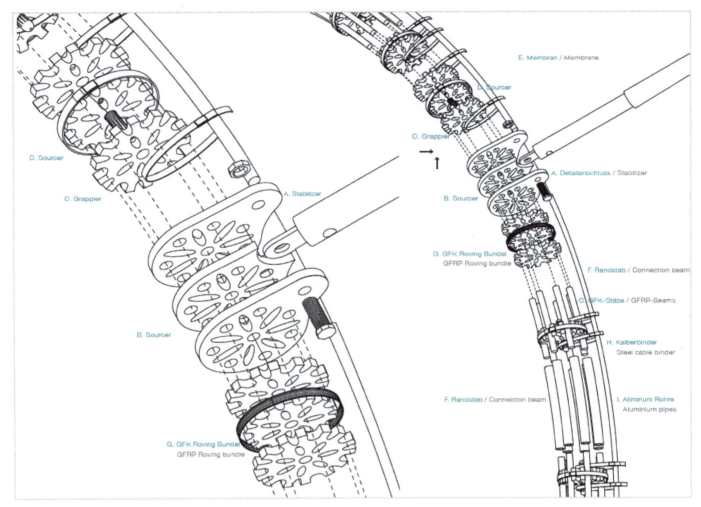

8 Digital detail for the central ring structure

ACKNOWLEDGMENTS

Student Team: Marcelo Acevedo Pardo, Fabrizio M. Amoruso, Vasileios Angelakoudis, Nick Dimke, Kaspar Ehrhardt, Luisa Höltig, Timo van der Horst, Tobias Hövermann, Michel Kokoruš, Dennis Mönkemeyer, Anies Ruhani-Shishevan, Gert Salzer, Anton Samoruko, Dino Tomasello, Zeliha Atabek, Björn Bahnsen, Niklas Dürr, Maria Fritzenschaft, Matthis Gericke, Mahmoud Ghazala Einieh, Can-Peter Grothmann, Moritz Seifert, Timo Volkmann.

Surveying: Erik Jensen, Dominik Trau.

Supervision: Lehrstuhl Tragwerksentwurf Prof. Michael Staffa, Wiebke Brahms.

Membrane Manufacturing workshop: Jakob Frick.

HCU Labs: Thomas Kniephoff, Jens Ohlendieck, Kai Schramme.

Fire Simulation: Ingenieurgesellschaft Stürzl GmbH.

Sponsors: MAX HOFFMANN, SOFiSTiK, Serge Ferrari, Textilbau GmbH.

REFERENCES

Ahlquist, Sean, Julian Lienhard, Jan Knippers, and Achim Menges. "Physical and Numerical Prototyping for Integrated Bending and Form-Active Textile Hybrid Structures." In *Rethinking Prototyping: Proceeding of the Design Modelling Symposium*, edited by Christoph Gengnagel, Axel Kilian, Julian Nembrini, and Fabian Scheurer. Berlin: Design Modelling Symposium.

Lienhard, Julian, and Jan Knippers. 2015. "Bending-Active Textile Hybrids." *Journal of the International Association for Shell and Spatial Structures* 56 (1): 37–48.

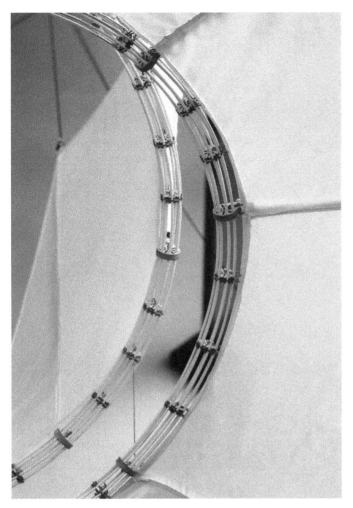

9 Ring structure after installation

10 Impression of the Textile Hybrid installation in the foyer of HCU Hamburg

Dr. Julian Lienhard completed his doctorate summa cum laude in April 2014 with his dissertation on bending-active structures at the Institute of Building Structures and Structural Design, University of Stuttgart. As an author of the specialist book *Construction Manual for Polymers + Membranes*, he has been honored by several awards during his academic career. Along with a number of different design studios, he has been teaching the Principles of Membrane Structures course at the University of Stuttgart, the Technical University of Vienna and since 2016 as a Visiting Professor at HCU Hamburg. His scientific interest in the principles of lightweight structures goes along with various realized experimental structures and prototypes along his academic and professional career. This forms the basis of his international structural engineering consultancy as a recognized specialist in membrane roofs and facades.

In 2008, Julian co-founded the engineering and design practice studioLD now str.ucture GmbH. Previously, he worked as a Structural Engineer at Knippers- Helbig and SL-Rasch in Stuttgart

Dr. Christian Bergmann is a senior architect and project architect at Hadi Teherani Architects in Hamburg, Germany. Previously he worked for Werner Sobek Stuttgart and UNStudio Amsterdam. He received his PhD in Architecture from the Institute for Lightweight Structures and Conceptual Design (ILEK) at the University of Stuttgart in 2013.

Dr. Riccardo La Magna is a structural engineer active both in research and practice. He received his doctor title from the Institute of Building Structures and Structural Design (ITKE) at the University of Stuttgart and is now project engineer at str.ucture GmbH. In his research he focuses on simulation technology, innovative structural systems, and new materials for building applications.

Jonas Runberger is an architect, researcher and educator with a special interest in the integration of computational tools into the architectural design process. He is Head of Dsearch, a Focus Lab for computational within White arkitekter AB . He holds a PhD in Architecture from KTH (Stockholm) and is a Professor in Digital Design at Chalmers Department of Architecture and Civil Engineering (Gothenburg).

Signal / Noise: Code and Craft in Architectural Drawing

Adam Marcus
California College of the Arts

1   *Rotated Arcs*, Seed 247/38 (detail)

This project consists of a series of parametrically generated and robotically produced drawings. The work explores overlaps between procedural design techniques, computer numerically controlled (CNC) machinery, conventions of architectural representation, and the craft of analog drawing. In today's paradigm of digital design and production, architects often eschew qualities of unpredictability and risk in the drawing process. In many practices, the act of drawing has been marginalized to merely an afterthought or a "deliverable;" the drawing becomes purely representational and no longer maintains any generative capacity. This project challenges this status quo by leveraging technology to subvert its own biases for precision and predictability, using computational design and fabrication techniques to reintroduce error in productive and measured ways that open up new and evocative aesthetic possibilities.

Each series of drawings begins by establishing an algorithm for producing fields of simple geometries in a regularly spaced grid. The geometries are then translated to G-Code instructions for a custom-made CNC drawing machine that paints ink on paper with a watercolor brush. Each of these acts of translation—from code to mechanical motion to the material deposition of ink on paper—introduces noise into the system: inaccuracies, glitches, and anomalies that compromise the fidelity of the original geometric information, but also generate unexpected and surprising visual effects.

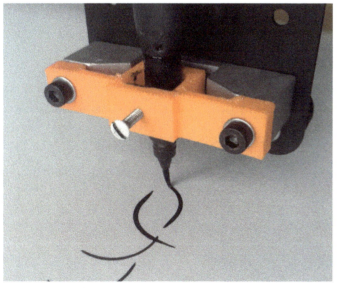
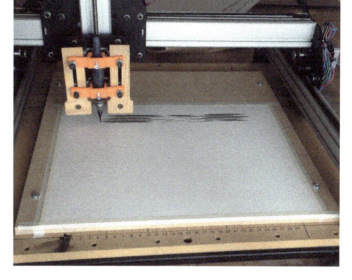

2   Custom-built robotic drawing machine with watercolor brush pen end effector.

The project channels the work of earlier procedural artists such as Anni Albers, Sol Lewitt, and Manfred Mohr in its use of gridded, primitive geometries such as lines and arcs. The relative neutrality of this geometry amplifies artifacts of error derived from medium and process, and provides a consistent framework for comparing the variation from one drawing to the next. Variations accumulate in layers as unexpected behaviors emerge at several points throughout the process. First, the initial procedural logics incorporate random seeds that allow for iterative variation of geometric parameters, such as rotation or length. Second, the translation of the virtual drawing to instructions for the CNC machine introduces issues of tolerance, calibration, and

mechanical imprecision that produce strange, accidental artifacts like bumpy lines and variable line weights. Finally, the delivery of ink onto the paper is entirely dependent upon the material parameters of the media, the brush quality, and even environmental factors like temperature and humidity.

Whether algorithmic, mechanical, or material in origin, the sources of noise are cumulative and contingent upon one another. Each moment of unpredictability echoes what furniture designer David Pye called the "workmanship of risk," a process of making in which "the quality of the result is continually at risk." Pye celebrated this risk as the source and locus of craft,

3 *Lines.* Clockwise from upper left: Seed 132; Seed 234; Seed 378; detail, Seed 378; Seed 345.

Signal / Noise: Code and Craft in Architectural Drawing Marcus

4   *Shattered Lines*, Seed 275.

in contrast to the more predictable "workmanship of certainty" that characterizes mechanical production (Pye 1968, 20). These drawings, produced by machines designed for precision, repetition, and certainty, recast Pye's notion of risk in the context of contemporary technologies. The introduction of risk and the modulation of this unpredictability contributes to a sense of craft that otherwise would not be present in drawings produced by typical plotters or printers. The drawings begin to demonstrate the opportunities that lie within translations from bits to motion to matter—and the possibility of finding craft in computational modes of design and fabrication.

ACKNOWLEDGMENTS

Design & Production: Adam Marcus, Frederico Leite Gonçalves

REFERENCES

Pye, David. 1968. *The Nature and Art of Workmanship*. London: Herbert Press.

 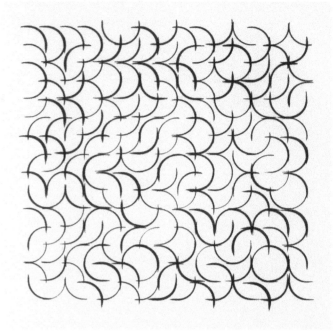

5   *Rotated Arcs*. Clockwise from upper left: Seed 116/38; Seed 213/56; Seed 247/38; Seed 239/12.

IMAGE CREDITS

All drawings and images by Adam Marcus / Variable Projects.

Adam Marcus is an Associate Professor of Architecture at California College of the Arts in San Francisco, where he teaches design studios in design computation and digital fabrication and collaborates with CCA's Digital Craft Lab. He has previously taught at Columbia University, the University of Minnesota, and the Architectural Association's Visiting School Los Angeles. He directs Variable Projects, an award-winning design and research studio in Oakland, California. Adam is a graduate of Brown University and Columbia University's Graduate School of Architecture, Planning and Preservation, and he currently serves on the Board of Directors for the Association for Computer-Aided Design in Architecture (ACADIA).

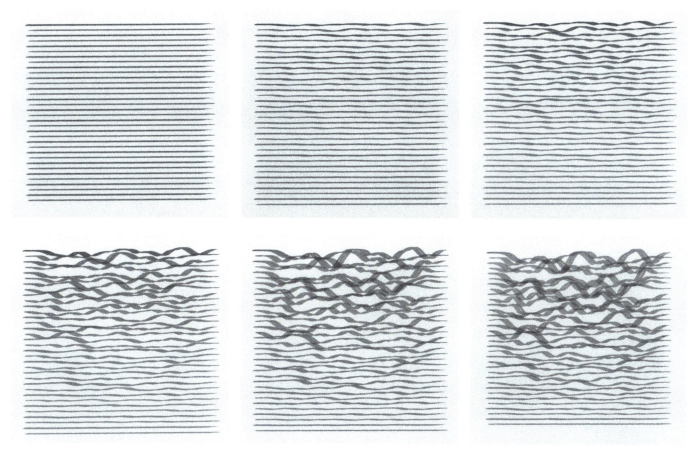

6   *Waves*, Seed 70, Increments 0 to 100.

7   *Pressed Splines*, Seed 227.

8   *Pressed Splines*, Seed 56 (detail).

Suggestive Drawing Among Human and Artificial Intelligences

Nono Martínez Alonso
Harvard Graduate School of Design

1   Hand drawing in collaboration with a bot that suggests textures.

We use sketching to represent the world. Design software has made tedious drawing tasks trivial, but we can't yet consider machines as equals in how we interpret the world, since they cannot perceive it. In the last few years, artificial intelligence has experienced a boom, and machine learning is becoming ubiquitous. This presents an opportunity to incorporate machines as participants in the creative process.

In order to explore this, I created an application—a suggestive drawing environment—where humans can work in synergy with bots that have a certain character, with non-deterministic and semi-autonomous behaviors. The project explores the user experience of drawing with machines, escapes the point-and-click paradigm with a continuous flow of interaction, and enables a new branch of creative mediation with bots that can develop their own aesthetics. A new form of collective creativity in which human and non-human participation results in synergetic pieces that express each participant's character.

In this realm, the curation of image datasets for training an artificially intelligent bot becomes part of the design process. Artists and designers can fine-tune the behavior of an algorithm by feeding it with images, programming the machine by example without writing a single line of code.

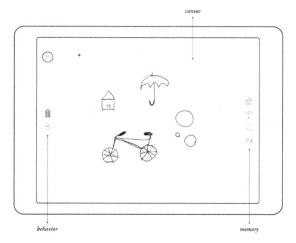

2   Behavior (humans and bots) and memory (stores and provides context).

3   Training sets a) edges2sketched trees, continuator, edge2daisies, edge2dress.

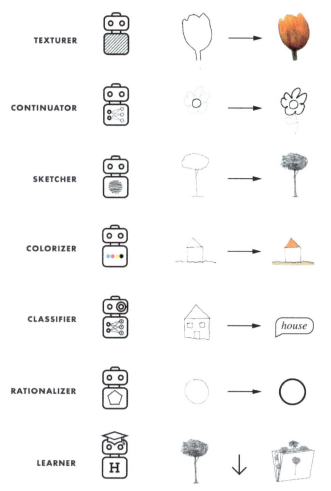

4   Each bot acquires a specific behavior during training.

The application incorporates behavior (humans and bots) but not toolbars, and memory—as it stores and provides context for what has been drawn—but no explicit layer structure. Actions are grouped by spatial and temporal proximity, which dynamically adjusts in order not to interrupt the flow of interaction.

The system allows users to access it from different devices, and also lets bots see what we are drawing in order to participate in the process. In contrast to interfaces of clicks and commands, this application features a continuous flow of interaction with no toolbars but bots with behavior.

What you can see in Figure 6 is a simple drawing suggestion: I draw a flower and a bot suggests a texture to fill it in. In this interface, you can select multiple human or artificial intelligences with different capabilities and delegate tasks to them.

I developed three drawing bots—texturer, sketcher, and continuator—that suggest texture, hand-sketched detail, or ways to

continue your drawings, respectively. Classifier recognizes what you are drawing, colorizer adds color, and rationalizer rationalizes shapes and geometry. Learner sorts drawings in order to use existing drawings for training new bots according to a desired drawing character, allowing the artist to transfer a particular aesthetic to a given bot. In training a bot, one of the biggest challenges is the need to either find or generate an image dataset from which bots can learn.

This project presents a way for artists and designers to use complex artificial intelligence models and interact with them in familiar mediums. The development of new models—and the exploration of their potential uses—is a road that lies ahead. As designers and artists, I believe it is our responsibility to envision and explore the interactions that will make machine intelligence a useful companion in our creative processes.

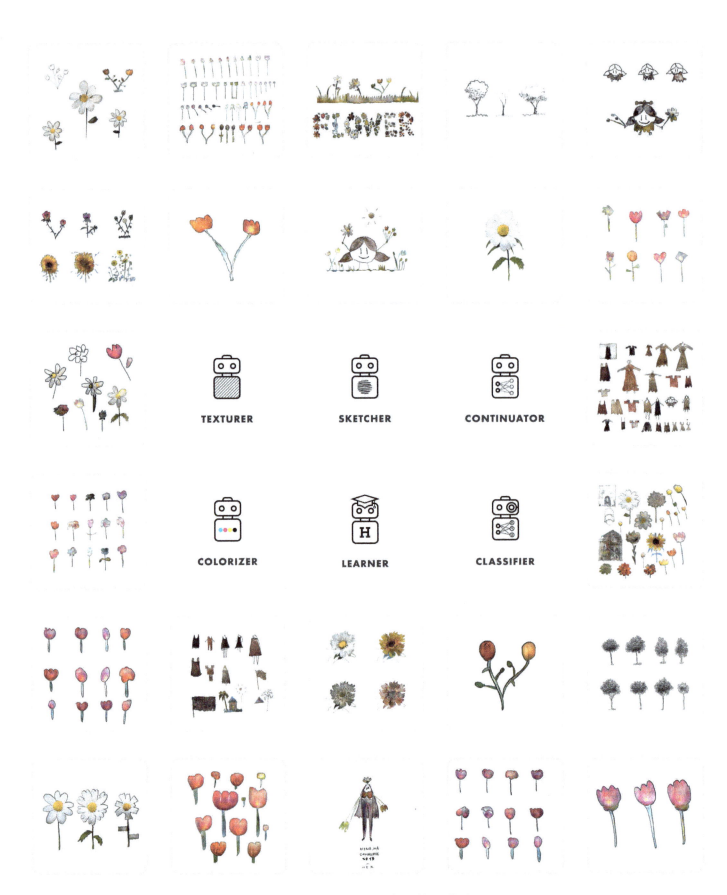

TEXTURER

SKETCHER

CONTINUATOR

COLORIZER

LEARNER

CLASSIFIER

5   The memory of the system provides drawing styles that then can be used to re-train new bots with specific character.

6   Input-output pairs. Top: **texturer** with edges2daisies. Bottom: **continuator** trees.

7   Suggestions of **texturer**, a bot that runs a pix2pix model trained with daisies.

8   Suggestions of sketcher, a bot that generates ink and watercolor drawings.

9   Drawings by artists, architects, and non-artists in collaboration with bots.

For further documentation, you can read the interactive web publication at www.nono.ma/suggestive-drawing or download it as a PDF at www.nono.ma/suggestive-drawing/pdf.

ACKNOWLEDGMENTS

I'd like to thank my advisor, Panagiotis Michalatos. His invaluable insights made this project a reality. The patience of my friend Jose Luis Garcia del Castillo and his input along the development of project have been more helpful than he can probably imagine. Thanks to Patrick Winston, Scott Kuindersma, Takehiko Nagakura, and many other academics for their valuable feedback. And thanks to Fulbright.

Mom. The artist. Thanks for being my friend. She sketched sixty four trees to train the sketcher bot. Other of her drawings also served for other training sets and for experimental purposes. You can take a look at her portraits and urban sketches on her site (www.lourdes.ac).

Bea. My girlfriend. She has been a great support and a huge inspiration in the development of this project. She is the original croquetilla, and all of my illustrations are inspired on her (http://nono.ma/croquetilla).

I'm extremely thankful to Phillip Isola, Jun-Yan Zhu, Tinghui Zhou, and Alexei A. Efros for their publication (and for open-sourcing their code), and to Christopher Hesse for porting the code to TensorFlow and making it dumb easy to use—pix2pix has made me discover and learn about new aspects of artificial intelligence and machine learning. TensorFlow has been a remarkably helpful library to get introduced to machine intelligence and develop intelligent bots.

Dress images belong to the The Metropolitan Museum of Art collection.

Disclaimer: The views and conclusions contained herein are those of the author and should not be interpreted as necessarily representing the official policies or endorsements, either expressed or implied, of Harvard University or the Harvard Graduate School of Design.

REFERENCES

Isola, Phillip, Jun-Yan Zhu, Tinghui Zhou, and Alexei A. Efros. 2016. "Image-to-Image Translation with Conditional Adversarial Networks."

Hesse, Christopher. 2017. "Image-to-Image Translation in TensorFlow." Affine Layer. https://affinelayer.com/pix2pix/

10 Drawing results by using **texturer** (top row) and **sketcher** (bottom row).

Nono Martínez Alonso (www.nono.ma) A computational designer and architect with a penchant for simplicity. After working in the design and delivery of complex architectural geometries at award-winning firms, such as AR-MA (Sydney) and Foster + Partners (London), he moved to Cambridge, where he studied a Master in Design Studies with a focus on Technology at the Harvard Graduate School of Design.

At Autodesk (Boston), he worked as a Research Engineer developing workflows for multi-material 3D printing, and currently works with the Generative Design Group developing tools for designers.

He is the writer of GettingSimple.com, co-founder of Viewtee.com, and developer of Axonometric, Lines, and Forces for iOS.

11 Illustration of Croquetilla without bot collaboration.

12 Illustration of Croquetilla with collaboration.

Unfindable Objects for BIM

Seth McDowell
University of Virginia /
mcdowellespinosa architects

Rychiee Espinosa
Cornell University /
mcdowellespinosa architects

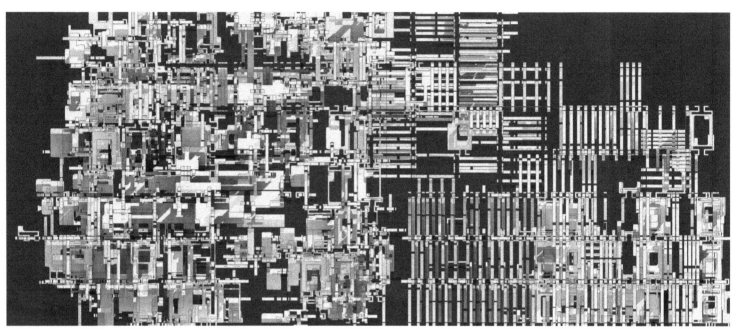

1   Elevation detail of Anomaly Exquisite Corpse BIM drawings, 2015. © mcdowellespinosa

Building information modeling (BIM) is not just a tool for project delivery and production. This research project seeks to identify new relationships between design processes and BIM that leverage computational resources for design objectives. The project outlines two approaches to breaking the constraints of BIM with more intuitive workflows for design. These include associative modules and conceptual massing with adaptive components. The work here highlights an exhibition created for the 2015 NY Architecture League Prize for Young Architects.

An unfindable object approaches and celebrates the exception, the special occurrence, the outlier. This project examines two conceptual model-making procedures aimed at creating spatial and material anomalies—those strange things that return no response from Google. The unfindable objects generated for the exhibition include a series of tangible objects and virtual BIM translations of the objects.

The exhibition presented a grouping of "spatial constructs." Using an identical set of material "ingredients," two different artists (Seth McDowell and Rychiee Espinosa), working from two separate locations (New York and Virginia), constructed a radically different set of physical objects utilizing abnormal construction techniques: linear threaded wads of chewing gum coated with dried spearmint leaves, and intricate modular constructions of laser-cut wood. Each of these objects are bound within a volumetric 12-inch cube and express the nature of tectonics and properties inherent to the

PRODUCTION NOTES

Architect: mcdowellespinosa
Sponsor: New York Architecture
             League
Type: Exhibition
Date: 2015

2   Anomaly Object 01, laser-cut basswood. © mcdowellespinosa

3   Anomaly Object 02, painted laser-cut masonite. © mcdowellespinosa

material. Drawings of these models executed in Autodesk Revit, translate the spatial constructs into architectural speculations—mysterious formations without context or utility.

The exercise presents two modalities of the exception. The methodology and exhibition was structured by two operations:

• Anomalous construct: the principle of variance. An anomaly is produced from the multiplicity of parts—parts that do not exactly fit together (wood clips).

• Clinamen construct: the principle of deviance. A material détournement is created (chewing gum and dried spearmint leaves).

The project addresses concerns about BIM's relationship to design workflow. BIM platforms frequently contain pallets of default/generic tools, which tend to result in architecture of a generic quality. Parametric objects are simply "dropped into" designs without careful consideration. Customization can be a cumbersome chore and only extremely patient or tech-savvy designers achieve provocative results. Thus, the agenda with these simulated BIM drawings is to transfer the spatial complexity and abstraction of the physical, unfindable objects into the heterogeneous BIM environment in an effort to break the boundaries present in the software. These abnormal objects are the tools used to dissect building information modeling.

ACKNOWLEDGMENTS

The drawings and objects where completed for the 2015 New York Architecture League Prize, focused on the theme of "Authenticity." The work was on display from June 23–August 1 in the Arnold and Sheila Aronson Galleries at the Shelia C. Johnson Design Center at Parsons School of Design at the New School.

The Architectural League Prize is one of North America's most prestigious awards for young architects and designers. The Prize, established in 1981, recognizes exemplary and provocative work by young practitioners and

4   Sectional perspective of Anomaly Exquisite Corpse BIM drawings, 2015. © mcdowellespinosa

5   Perspective of Anomaly Exquisite Corpse BIM drawings © mcdowellespinosa

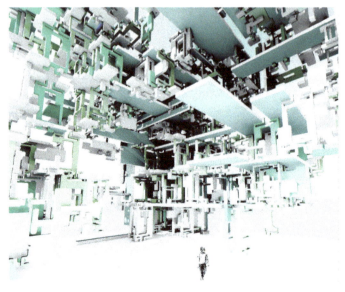

6   Perspective of Anomaly Exquisite Corpse BIM drawings © mcdowellespinosa

Unfindable Objects for BIM McDowell, Espinosa

7 Anomaly Exquisite Corpse BIM drawings, 2015. © mcdowellespinosa

provides a public forum for the exchange of their ideas. Each year, The Architectural League and the Young Architects + Designers Committee organize a portfolio competition. Individuals representing six winning practices are then invited to present their work in a variety of public fora, including lectures, an exhibition, and on the League's website.

REFERENCES

Carelman, and René Claire. 1984. *Objets Introuvables: A Catalogue of Unfindable Objects.* London: Frederick Muller.

Bök, Christian. 2002. *'Pataphysics: The Poetics of an Imaginary Science Avant-Garde & Modernism Studies.* Chicago, IL: Northwestern University Press.

Seth McDowell is an Assistant Professor of Architecture at the University of Virginia. McDowell is the co-founding partner of mcdowellespinosa, an experimental architectural practice focused on the transformation of waste, excess, and the ordinary into new spatial and material realities. National and international recognition for his design work include: the 2015 NY Architecture League Prize on the topic of Authenticity; "Layered Intelligence," a winning proposal for The Chicago Architecture Foundation's 2015 ChiDesign Competition; "My Hair is at MoMA PS1," a finalist in the 2012 MoMA PS1 Young Architects Program; and "Water Fuel: The Plan for a Self-Sustaining New York," the first place submission in the 2010 Self-Sufficient City competition. McDowell holds a Master of Architecture from Columbia University's Graduate School of Architecture, Planning, and Preservation and a Bachelor of Science in Design from Clemson University.

Rychiee Espinosa is a Strauch Visiting Critic, focusing on issues of sustainability and environmental impact within the field of design at the Cornell University College of Architecture, Art and Planning. She is also

8   Clinamen Exquisite Corpse BIM Drawing, 2015. © mcdowellespinosa

Unfindable Objects for BIM McDowell, Espinosa

9 Clinamen Object 01, 2015. Spearmint chewing gum, wrappers and leaves. © mcdowellespinosa

10 Clinamen Object 02, 2015. Spearmint chewing gum, wrappers and leaves. © mcdowellespinosa

an Associate Architect at Steven Holl Architects where she has served as Project Architect for the Glassell School of Art at the Museum of Fine Arts Houston in Houston, Texas and the University of Iowa School of Art and Art Historyís Visual Arts Building in Iowa City, Iowa.

Espinosa received a Master of Architecture degree from Columbia Universityís Graduate School of Architecture, Planning and Preservation in 2009, a Bachelor of Science degree in Architecture from Lawrence Technological University in 2006, and a Bachelor of Science in Biology with a focus in Kinesiology and Psychology from Indiana University in 2001.

Surface Ornamentation as Byproduct of Digital Fabrication

Ashish Mohite
Aalto University School of
Architecture

Mariia Kochneva

Toni Kotnik
Aalto University School of
Architecture

1   12 ribs at 120° and -120°, extrusion 5 mm and 10 mm, Vrib: 400 mm/min, Vcyl: 800 mm/min.

Introduction

This project consists of a series of experiments directed towards devising a methodology to use a
3D printer as a generative constituent of the design process. The thesis is that the manipulation of
manufacturing parameters could lead various architectural facets to be informed by the process of
making. A method to manipulate G-code, an interface between digital parametric design and digital
manufacturing, was developed in order to instigate the emergence of controlled yet indeterminate
textural patterning directly out of a fabrication process.

The objective of the project is derived from a concept of surface ornamentation as an indirect
material trace of the process of formation. This line of thought touches upon several themes.
Among them is an idea of ornament as a behavior, immanent to an object, made manifest through
the construction process (Moussavi 2008). That behavior is referred to as the internal structuring
of an object's materiality when exposed to external forming forces (Spuybroek 2016). The process
of formation is therefore informed by the relationship between material logic and machine logic,
wherein surface variation is an expression of that interaction.

The methodological foundation of the research is based on such principles of "digital craft" as the
continuity between design and production through the translation of algorithmic logics from stage
to stage, the integral involvement of an architect at all aspects of actualization, and an element
of "risk," in which the ability to modify production parameters converts the space of making into a

2   24 ribs at 120 °, Vrib: 400 mm/min, Vcyl: 800 mm/min

3   6 ribs at 30°, extrusion 5 mm, Vrib: 800 mm/min, Vcyl: 800 mm/min

4   12 ribs at 60°, extrusion 5 mm, Vrib: 400 mm/min, Vcyl: 800 mm/min

5   18 ribs at 120°, extrusion 5 mm, Vrib: 400 mm/min, Vcyl: 800 mm/min

space of discovery that is resistant to totalizing control (Kolarevic 2008).

The idea of heterogeneous surface ornamentation as a negotiation of internal and external forming forces was translated into the design of a production process in which the surface was informed by printing parameters, such as speed of material deposition, toolpath, and disabled retraction, and actualized in a material medium of plastic.

Method

In order to set a controlled experimental space, it was decided to use a single geometry, a single printer and a single material. For all printed models the digital model is a simple cylinder, the geometry of which is kept stable throughout experimentation. Surface ribbing, a technique to add or subtract mass from a surface, was programmed in G-code, allowing for an iterative process and a range of effects to materialize. These effects (ornamental manifestations), while designed and reproducible,

are not entirely uniform or predetermined, and result in pattern heterogeneity and unexpected deviations. While some spontaneous variation is encouraged, the research seeks to develop an understanding of the relationship between all constituent elements so that a system of controls can be devised.

Model Set 1: Accumulating Mass by Ribbing

Figure 2 illustrates the programming of the speed of deposition with disabled retraction. In G-code lower and upper cylinder bases are subdivided into segments, endpoints of corresponding segments are connected, and then the top base is rotated around its z-axis. At points located on connecting curves, the printer is set to print with speed of 400 mm/min, whereas the regular speed is 800 mm/min. Slower speed translates into higher flow rate, so more material is deposed. At 24 ribs clear boundaries between the thicker and thinner surfaces are blurred and the printer starts to fill the in-between space with fine filaments (an occurrence known as stringing), producing minute variation throughout.

6   6 ribs at 60°, extrusion 5 mm, Vrib: 400 mm/min, Vcyl: 800 mm/min

7   6 ribs at 60° and -60° extrusion 5 mm, Vrib: 400 mm/min, Vcyl: 800 mm/min

8   12 ribs at 60° and -60° extrusion 5 mm, Vrib: 400 mm/min, Vcyl: 800 mm/min

9   12 ribs at 60° and -60° extrusion 5 mm, Vrib: 800 mm/min, Vcyl: 1600 mm/min

In order to further explore stringing, ribs were extruded 5 mm outwards in G-code. In these experiments the number of ribs is 6, 12, and 18; and the angles are 30°, 60°, and 180° (Figures 3–5). The 180° model (Figure 5) approaches the limit of controlled variation, because each printing layer of the cylinder is rotated in relation to the previous one, while ribs are perpendicular to each layer. When rotation, and therefore displacement, becomes too severe, each following layer of rib slightly shifts and loses support from below, causing the falling of matter downwards. The model's surface can no longer be determined as singular and continuous. That, combined with less than parallel strings, produces a dense space of webbed matter all around the surface of the cylinder. Figure 6 shows a failed model, because that deformation exceeds predetermined limits of variation and it can not be reproduced.

Further experimentation involved the programming of intersecting extruded ribs as an attempt to see what kind of difference might result from the addition of geometric complexity. The orientation of ribs clearly plays a significant role, and comparing a model with one-directional ribs (Figure 5) to one with two-directional ribs (Figure 8) shows that stringing filaments in an opposite direction induces their merging in the center, which produces a branching superstructure. At this point, one more parameter was taken into consideration, namely the printing toolpath (Figure 9). All preceding models are produced with a default toolpath that amounts to printing the rib and cylinder surfaces continuously, while ribs are treated as a secondary geometry and the printer "returns" to them. The adjustment of the toolpath consisted in a topological split of the geometry in G-script, so that one layer of cylinder was printed first and then the ribs were continuously printed in the same layer (Figure 9).

Model Set 2: Shedding Mass by Ribbing

In model set 1, the speed of deposition was decreased for the ribs, while the surface of the cylinder itself was printed with regular speed. In the following cases (Figures 10 and 11), the

10 12 ribs at 60°, Vrib: 400 mm/min, Vcyl: 1600 mm/min

11 18 ribs at 120°, Vrib: 400 mm/min, Vcyl: 1600 mm/min

speed of deposition for rib areas remained 400 mm/min, whereas the cylinder surface was printed at a rate of 1600 mm/min. As retraction was still disabled, the material continued to pour, filling the space between ribs with porous, semi-directional matter. The action of thinning the cylinder's surface results in ribs becoming more pronounced as structural elements.

G-code of models, represented by Figures 12 and 13, is a diagonal mesh, where solid parts are set to be printed with a regular speed of 800 mm/min and voids at 1600 mm/min. The difference between three models is the length of voids; 5 and 10 mm respectively. Similarly to experiments with extruded ribs, a consistent shift of a certain parameter value indicates the limits of controlled variation. Figure 13 shows a model that is too structurally unstable, even though it exhibits a promising effect, akin to crochet.

Results

Research is beginning to accumulate data on the correlation between specific parameters, their manipulation, and resulting deformation. Models show that it is possible to program controlled surface variation by working closely with printing settings. The value of the presented experimentation is seen in a potential contribution to the discourse and practice of digital ornamentation. At the same time, it is a technique that allows a manufacturing machine to act as a "making hand" in the design process. Further research will continue to focus on shedding and accumulation of matter through various techniques. Simultaneously, presented experiments and future ones will be reproduced using different printers and materials in order to study the influence of material composition and behavior on the outcome of the process.

REFERENCES

Kolarevic, Branko. 2008. "The (Risky) Craft of Digital Making." In *Manufacturing Material Effects: Rethinking Design and Making in Architecture*, edited Branko Kolarevic and Kevin R. Klinger, 119–128. London: Routledge.

12 Vrib: 800 mm/min, Vcyl: 1600 mm/min

13 Vrib :800 mm/min, Vcyl: 1600 mm/min

Moussavi, Farshid, and Michael Kubo, eds. 2006. *The Function of Ornament*. Barcelona: Actar.

Spuybroek, Lars. 2016. *The Sympathy of Things: Ruskin and the Ecology of Design*. London: Bloomsbury Publishing.

IMAGE CREDITS
Ashish Mohite

Ashish Mohite is a researcher and doctoral candidate at Aalto University. His research topic revolves around the notion of craft in the digital fabrication process. Before starting his doctoral studies, he has worked, taught, and exhibited in India and Europe. He was recipient of Charles Correa gold medal for best bachelor thesis in India in 2007.

Mariia Kochneva is an independent researcher based in Helsinki, Finland. After receiving her Master's Degree from Städelschule, Frankfurt am Main, she has worked and done research on infrastructure as a natural system in Russia, India and Europe. Her current work is focused on the phenomenon of digital architectural ornament.

Toni Kotnik is Professor of Design of Structures at Aalto University. He studied architecture and mathematics in Germany, Switzerland and the US and taught at the Architectural Association in London, the Institute for Experimental Architecture at the University of Innsbruck, the Swiss Federal Institute of Technology (ETH) in Zurich, and the Singapore University of Technology and Design. Toni Kotnik has been lecturing worldwide and his practice and research work has been published and exhibited internationally, including the Venice Biennale, and is centered on the integration of knowledge from science and engineering into architectural thinking and the design process.

Thermoplastic Concrete Casting

Tsz Yan Ng
University of Michigan,
Taubman College of Architecture
and Urban Planning

Wes McGee
University of Michigan,
Taubman College of Architecture
and Urban Planning

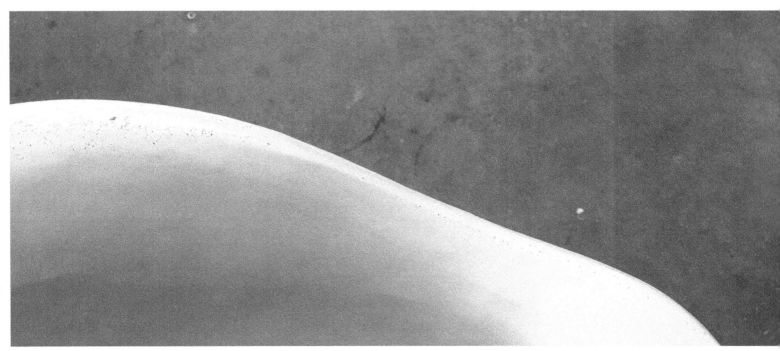

1   Detail of Eames's Molded Chair in GFRC.

Thermoplastic Concrete Casting explores molding techniques for glass fiber reinforced concrete (GFRC) utilizing non-woven thermoplastic textiles. Generating complex geometries in concrete typically incurs a high cost in time, material, and labor to produce the molds. Given that concrete is one of the most ubiquitously used building materials in the world, this research seeks to develop novel ways of creating formwork that would eliminate heavy, rigid molds and scaffoldings for support. Incorporating sartorial techniques of tailoring and patterning, the thermoplastic textile is cut, felted together (a process of needle punching where textile fibers are entangled together), heat stiffened, and surface finished, ready for GFRC casting.

We explored this technique at two scales: first, at object scale with the reproduction of Eames's molded fiberglass armchair and Saarinen's Womb Chair, and second, at architectural scale with the installation of an 11′ x 7′ wall composed of five modules with an adjoining table surface. Both scales were designed as prototypes to test the viability of this technique to efficiently and accurately produce complex curvatures. The full-scale wall was an opportunity to explore structural conditions related to joining discrete panels, as well as to understand spatial and experiential effects.

A key component of this research was to incorporate the use of physics-based design tools, such as the Kangaroo plugin for Rhino/Grasshopper. Utilizing a physics-based modeling approach enables

PRODUCTION NOTES

Designers:	Tsz Yan Ng, Wes McGee
Site:	Ann Arbor, MI
Location:	Annex Gallery
Year:	2017

2   Front view.

designers to simulate material behaviors in real time, while simultaneously enforcing geometric constraints. In this case the technique was applied to enable modifications to the global form while enforcing the developability of the resulting textile patterns. These were then unrolled and modified parametrically to account for the shrink rate during the stiffening process, as well as allowances for the felted seams. Another ongoing area of experimentation was the use of needle felting to seamlessly join nonwoven textiles together.

Thermoplastic Concrete Casting aimed to challenge the typical processes for forming complex geometries in concrete. The project comingles sartorial techniques with architectural methods of making to address construction challenges. By reducing the waste associated with typical subtractive mold making techniques, it presents the potential for large scale GFRC casting with minimally supported surfaces. Through a discursive process of full-scale prototyping and parametric design, the project links computational design and fabrication processes with heuristic

knowledge of building to inform the design and production at different scales.

ACKNOWLEDGMENTS

Thermoplastic Concrete Casting was made possible through the generous support from the Taubman College of Architecture + Urban Planning, University of Michigan. Additional support was received through the University of Michigan Office of Research.

Design Team

Tsz Yan Ng and Wes McGee

Fabrication/Installation Assistance

Simon Anton, Drew Bradford, Scott Chriss, Kristen Gandy, Layth Adulameer M Mahadi, Asa Peller, Jaemoon Rhee, and Andrew Thompson.

3   View of cast GFRC wall with table extension.

4   Close-up of cast panels.

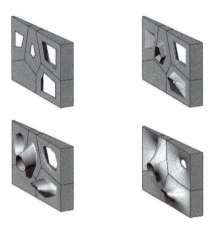

5   Mesh is relaxed with differential warp/weft stiffness, combined with planarization constraints to force individual panels to remain developable.

6   Plan view showing the final subdivision of individual mesh faces.

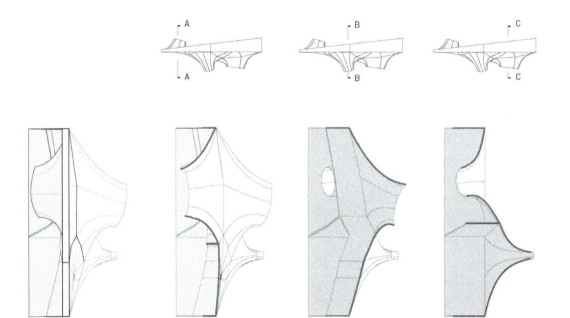

7   (left) Side elevation from 2" side, (right) Section A, B, and C.

Thermoplastic Concrete Casting Ng, McGee

8   Eames's molded armchair in GFRC.

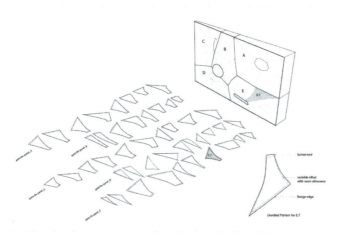

9   Once patterned, the individual panels are unrolled, and seam offsets and shrinkage allowances are added to each edge.

10   View of wall from tapered side.

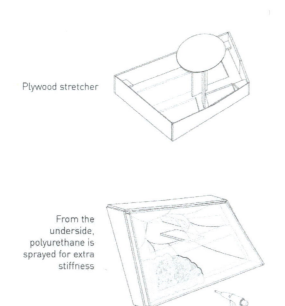

Plywood stretcher

From the underside, polyurethane is sprayed for extra stiffness

Thermoplastic textile, patterned, felted together, fastened with staples on stretcher, and heat stiffened

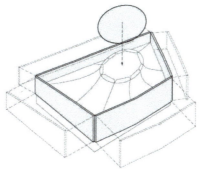

After mold surface is prepped, cap for funnel end is attached, along with the flanges. Edges are then siliconed.

11   Diagram of mold assembly.

12 (clockwise from top left) Prepared molds of chairs, patterned nonwoven thermoplastic textile, underside of stretcher with thermoplastic stiffened on top, demolding process, spraying process for Womb Chair, bolting of wall panels, prepared mold of wall panel, heat shrinking on stretcher, and spraying process of wall panel.

Thermoplastic Concrete Casting Ng, McGee

13 Overall dimensions of wall: 11 ft wide x 7 ft tall x 5.4 ft deep (without table extension).

14 Saarinen's Womb Chair in GFRC. (Model: Ellie Abrons)

Tsz Yan Ng is an Assistant Professor in Architecture at Taubman College, University of Michigan. She was the Walter B. Sanders Fellow at the University of Michigan (2007-08) and the Reyner Banham Fellow at the University of Buffalo (2001-02). Ng's practice includes architectural designs and installations in visual art. Common to both practices are projects that deal with questions of labor in its various manifestations, with special focus on techniques in clothing manufacturing and concrete forming. Her design work has been exhibited in both solo and group exhibitions in Detroit, Los Angeles, Ann Arbor, Montréal, Ithaca, and Buffalo.

Wes McGee is an Assistant Professor and the Director of the FABLab at the University of Michigan Taubman College of Architecture and Urban Planning. His work revolves around the interrogation of the means and methods of material production in the digital era, through research focused on developing new connections between design, engineering, materials, and manufacturing processes as they relate to the built environment.

Punctual Urban Redevelopment in Informal Urban Contexts

Trevor Ryan Patt
Singapore University of
Technology and Design

1   Perspective view of model after simulation has run for 5000 cycles.

This project develops an alternative approach to masterplanning within informal urban sites using the urban village of Xiaozhoucun, Guangzhou as a case study. In contrast to the *tabula rasa* approach that currently dominates, this project adapts to the dynamic metabolism of the village and, rather than replacing, can develop alongside it .

Enabling this approach is a computational engine that enacts three actions concurrently: distributed analysis of the circulation network, identification of potentiality in the urban fabric, and generation of new urban form. A multi-agent system of weighted random walks (Figure 6) continuously traverses the streets and alleys of the village, accumulating traces of clustering and bottlenecks. Each agent analyzes the idiosyncrasies of its localized network, particularly accessibility and geodesic depth. Through this, the model identifies locations where punctual interventions might improve the network connectivity or insert a small public space without disturbing the integrity of the urban fabric and its tangle of warren-like alleyways. These potential interventions are compared to an information model of the built form—existing building volumes, the age of buildings as they creep toward obsolescence, availability of reclaimed building material (Figure 2)—to find overlaps where redevelopment of a building can coincide with modifications to public space adjacent to the building footprint.

PRODUCTION NOTES

Site Area: 15 ha

Location: Xiaozhoucun, Guangzhou

Date: 2016-2017

2   Sociomaterial processes in Xiaozhoucun: informal construction benefits from salvaging and recycling brick during demolition.

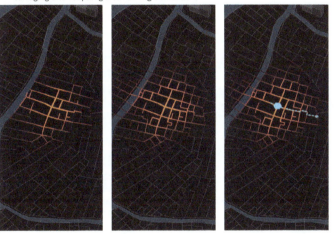

4   During the random walk, agents analyze their existing local network (left) and compare to a potential expanded network (center) to identify shortcuts (right) that would improve circulation and network accessibility.

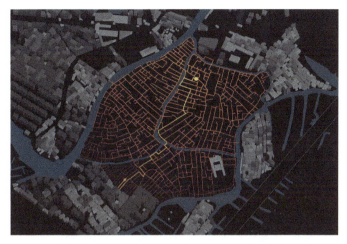

3   Geodesic distance from as starting point to every part of the existing circulation network. The length of the longest path (in yellow) is the point's eccentricity.

5   A screenshot of the simulation in progress. Thirty-five agents are visible (blue dots) showing potential shortcuts (see Figure 4). At the moment of this image, two buildings had already been selected for redevelopment (yellow polygons).

Thus the model disrupts the conventional scalar and temporal hierarchies of masterplanning. It manages to advance a coherent urban goal through incremental methods and limited vision instead of a wholistic, authored image of the final state. The avoidance of a complete or totalizing masterplan was designed into the process intentionally so that the model is able to react to the rapid turnover of the built environment of the village, even to utilize it as a mechanism of implementation. The benefit of this method is its flexibility in the face of the changing and unpredictable conditions that cannot be entirely regulated in the context of informal urbanism. Because of the stochastic nature of the multi-agent random walk and the restriction of each analysis to a localized portion of the network, the model is generally useful even if aspects of the village develop independently of the model. In this way the model simulates the potential for such a tool to be used over a long timespan, updated with empirically gathered data as the village develops, and providing feedback to guide future development without necessarily controlling it.

A framework like this, which goes beyond phased development into truly time-based planning, can also be compelling in more formal urban planning because it allows the masterplan to develop alongside the city, and to integrate early or intermediate results adaptively rather than relying on pre-given development targets.

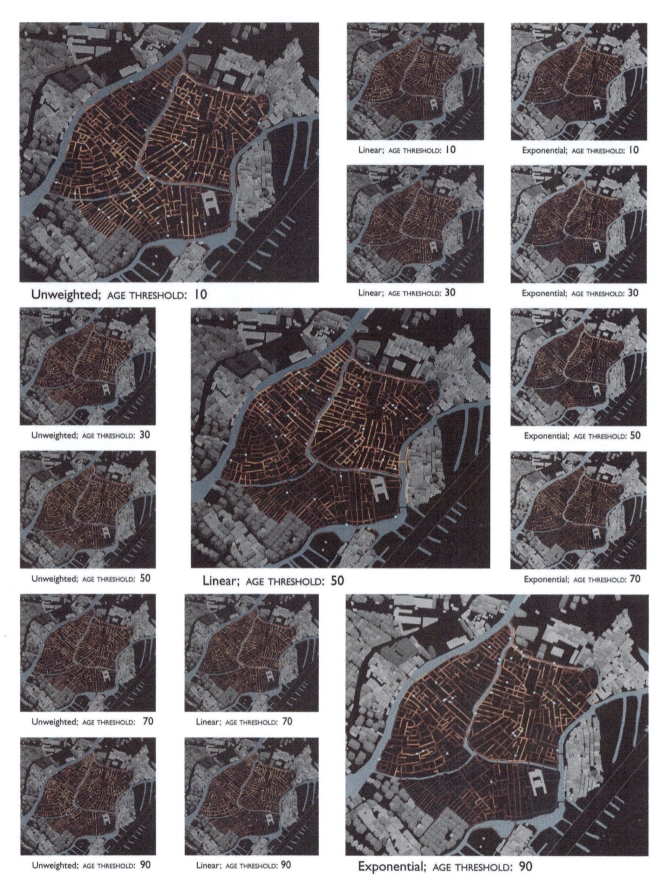

Unweighted; AGE THRESHOLD: 10

Linear; AGE THRESHOLD: 10

Exponential; AGE THRESHOLD: 10

Linear; AGE THRESHOLD: 30

Exponential; AGE THRESHOLD: 30

Unweighted; AGE THRESHOLD: 30

Exponential; AGE THRESHOLD: 50

Unweighted; AGE THRESHOLD: 50

Linear; AGE THRESHOLD: 50

Exponential; AGE THRESHOLD: 70

Unweighted; AGE THRESHOLD: 70

Linear; AGE THRESHOLD: 70

Unweighted; AGE THRESHOLD: 90

Linear; AGE THRESHOLD: 90

Exponential; AGE THRESHOLD: 90

6   Testing the random walk parameters. The highlighted condition at center was chosen for resultant coverage and density comparable to eccentricity values.

7   After 5000 cycles, the simulation model proposed widening or opening these
    edges, adding around 4.56 km of new alleyways.

9   Eccentricity values (see Figure 3) of the existing urban network. At left, the
    values are plotted, with quartiles labeled.

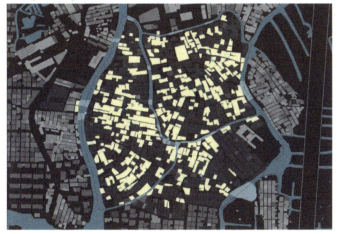

8   At the same time 379 parcels were reconfigured (29.5% of the village by
    footprint), nearly doubling the FAR from 1.27 to 2.48 (see Figure 11).

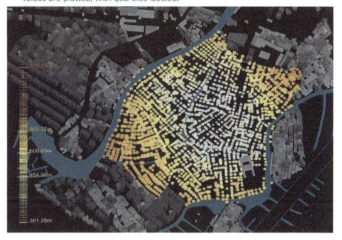

10 Impact of simulation model on eccentricity as a result of introducing shortcuts
    (as described in Figure 4).

Despite the lack of centralized coordination, this project demonstrates
the capacity to guide development in an informal context, even as an
exploratory study with only a few initial parameters. In one typical
example (Figure 10), the model reduced the diameter and average
eccentricity of the circulation network by 10% (from 776 to 702 meters
and 565 to 509 meters, respectively). Consistent with the aims of a
punctual redevelopment, the length of an average intervention was
only 7.6 meters (Figure 7). At the same time, the model proposed 62
new pockets of open space while nearly doubling the FAR (from 1.27 to
2.48). From the built floor area, 70,000m2 of the original 190,000 were
replaced and 317 buildings were extended vertically, resulting in a total
built area of 370,000 m^2 (Figure 8).

Ultimately, this project points to how a disruption of the object and
processes of masterplanning can enable masterplanning to engage with
a new set of informal processes, and how relinquishing control of the
outcome can be offset by the agency of a collection of opportunistic
reactions, temporal sequences, and localized procedures.

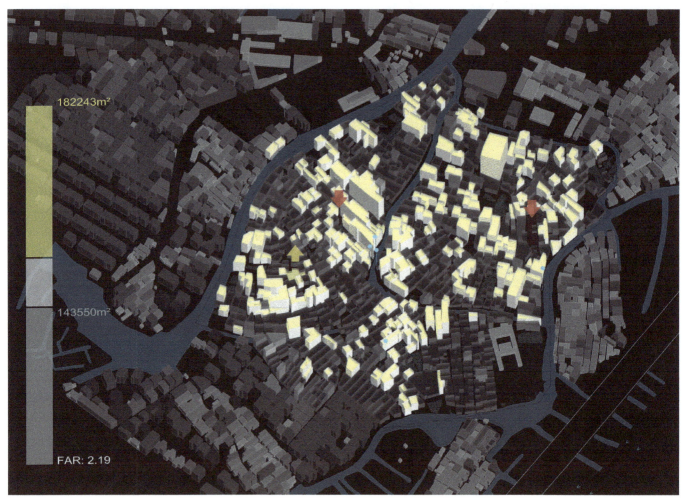

182243m²

143550m²

FAR: 2.19

11 A screenshot of the simulation in progress. Red arrows indicate ongoing demolition, while yellow arrows indicate reconstruction.
Total measures of the building stock (in m²) are tracked at left—existing, undeveloped area in dark grey, redeveloped area in light grey, and new contruction in yellow. .

ACKNOWLEDGMENTS

This research was begun as part of a PhD completed at the M×D Lab at EPFL. Cadastral data was supplied through a partnership with Kongjian Yu at PKU. The research is continued with support from SUTD's Startup Research Grant.

Trevor Ryan Patt is an Assistant Professor at Singapore University of Technology and Design. His research focuses on the point of contact between architecture and urbanism, with an emphasis on the ways that advanced computational techniques can reshape the approach to urban design and how we fundamentally think about the city. He completed his PhD, *Assemblage Form: An ontology of the urban generic with regard to architecture, computation, and design*, at the École polytechnique fédérale de Lausanne.

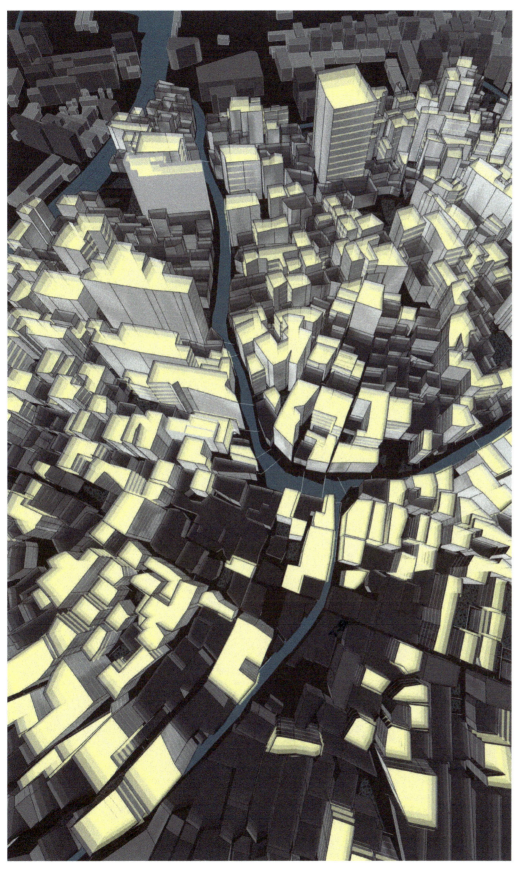

12 Perspective view of model after simulation has run for 5000 cycles.

(ultra) light network

Felix Raspall
Singapore University of
Technology and Design

Carlos Bañón
Singapore University of
Technology and Design

1   (ultra) light network installation in the context of Marina Bay, Singapore (Carlos Bañón, © 2017).

INTRODUCTION

In architecture, the use of additive manufacturing (AM) technologies has been primarily limited
to the production of scale models. Its application for functional building components has been
typically undermined by the long production time, elevated cost to manufacture parts and the low
mechanical properties of 3D-printed components. As AM becomes faster, cheaper and stronger,
there are emerging opportunities for architects to make creative use of AM to produce functional
architectural pieces. Our research investigates the feasibility of AM to produce architecture that
is functional and centered in space frame assemblies. It advances custom digital design tools,
enhances our understanding of the manufacturability of complex geometry parts, integrates
structural and information systems in architecture, and permits the assembly of complex structures.
Our ongoing project started in late 2015, and consistent of two full-scale projects. The first project,
vMesh, completed in 2016, sets the basic instruments that are needed to design, manufacture and
assemble a complex 3D structure.

(ultra) light network

The second project is "(ultra) light network," designed and built for iLight Marina Bay 2017. It
was a light art installation, a mesh that combines structure and interactive light. As a research
project, it focuses on enlarging the scale, durability and complexity of space frame structures
using 3D-printed components, and its main innovation relies on the integration of data and power

PRODUCTION NOTES

Architects:	Felix Raspall and Carlos Bañón
Client:	iLight
Status:	Completed
Site Area:	30,000 sq. ft.
Location:	Marina Bay, Singapore
Date:	2017

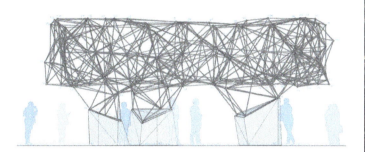

2   Elevation (Felix Raspall and Carlos Bañón, © 2017)

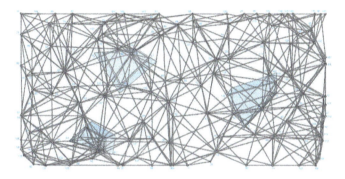

3   Plan (Felix Raspall and Carlos Bañón, © 2017).

4   Side view (Carlos Bañón, © 2017)

transmission into the structural frame. The main objective was to test how AM manufacturing enable the creation of very complex parts that can be used to solve multiple architectural problems concurrently. Our methodology covered all stages in the design and manufacturing process.

I.   Associative Model

A robust parametric script was developed to accurately manage the geometric complexity of both the space frame and its nodes. The modeling and programming platform was McNeel's Rhinoceros and Grasshopper. The algorithm first generates a tetrahedral three-dimensional mesh from an input 10 x 5 x 2.5 m prismatic volume. This basic form meets our initial concept of a floating prism hovering on top of three vertical supports. The result, a three-dimensional wireframe model, contains the basic graph of the space frame and the topology of every node. The naming system of nodes and bars, which will be used for the assembly, is also defined at this stage. (ultra) light network consists of 152 nodes and 715 bars. The conceptual and visual

lightness of the design was complemented by the actual light weight of the physical structure, for which we favored very slender linear elements arranged into a hyper-redundant mesh. The total weight of the structure, which covers 50 m2, was 150 kg. We conducted structural analysis of the structural frame directly in the same modeling and programming platform.

Our script, then, defines the geometry of each node and produces the file for printing. The main steps of this script are described in Figure 10. The first step involves the creation of the basic topology, where the length of the branch in each node is determined by the angle with its closest neighbor branch. Branches that are very close together will be longer to avoid self-intersections. The length of the branches is then further adjusted to ensure that the bars are all standard lengths. The script then generates the solid, using truncated pyramids with a wall thickness of 3 mm. The connectors that will receive the bars are then generated and added to the model. The final step is the addition of the ID of the node and of each bar reaching the node.

5   Public engagement with (ultra) light network (Kazry Kas Kazan, © 2017)

(ultra) light network Raspall, Bañón

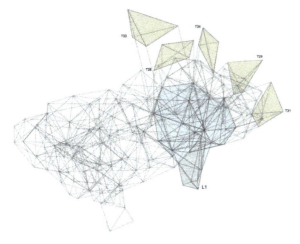

6   Diagram of tethrahedral topology (Felix Raspall and Carlos Bañón, © 2017).

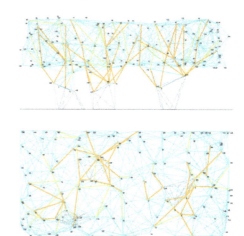

7   Structural analysis (Felix Raspall and Carlos Bañón, © 2017).

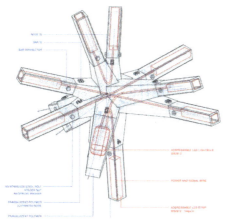

8   Node detail (Felix Raspall and Carlos Bañón, © 2017).

9   Closeup of a node (Carlos Bañón, © 2017).

For the bars, the procedure is simpler. The initial tetrahedral mesh has bars of all different lengths, which makes the assembly process tedious. Therefore, the bars are adjusted to standard lengths in increments of 5 cm.

II.   Interactive lighting system

The project integrates an interactive lighting system that illuminates the structure in response to the public behavior. LED strips were placed inside of the bars and nodes, where the electronic components such as wires, LEDs, connectors, and controllers are hidden inside the translucent structure. Organized in 35 individual linear circuits, the 50.000 individually addressable LED dots are controlled by a bespoke algorithm running simultaneously on five Teensy micro-controllers. The program uses the information from three ultrasonic sensors to detect the presence of visitors and trigger light pulses through the structure, emulating the firing of neurons in the brain. Figure 11 illustrates the diagram of circuits, which maps the individual address of each of the 50,000 pixels into its physical location in the structure.

III.   Manufacturing of structural elements

Because of the translucent properties required for the desired light effect, all the elements in the mesh are made of translucent polymers. The 715 bars are polycarbonate square tubes with high density LED strips embedded within. This material evenly diffuses and smooths the individual light sources.

For the 152 unique nodes, we tested two printing technologies. We manufactured 70 nodes using FDM printing of clear ABS, and 82 nodes using SLS printing of polyamide (PA). Both AM technologies were satisfactory, but we identified some differences between them. The optic properties of clear ABS were superior in the amount of light that it let pass through, but its transparency also made the LED points more visible. On the other hand, the PA node emitted less light, but the light was very even. The printing quality has higher resolution with SLS, but the FDM process was good enough. We conducted tensile tests of the connectors using an UTM, and we estimated that the tensile capacity of each node was over 2 kN for both materials. The lead time for the 152 nodes was one month.

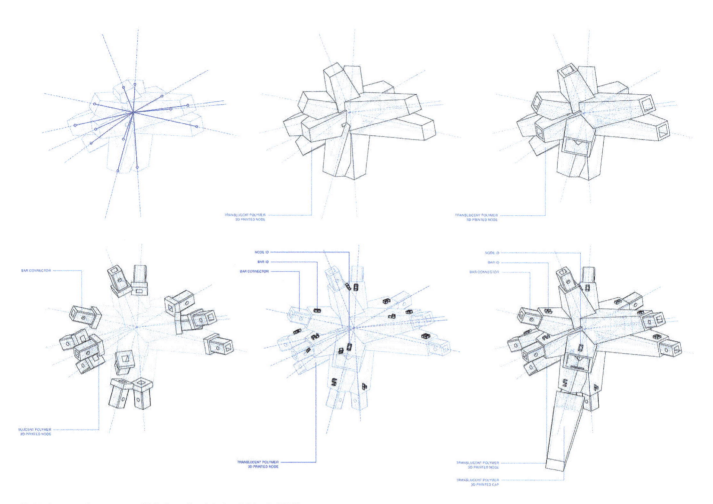

10 Node generation sequence (Felix Raspall and Carlos Bañón, © 2017).

IV. Assembly process

Contrary to its complex appearance, the assembly sequence was relatively undemanding and speedy. Simple equipment was required throughout the entire process, thanks to a straightforwardly designed bar–node mechanical connection, which only required a single bolt and nut. The millimetric precision in both bars and nodes made the construction easy. The electronic connections were more onerous, because each bar and node requires ground, power and signal, totaling over 2000 connections. Three main parts of the structure were pre-assembled in our lab, but due to transportation constraints, a substantial part of the assembly was conducted on-site. The assembly process took 10 days.

At first, the structure felt wobbly and unsteady, due to its extremely slender elements, which had a 30:1 to 135:1 aspect ratio. However, and unlike other systems now in use, its hyper-redundancy enabled the network to absorb stresses and evenly respond to expansion, contraction and distributed and punctual loads, and made it highly resilient to damage to members. Three polygonal heavy bases, machined in 18 mm plywood and cladded in 10 mm white opal polycarbonate panels, served as a necessary ballast to grant the stability of the lightweight mesh and house the power boxes.

REFLECTION

The results of the (ultra) light network project demonstrate that AM can be successfully used to produce functional elements in architecture, and open new paths for designers to deal with complex geometries where lightness, continuity and sleekness play an important role. The resulting hyper-redundant structure is not only structurally functional, but also reinforces a narrative of lightness, both conceptually and literally.

The complexity of the project was successfully managed through the custom programming of an associative model that automatically solves the structure graph, standardizes the bars lengths, produces each node geometry and validates the structural performance. The manufacturing process of bars and nodes was straightforward, as the associative model produced the print files and cut sheets automatically.

The assembly process was very smooth for a structure of such complexity.

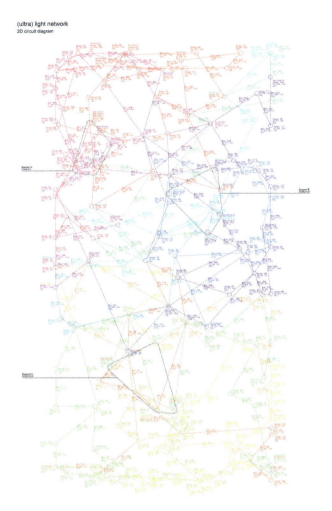

(ultra) light network
2D circuit diagram

11 Circuits diagram (Felix Raspall and Carlos Bañón, © 2017).

12 Performance under the installation (Kazry Kas Kazan, © 2017).

The precision of nodes and bars and well-designed node–bar connections simplified the process. We experienced some challenges during the assembly stage related to the accessibility of the higher nodes. The electric connections between nodes and bars were the most time-consuming, and improved detailing will mitigate this bottleneck.

ACKNOWLEDGEMENTS

Design Concept: Felix Raspall and Carlos Bañón; Project Lead: Felix Raspall, Carlos Bañón, Manuel Garrido, Felix Amtsberg and Mohan Elara.; Research Team: Tay Jenn Chong, Pan Shiqian, Gowdam Sureshkumar, Thejus Pathmakumar, Joei Wee Shi Xuan, Liu Hong Zhe, Yiping Goh, Mohit Arora and Naik Hiong Chiang.

Sponsors: Stratasys, Center for Digital Design and Manufacturing at SUTD, and SUTD.

Felix Raspall is an architect and design researcher investigating the relationships between design, materiality and technology. He is an Assistant Professor at SUTD, holding a Doctor of Design from Harvard University, a Master of Architecture from Yale University, and a B.Arch. from the University of Buenos Aires. He leads his own professional practice in Argentina. Felix's work explores modes of design production in which material constraints creatively inform designs through digital technologies. Before joining SUTD, Felix conducted teaching and research in several institutions, including Harvard University, Graz University of Technology, and the University of Buenos Aires. His design and research work has been published in books and journals and was the recipient of several awards.

Carlos Bañón, prior to joining SUTD, was an Assistant Professor of Architecture at Polytechnical School of Alicante. There he taught graphical procedures and parametric design strategies and co-founded FAB-LAB Alicante, where he conducted a variety of workshops and seminars related to form-finding and advanced geometries. Furthermore, as invited professor, he took part in architectural workshops and lectures at EPFL Lausanne, ETSAM Madrid, UPV Valencia and UIC Catalonia. Besides his academic activity, he co-founded Subarquitectura Office along with Andrés Silanes and Fernando Valderrama, in Spain, where he currently searches for new architectural forms and systems, obtaining acknowledgement and international awards for their built production, highlighting amongst others, the Tram Stop in Alicante, the 3D Athletics Track in Elda, the 360° House in Madrid and YHIWA Prototypes in West Africa.

Expressive Robotic Networks

Benjamin Rice
Univeristy of Texas at Austin

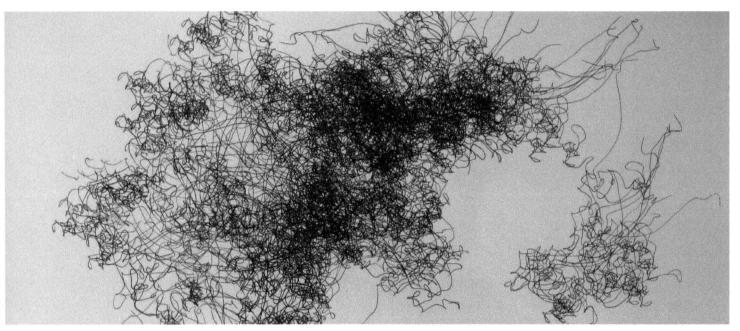

1   1036 (Benjamin Rice, 01/13/2017, ©).

The related acts of creation and expression have long been considered fundamentally anthropocentric in both form and nature. So much so, in fact, that they are often prefixed with the word "human" as a way of qualifying their existence and significance—as in "human creation" and "human expression." The Oxford Living Dictionary even goes so far as to define art as "the expression or application of *human* creative skill and imagination" (emphasis added). But at what point does the agency of the rapidly developing technological "other" begin to reshape this anthropocentric position? It is precisely this question that provides the basis for this project, which attempts to challenge the historical and disciplinary underpinnings of what it means to draw.

The technological other in this case is a robotics network that can simultaneously learn, compare, decide, and produce, allowing traditionally human acts of expression to not only be automated, but be fully assimilated into an autonomous environment that exists independent of most human involvement. This evolves the long-held hierarchy between human and tool, with the machine gaining an autonomy to think and create outside the confines of immediate human direction. The result is a reexamining of the disciplinary act of drafting not as an anthropocentric depiction of figure or communication of instructions, but rather as a generative act of autonomous representation.

For the two drawing series presented here the network pulled from the vast history of recursive multiplication and grid making (both fundamental concepts within architectural conception and production), including imagery of countless natural phenomena as well as the work of both artists and architects, and developed its own repetitive visual languages. By harnessing machine-learning techniques, including object detection and linear

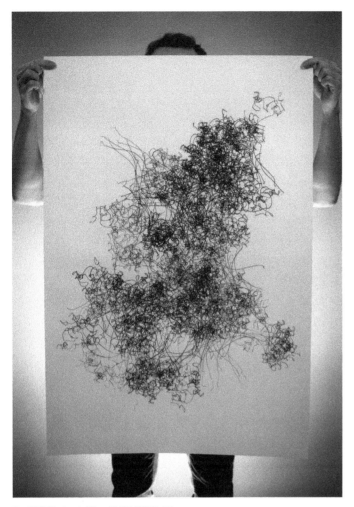

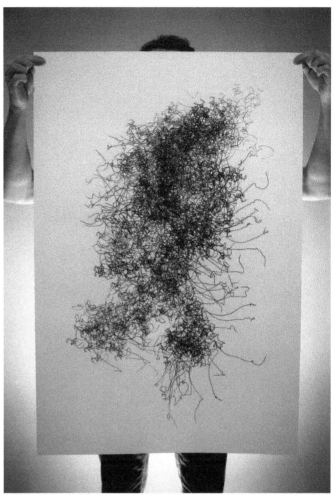

2 733 (Benjamin Rice, 01/13/2017, ©).

3 1112 (Benjamin Rice, 01/13/2017, ©).

regression models with various fit methods, initial plotting could then be aggregated into compositions by a KUKA KR60 robotic arm. These drawings can be seen both as a final, precedent-based designed product, or as the first step in an autonomous generative design process. In either case, the creation of an autonomous network capable of producing such expressions presents a far more nuanced understanding of how technology is shaping and disrupting the relationship between design and making, real and virtual, architecture and engineering, on site and remote, professionals and crowds, as well as physical and digital data, as such concepts relate to the discipline of architecture.

REFERENCES

"Art." *Oxford Living Dictionaries*. Available at https://en.oxforddictionaries. com/definition/art

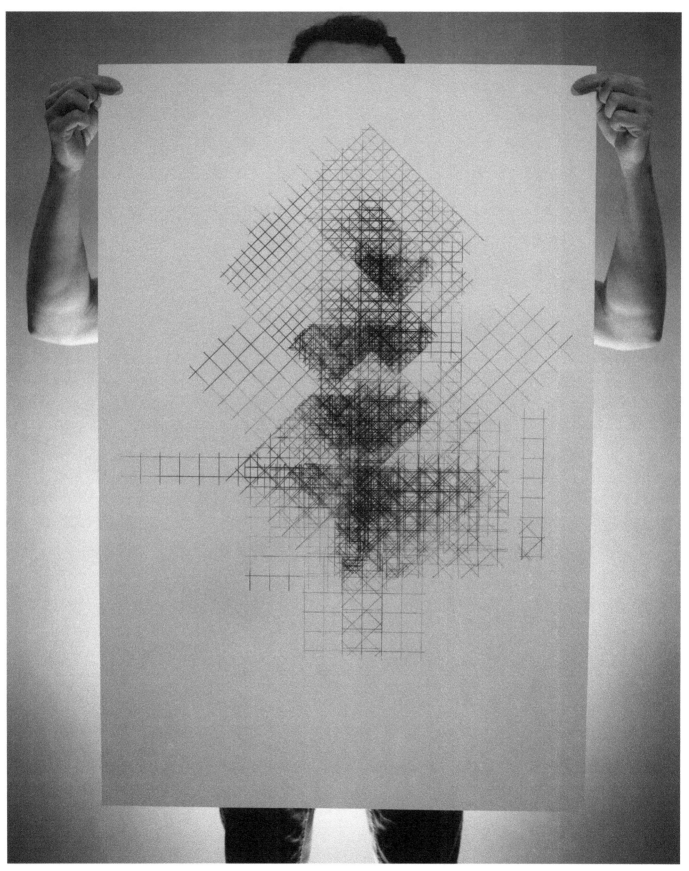

4   65 (Benjamin Rice, 01/13/2017, ©).

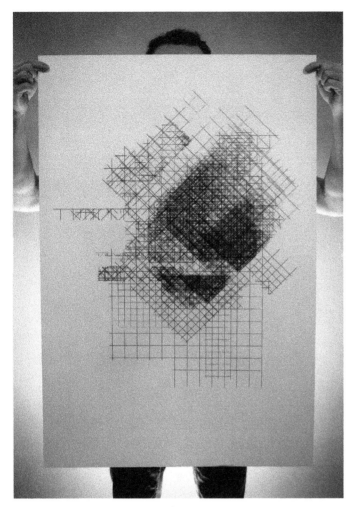

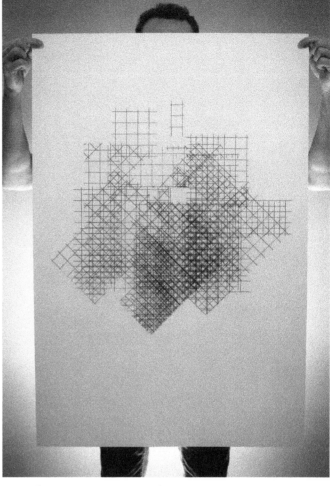

5   204 (Benjamin Rice, 01/13/2017, ©).

6   912 (Benjamin Rice, 01/13/2017, ©).

Benjamin Rice is a principal of MTTR MGMT. Before joining MM Benjamin helped deliver high profile architectural projects and competitions for some of the worlds leading architectural firms.

Benjamin's work, both personal and professional, has been published and exhibited widely. Recent exhibitions include the A+D Museum in Los Angeles, the Storefront for Art and Architecture in New York, and the Denver Art Museum. Recent publications include On Ramp, Pidgin Magazine, TARP, eVolo Magazine, and the recent Actar book Critical Prison Design: Mas d'Enric Penitentiary by AiB arquitectes + Estudi PSP Arquitectura.

Benjamin is currently a Research Scientist Assoc. the University of Texas at Austin. He has taught previously at the Virginia Tech School of Architecture + Design, the UC Berkeley College of Environmental Design, the California College of the Arts, and as an assistant at the Southern California Institute of Architecture and the Princeton University School of Architecture. He received his Bachelor of Architecture from the Southern California Institute of Architecture and his Master of Architecture from the Princeton University School of Architecture.

LightScale II
arc/sec Lab

Uwe Rieger
The University of Auckland

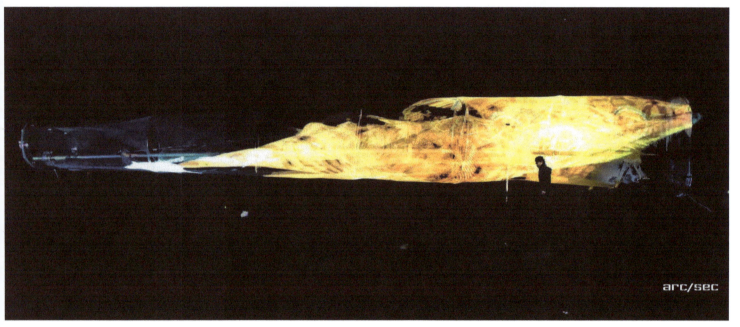

1   Installation LightScale II (photo: Uwe Rieger, 2017).

Slowly rotating and dipping its immense translucent bulk, the kinetic installation LightScale II floats through a virtual ocean like a giant whale while it processes and materialises environments, events and user interactions. LightScale II generates a mysterious tactile experience of three dimensional data through the projections that fall on its multiple layered gauze skin.

The kinetic structure is formed from a 20-metre-long carbon fibre mast construction, surrounded by multiple layers of black mesh. Mounted asymmetrically on a single pin-joint, the structure is held in a fragile balance with a set of counterweights. A single touch from a visitor allows the form to oscillate freely in space with little friction. A motion tracking system combined with ultrasound sensors recognises the touch, position and movement of LightScale, and a live-render program overlays the physical construction with projected digital information. The installation combines three types of datasets: firstly, place-bound information which only appears in specific positions; secondly, kinetic data which follows the moving object; and thirdly, responsive sets of data which correspond to user interaction with LightScale II.

The principle of projecting onto a layered surface to generate spatial appearances is well known. It is used in both spectacular entertainment shows and refined artistic projects. Examples for this are the mesh projections by Nonotak Studio, such as Daydream V2 1, and Anthony McCall's Solid Light Works2, which illuminates fog particles. What makes the LightScale II project distinct is the

PRODUCTION NOTES

Architect: Uwe Rieger
Status: First presentation 09/2017
Site Area: 30 m x 30 m x 6 m
Location: Mariendom Linz, Austria
Date: 2017

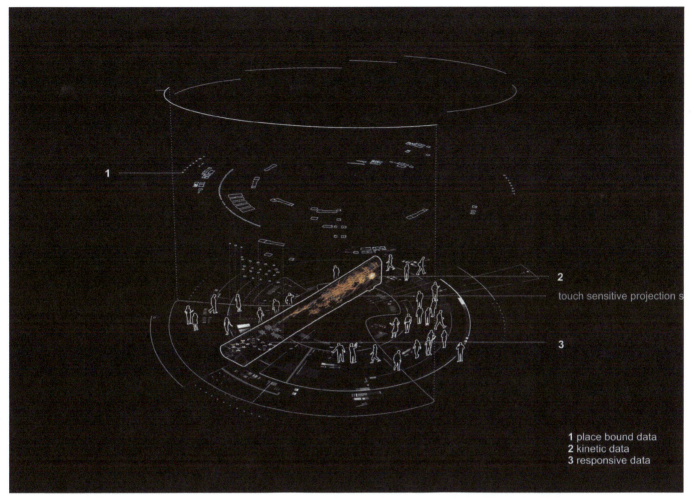

Within the image:
1
2 touch sensitive projection s
3

1 place bound data
2 kinetic data
3 responsive data

2   Tactile data sets (drawing Yiqiu Hong, 2016).

1:1 calibration of an interlinked virtual world with a physical setup. The space generated is not a 2D animation creating a 3D effect, rather it is a precisely calculated environment, defined in three dimensions by using spatial sensors and an array of data projectors.

The principle of visualizing place-bound data is comparable to AR head mounted displays such as the Microsoft HoloLens. The difference is that the LightScale II does not require any additional viewing device. From the beginning, the design process integrates physical and digital reality and the outcome is a fusion of both worlds, creating a new form of haptic-digital materiality and responsive architecture. The project has its conceptual roots in a design by kunst und techink3 (Rainer Hartl, Martin Janekovic, Uwe Rieger and Helle Schroeder) developed in Berlin in the late 1990's.

Equipped with new digital spatial technologies, LightScale II becomes an intelligent navigation tool that creates responsive haptic-digital constructions and materializes spatial narratives.

The technical principle was developed and designed by Associate Professor Uwe Rieger at the arc/sec Lab for Digital Spatial Operations at the School of Architecture and Planning at the University of Auckland. The Lab investigates concepts for new building and urban conditions in which digital information is both connected to spatial appearance and linked to material properties. The approach focusses on the step beyond digital representation and digital fabrication, working to the point where data is reconnected to the human perception of the physical world. The research at the Lab is conducted in a cross disciplinary design environment and is based on experiential investigations. The Lab utilizes large-scale interactive installations as the driving force for the exploration and communication of new dimensions in architectural space. Experiments are intended to make data tactile and to demonstrate real time responsive environments. They are the starting point for both the development of practice-oriented applications and also experiments that enable speculation on the future of our cities and buildings.

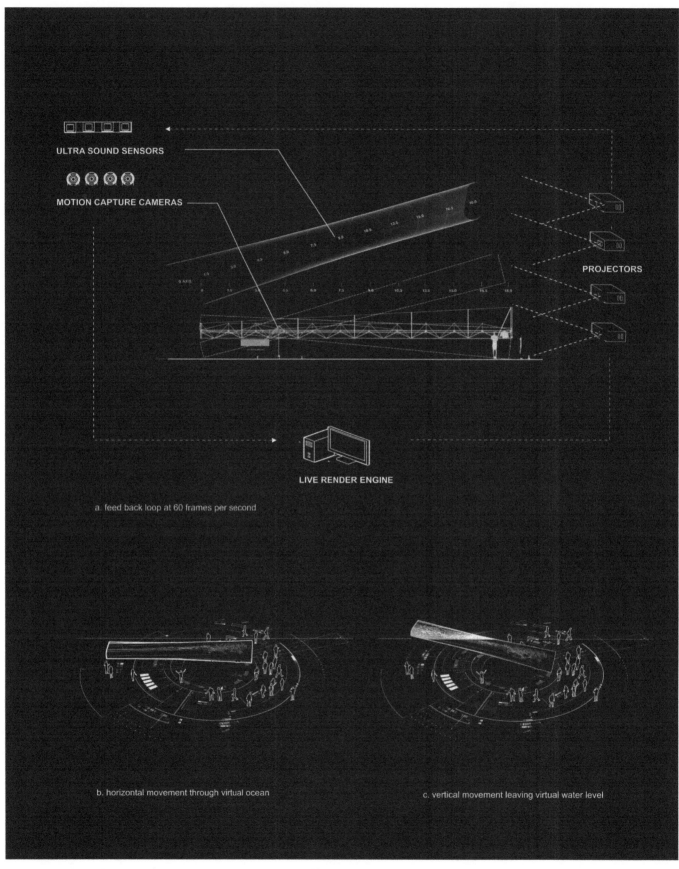

ULTRA SOUND SENSORS

MOTION CAPTURE CAMERAS

PROJECTORS

LIVE RENDER ENGINE

a. feed back loop at 60 frames per second

b. horizontal movement through virtual ocean

c. vertical movement leaving virtual water level

3   Digital spatail operations concept (drawing Uwe Rieger, Yiqui Hong, 2016/17).

4   LightScale II Structure (photo Uwe Rieger, 2017).

5   LightScale II Structure (photo Uwe Rieger, 2017).

6   LightScale II Carbon Fibre Mast (photo Uwe Rieger, 2017).

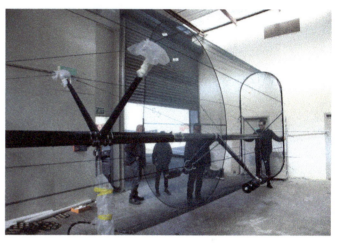

7   LightScale II Structure (photo Uwe Rieger, 2017)

The underlying research question for the Lab's projects asks what are the functional, programmatic and aesthetic design parameters for haptic-digital architecture and their user interaction?

The full setup of the installation LightScale II requires a space of 30 m x 30 m x 6 m. The first public test and presentation is scheduled for September 2017.

PROJECT CREDITS

Design and Concept: Uwe Rieger

Programming: Yinan Liu

Technical Support: Karl Butler

With contributions and graphics from: Don Aualiitia, Louise Burling, Anne Buttle, William Challacombe-King, Jamikorn Charoenphan, Catherine Cruz, Ying Feng, Alex Goh, Zijia Ge, Michael Hori, Taryn Korent, Alexei Matene, Emilio Ocampo, Inosia Paea, Patrick Sherwood, Clement Wilson, Celine Xiang, Levi Shim;

Construction: C-TECH lmtd, Auckland, NZ

Textile Engineering: Structure Flex, Auckland, NZ

Textile Fabrication: Nautilus Sails, Auckland, NZ

REFERENCES

"Daydream V.2." Nonotak Studio, accessed July 19, 2017, http://www.nonotak.com/_DAYDREAM-V-2

McCall, Anthony. "Current and Upcoming." Anthony McCall, accessed July 19, 2017, http://www.anthonymccall.com/

Rieger, Uwe. 2002. "Kunst und Technik." In *Uncertainty Principles-Unschaerfe Relationen*, edited Karin Damrau and Anton Markus Pasing, 79–83. Wiesbaden, Germany: Nelte.

8   Test projection on 1:10 model (photo Uwe Rieger, 2017)..

Uwe Rieger studied physics and architecture in Germany. He was the co-founder of the interdisciplinary group kunst und technik e.V. and the architecture office XTH-berlin. His work on Reactive Architecture is based on mixed reality concepts. Since 2006 he has been Associate Professor for Design and Design Technology at the University of Auckland, where he has established the arc/sec Lab for Digital Spatial Operations.

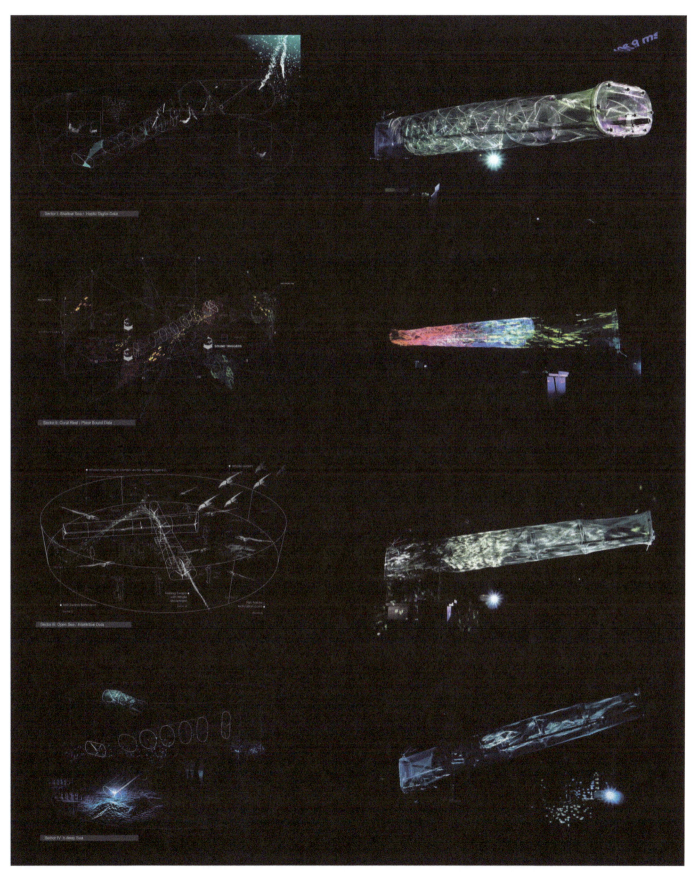

9   Virtual Ocean Sectors I–IV (drawings by Anne Buttle, William Challacombe-King, Ying Feng, Taryn Korent, el al.; photos Uwe Rieger).

WAVE/CAVE

William Sharples
SHoP Architects

Christopher Sharples
SHoP Architects

Sameer Kumar
SHoP Architects

Andrea Vittadini
SHoP Architects

Scott Overall
SHoP Architects

Clinton Miller
SHoP Architects

Victoire Saby
SHoP Architects

John Paul Rysavy
SHoP Architects

1   Exterior, Day (Tom Harris, 2017, © Tom Harris).

We live in hectic times. Our attention gets scattered by new wonders that are swept away before they can become familiar. What results is a pervading sense of unease, an internal agitation. SHoP's contribution to Interni's MATERIAL IMMATERIAL exhibition at FuoriSalone 2017 is a study of this dilemma we all experience—a slow, quiet commentary on solidity, deep time, and the contemporary pace of change. WAVE/CAVE is presented as an extended architectural experience in two acts. In year one, the system of 1,670 fluted terracotta blocks were arranged as a soaring sculptural enclosure, open to the action of life around it but accessible only to the imagination and the gaze. At a future date, the exact same composition will be rebuilt in the inverse, creating a meditative space that welcomes inhabitation and rewards our wait with silence. A purposefully massive construction, calling out to and evoking the timeless constant of gravity, WAVE/CAVE first looks to the sky to complete its form, then, inverted in its final state, it invites us to look within.

WAVE/CAVE is a 55 square meter topographic composition of unglazed terracotta blocks. The blocks are extruded through a custom die and CNC cut into 797 profiles. Stacked in three tiers, the interior faces of the blocks reveal a surprising ornamental richness as they describe a smoothly curved surface inscribed within a 3.6 m high perimeter wall. Developed in collaboration with NBK Terracotta in Emmerich, Germany, the unique extrusions feature regularly fluted exterior faces and a webbed cross-section that exposes its full geometrical complexity when cut at various inclinations.

PRODUCTION NOTES

Architect: SHoP Architects
Client: Interni
Status: Built
Location: Milan, Italy
Date: 2017

2   Exterior, Night (Tom Harris, 2017, © Tom Harris).

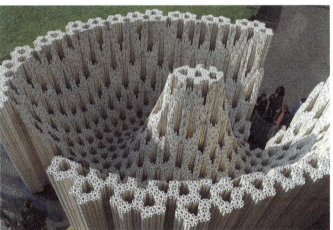

3   Overhead (Spirit of Space, 2017, © Spirit of Space).

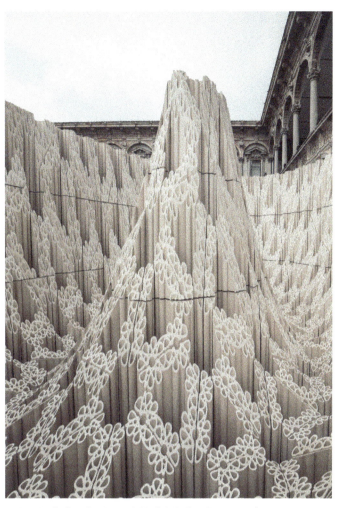

4   Interior (Delfino Sisto Legnani, 2017, © Delfino Sisto Legnani).

A system of 12 mm diameter steel rods is grouted with Sikabond T2 resin to connect each block vertically. A series of 4 mm thick steel rings links clusters of blocks together to ensure lateral stability. The entire assembly weighs over 60 tons and rests on an 8 mm steel plate over HEA120 structural steel framing. Engineered by Arup, the structural solution was conceived, produced, and installed by Metalsigma Tunesi.

The lighting design by PHT Lighting Design features over 70 Flori 1.0 projectors by Luce&Light, integrated in the platform and illuminating the perimeter wall as well as the sculptural interior surface

Leveraging our practice's expertise with handling direct-to-fabrication project delivery for complex geometries, SHoP took on the responsibility of documenting and managing each individual terracotta tile. Expanding on this previous research, the project team set out to fully realize an entirely automated process of design and documentation that had previously been performed

semi-manually, bringing the benefits of total automation to a traditional fabrication from paper documentation. With this approach, we could efficiently manage the fabrication and construction of complex, unique geometries without directly accessing CNC inputs.

With WAVE/CAVE, we were ultimately able to fulfill the technical requirements of the NBK, including drawing sets, automatically without the need for human post-processing. In total 3,193 drawings and 797 3D models were delivered to fabricate the 1670 terracotta tiles. The design was conceived and modeled with tight adherence to fabrication restrictions, embracing the processes available to the fabricators rather than letting the fabrication process neuter the design intent.

What makes WAVE/CAVE unique is not just the creation of parametric 3D geometries, but also the delivery of a fully parametric 2D fabrication drawing set. While it may be that the delivery of a purely 3D set may be the future, a great deal of

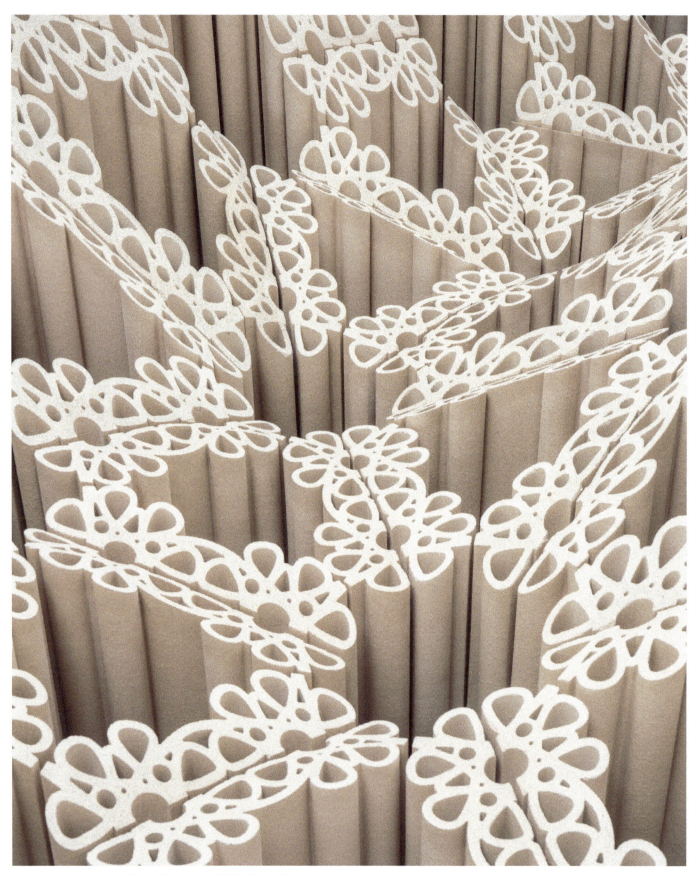

5   Terracotta Detail, Interior (Delfino Sisto Legnani, 2017, © Delfino Sisto Legnani).

WAVE/CAVE Sharples, Sharples, Kumar, Vittadini, Overall, Miller, Saby, Rysavy

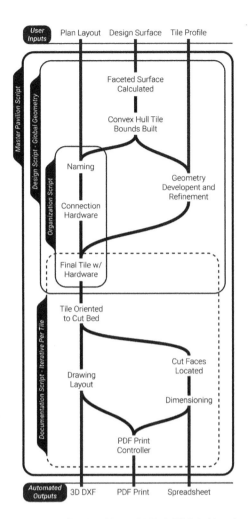

6   Script Process Diagram (SHoP Architects, 2017, © SHoP Architects).

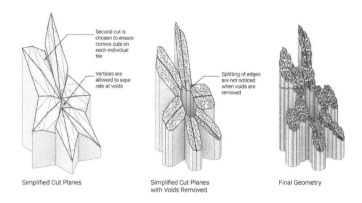

7   Geometry Development (SHoP Architects, 2017, © SHoP Architects).

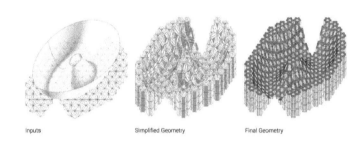

8   Script Inputs and Output Geometry (SHoP Architects, 2017, © SHoP Architects).

change will need to take place in the construction and fabrication industries as well as in the legal environment to phase out the 2D drawing (Sharples 2010). Instead of waiting for change, we have bent the 2D set to our needs in the present.

To achieve automation, it was necessary for us to develop a suite of new tools for the creation of high resolution geometry and accurate, legible documentation. The design and documentation script was built on top of Grasshopper for Rhinoceros 5, taking advantage of its ability to quickly prototype as well as giving us the necessary tools to build out more robust C# based scripts which interfaced with Rhino's back-end API for more custom processes. The entire master script only requires a minimal set of design inputs and once in place runs itself until all fabrication geometry and documentation are produced.

Custom tools include geometric operations such as a bespoke convex hull script to perform much faster boolean operations on solids with planar faces as well as scripts to create high resolution and visually consistent PDF prints directly from the Grasshopper interface, among others.

The developed process ultimately proved invaluable to the completion of the project. The timely completion on an extremely tight schedule with a small team serves as testament. Further, modifications to the design were possible until the day of documentation delivery because of new information regarding fabrication constraints and site conditions without disrupting the project schedule.

ACKNOWLEDGMENTS

WAVE/CAVE was designed and built for Interni's MATERIAL IMMATERIAL exhibition at FuoriSalone 2017 in collaboration with NBK Terracotta, Metalsigma Tunesi, Arup, PHT Lighting, and Luce&Light.

REFERENCES

Sharples, Coren D. 2010. "Technology and Labor." In *Building (in) the Future: Recasting Labor in Architecture*, edited P. Deamer and P. Bernstein. New York: Princeton Architectural Press. 91-99.

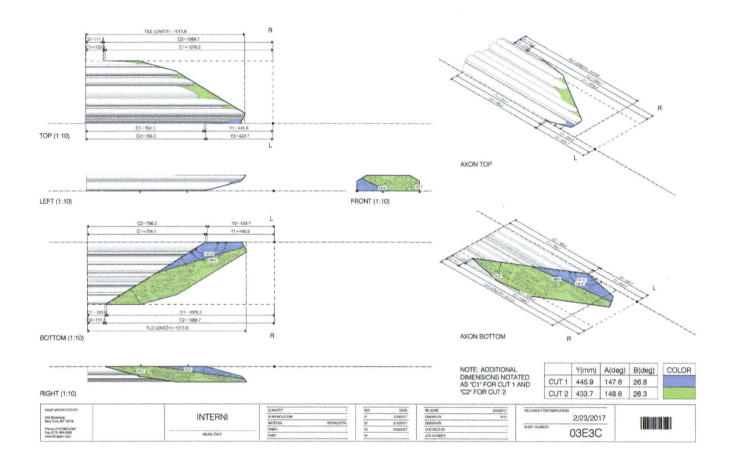

9 Example Automated Cut Sheet (SHoP Architects, 2017, © SHoP Architects).

William Sharples Principal, SHoP. William holds a Bachelor of Engineering from Pennsylvania State University, and his Master of Architecture from Columbia University. He has led SHoP's major institutional and commercial work with clients such as Columbia University, Fashion Institute of Technology, Botswana Innovation Hub, and Google Inc. He lectures widely at academic institutions and has held teaching positions at Cornell University, Yale University, and the Parsons School of Design.

Christopher Sharples Principal, SHoP. Christopher holds Bachelor of History and Bachelor of Fine Arts degrees from Dickinson College, and his Master of Architecture from Columbia University. He has taught at Cornell University, Parsons School of Design, The City College, City University of New York, Columbia University, and the University of Virginia. Chris has served as Principal for many significant projects including the Barclays Center, SITE Santa Fe gallery expansion, Google Headquarter Offices, and currently, Uber Headquarters in San Francisco.

Sameer Kumar Director of Enclosure Design, SHoP. Sameer holds a Bachelor of Architecture from CEPT University and a Master of Architecture from the University of Pennsylvania. He has led facade direction on many of SHoP's most high-profile projects including 111 West 57th Street, South Street Seaport, and Domino Sugar Refinery Development. Sameer currently serves as a Visiting Lecturer at Princeton University and the University of Pennsylvania.

Andrea Vittadini Project Director, SHoP. Andrea received a Bachelor of Architecture from Politecnico di Milano in Milan, Italy, and a Master of Architecture from Yale University. Andrea has played a key role as project director on several important projects including the Botswana Innovation Hub, a master plan for the LaGuardia Airport, Orlando International Airport, Konza Technology City Master Plan and Pavilion in Nairobi and 447 Collins Street in Melbourne. Andrea has co-taught at Cornell University with William Sharples.

10 Uncut Extruded Terracotta (SHoP Architects, 2017, © SHoP Architects).

11 Cutting Process (SHoP Architects, 2017, © SHoP Architects).

12 Terracotta Compared to 3D Model (SHoP Architects, 2017, © SHoP Architects).

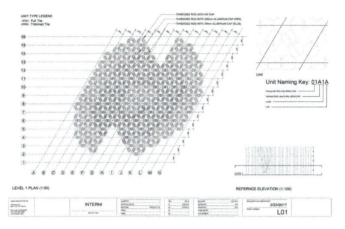

13 Level 1 Unit Plan (SHoP Architects, 2017, © SHoP Architects).

Scott Overall Associate, Computational Design, SHoP. Scott holds a Bachelor of Science in Civil Engineering from the University of Kentucky and a Master of Architecture from Columbia University. His work focuses on applied computation in design and construction, playing an integral role in executing projects such as the Botswana Innovation Hub and Uber Headquarters. He currently teaches Virtual Design and Construction at Columbia University.

Clinton Miller Director of Computational Design, SHoP. Clint received a Bachelor of Science in Architecture and a Bachelor of Arts in Mathematics from the Ohio State University and a Master of Architecture from the Columbia GSAPP. Clint has worked on a number of SHoP's projects, including Atlantic Yards B2, Pier 17, and the Uber Headquarters.

Victoire Saby Senior Associate, SHoP. Victoire holds a Master of Architecture from ENSAPLV in Paris and a Master of Engineering from Ecole des Ponts et Chausses. Victoire has worked on several of SHoP's high-profile jobs including the Hudson's Site Project in Detroit, and the SITE museum in Santa Fe. She specializes in interdisciplinary design that spans across architecture, engineering, computation, and construction. Victoire has taught and lectured at institutions in France and the US.

John Paul Rysavy Senior Associate, SHoP. John Paul received a Master of Architecture from The University of Texas at Austin following study at L' École nationale supérieure d'architecture de Versailles and The Illinois School of Architecture. John Paul has worked notably on the Botswana Innovation Hub and Uber Headquarters. He has held teaching positions at the University of Texas and has served as a guest critic at several academic institutions.

The CorkCrete Arch

José Pedro Sousa
DFL - CEAU/FAUP

Pedro de Azambuja Varela
DFL - CEAU/FAUP

Pedro Martins
DFL - CEAU/FAUP

1   The CorkCrete Arch assembled in the Faculty of Architecture of the University of Porto.

Developed by the Digital Fabrication Lab (DFL-FAUP), the CorkCrete Arch was a design-based research work concerned with using robotic fabrication technologies as design drivers for the production of a novel building system (Brookes 2018). By exploring the combination of two different materials – cork and concrete (GRC - glass-fiber reinforced concrete) - the goal was to merge the sustainable and insulation properties of the first with the structural efficiency of the second (Sousa et al. 2015, Sousa et al. 2016). The result is a lightweight and performative material system suited for customized prefabrication and easy on-site installation. From the production point of view, this project represented a complex challenge. Since it is not a single material installation, as many robotic experiments are, the process had to coordinate the different physical tolerances resulting from employing diverse materials and fabrication processes (i.e. robotic and manual).

To do so, the design and material deployment of the Arch were envisioned from the beginning in an algorithmic fashion. This allowed its full development in a single parametric design environment, from conception to materialization. Based in the catenary curve, the geometry of the arch was conceived to challenge the different fabrication processes required for its material production. Aiming at employing a milling process, the outer face of the cork panels was designed as a double curved surface with a customized engraved texture. The inner surface was kept flat in order to avoid an extra milling process and production time. This decision explains the emergence of a segmented line in the arch, separating the cork and the GRC materials. Aiming at using hotwire

PRODUCTION NOTES

Project: José Pedro Sousa

Team: Pedro de Azambuja Varela

               Pedro Filipe Martins

Production: DFL - CEAU/FAUP
               Digital Fabrication Lab
               Faculty of Architecture
               University of Porto

Partners: Amorim Isolamentos

               Mota Engil

Materials: Concrete (GRC)

               Cork (MDFacade)

Location: Porto

Date: 2015

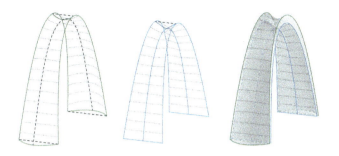
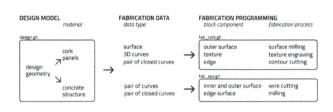

2   Geometry generator lines. In green, the cork surface, in blue the GRC surface.

3   The digital continuum process from design to manufacturing with Rhinoceros / Grasshopper / KukaPrc.

4   Simulation of the separation of the arch in its constituent parts. Cork is represented in brown and concrete (GRC) in gray.

5   Simulation of the complete CorkCrete Arch.

cutting (Feringa and Søndergaard 2014), the inner surface of the GRC panels was designed as a ruled surface featuring a subtle crease effect in the top. Although it resembles a classic form, the shape of the structure has thus specific geometry details that challenge the use of robotic fabrication technologies.

All the robotic works for fabricating the cork panels and EPS molds took place at the DFL laboratory. The fabrication of the cork panels involved a sequence of 3 steps: machining the double-curved surface, engraving the variable texture, and finally cutting the skewed contour. Regarding the fabrication of the EPS molds for the GRC panels, a more elaborated process was followed. Using robotic hot-wire cutting, two curved slices were cut from EPS blocks and the perimeter contour was cut through robotic milling. While the resulting outer part was glued to the bottom curved surface to define a frame for the projection of the GRC, the inner part was saved to be later inserted inside the GRC panel. The wasted material from the molds production was thus embedded in the final structure to provide a smooth surface

for fixing the cork panels. The EPS molds were then shipped to the precast Factory of Mota Engil and used for the manual projection of a 15mm thin layer of GRC material.

Once completed, the CorkCrete Arch was manually assembled several times, and in different places, which proved the ease of construction due to the lightness of this building construction system. From the structural point of view, it was stable enough to be installed on the FAUP garden without any fixation to the ground. From the aesthetic point of view, the contrasts between the cork and the concrete materials (e.g. dark/bright, textured/smooth, soft/hard...) triggered the curiosity of the people who felt compelled to visit and touch it. From the technological point of view, robotic fabrication proved to be a flexible and precise process to manufacture building components. The techniques employed in the production of the CorkCrete Arch opened possibilities for real industrial implementations. Future research avenues will explore the CorkCrete system in the design and construction of larger structures.

6   Robotic hotwire cutting of the EPS moulds surfaces.

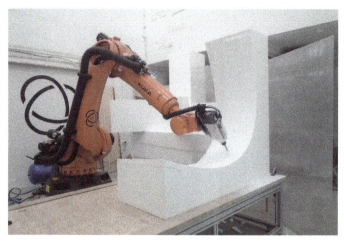

7   Robotic trimming the contours of the EPS moulds.

8   Manual spray of GRC into the mould.

9   Final GRC panel suspended after demoulding.

REFERENCES

Sousa, J. P., Martins, P., and Azambuja Varela, P.. 2016. "The CorkCrete Arch Project: The Digital Design and Robotic Fabrication of a Novel Building System Made out of Cork and Glass-Fiber Reinforced Concrete." In Proceedings of the 21st CAADRIA – Computer Aided Architectural Design Research in Asia Conference. Univ. of Melbourne, 735-744.

Sousa, J.P., Veiga, G., Moreira, A.P. 2015. "Robotic fabrication of Cork. Emerging opportunities in architecture and building construction." In Proceedings of the 35th Annual Conference of the Association for Computer Aided Design in Architecture, ACADIA, 250–259.

Brookes, A.J. and Meijs, M. 2008. Cladding of Buildings. 4th Ed. Taylor & Francis.

Feringa, Jelle and Søndergaard, Asbjørn. 2014. "Fabricating architectural volume: Stereotomic investigations in robotic craft" In Fabricate: negotiating design & Making. Edited F. Gramazio, M. Kohler and S. Langenberg. GTA Publishers. 76-83.

ACKNOWLEDGEMENTS

The CorkCrete Arch was developed by the Digital Fabrication Laboratory (DFL), of the Center of Studies in Architecture and Urbanism (CEAU) of the Faculty of Architecture of the University of Porto (FAUP). It was part of the research project with the reference PTDC/ATP- AQI/5124/2012, funded by FEDER funds through the Operational Competitiveness Programme (COMPETE) and by national funds through the Foundation for the Science and Technology (FCT).

The authors would like to thank the industrial partners Amorim Isolamentos (cork) and Mota Engil (concrete) for their parnership in the project.

All figures produced by the DFL - CEAU/FAUP, 2015.

10 Robotic milling the outer surface of the cork panels.

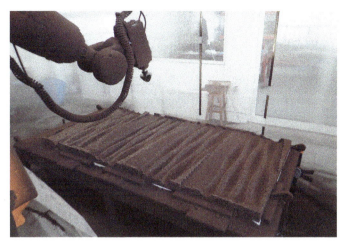

11 Robotic engraving of the texture.

12 Robotic cutting the panels' contour.

13 Aspect of the finalized cork panels.

José Pedro Sousa is Assistant Professor and the Director of the Digital Fabrication Laboratory (DFL), at the Faculty of Architecture of the University of Porto (FAUP). Graduated in Architecture from FAUP, he has a Master in Genetic Architectures from ESARQ-UIC (Barcelona), a PhD in Architecture from the University of Lisbon, and was a Special Student at MIT and a Visiting Scholar at UPenn (USA). He has developed an intensive professional activity merging the realms of teaching, research and practice, with a focus in exploring the conceptual and material opportunities in architecture emerging from the use of computational design and digital fabrication technologies.

Pedro de Azambuja Varela is an architect and PhD researcher with the Digital Fabrication Lab (DFL), at the Faculty of Architecture of the University of Porto (FAUP). After working in architecture offices in Vienna and New York and developing his own practice AZVAvisuals mainly focused in visualization for architecture, completes a post-graduation in Digital Architecture (CEAAD) in 2013 and in 2014 enrolls in the PhD program of FAUP. Concurrently to the development of various cork vaulted experiments and pavilions, Pedro is actively developing his PhD thesis in the Digital Fabrication Laboratory at FAUP, where he regularly publishes papers on Stereotomy.

Pedro Filipe Martins is an architect and PhD researcher with the Digital Fabrication Lab (DFL), at the Faculty of Architecture of the University of Porto (FAUP), focusing on the application of robotics in concrete construction. Graduated from the Architecture Department at the University of Coimbra in 2006, where he also currently teaches, in the MSc program. After developing experience in several architectural practices, received a PhD grant for graduate studies at FAUP. His research is being developed on the integration of digital fabrication technologies in concrete construction and architecture, with an emphasis on the use of robotic strategies for complex, non-standard concrete prefabrication.

14 Assembly of the GRC panels.

15 Fixation of cork panels.

16 Underneath view of the GRC geometry.

17 View of the outer cork texture.

The CorkCrete Arch Sousa, Azambuja Varela, Martins

18   View of the CorkCrete Arch in the Faculty of Architecture of the University of Porto.

AUGMENTED CORAL

An Installation Using Digital Fabrication and Mixed Reality

Ming Tang
University of Cincinnati

Mara Marcu
University of Cincinnati

1   In an immersive mixed reality world, augmented reality supports the spectator's perception, decision, and action looped through various sensory and motor interfaces. Photograph by Ming Tang. 2016.

Background

Today, as a paradigm shift, headmounted displays (HMD) such as Google Glass, Microsoft HoloLens, both forms of virtual reality (VR) and augmented reality (AR), are being reintroduced as mixed reality (MR) instruments into the art installation. MR has provided artists and designers with the technologies that allow the audience to interact with and experience the physical and virtual world simultaneously in an immersive environment. In a 1995 essay, "The Vision of Virtual Reality," Biocca, Kim, and Levy (1995) argued that the "essential copy" and "physical transcendence" were important drivers in the generation of mixed realities. They described the search for the "essential copy" as seeking a "means to fool the senses—a display that provides a perfect illusory deception," while "physical transcendence" is rooted in an "ancient desire for escape from the confines of the physical world, [to] free the mind from the 'prison' of a body" (Biocca, Kim, and Levy 1995, 7). This theoretical foundation, with the latest mixed reality technology, has inspired the researchers to invest new meaning in digital arts, and to explore the relation between the separator and the physical space, the perception of action, time, space, and our own body.

2　The installation consists of 330 polypropylene surfaces using algorithm modeling, laser cutting, and 1556 rivet connections. Photograph by Ming Tang. 2016

Project Brief

The "Augmented Coral" project is an installation that curates and expands on digital fabrication and mixed reality work, which is produced by the team at the School of Architecture and Interior Design at the University of Cincinnati. The designers constructed this mixed reality art installation with a physical sculpture and its animated holographic form. The project employed a computational process to design and fabricate an abstract coral sculpture. Then the Microsoft HoloLens near-eye light-field display is used to project an animated holographic simulation. Through sensory perception and the motor response of users, the HMD helps a person to perform a sensorimotor and cognitive activity in a mixed reality world.

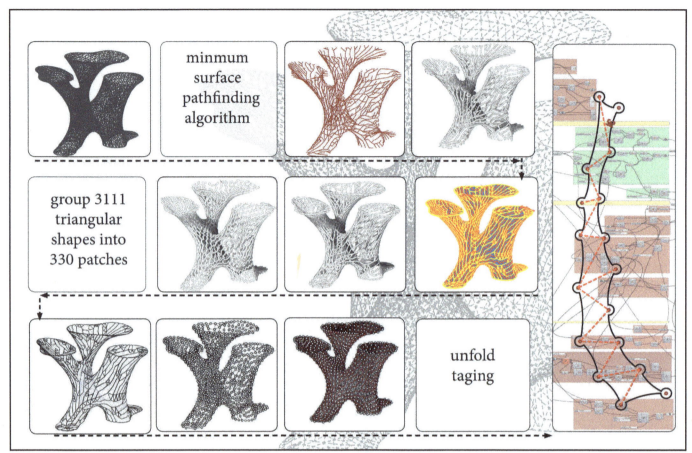

3   Process of digital fabrication.

Process: From Essential copy to Symbolic Form.
Method: Digital Fabrication

First, the designers applied parametric design methods to generate a minimum surface representing a coral form. Using various form optimization algorithms in Kangaroo and mesh-machine in Grasshopper, the minimum surface was converted into 3111 triangular shapes. Then a pathfinding algorithm was applied to group the triangular shapes into 330 patches, which represent the geometrical pattern across a coral surface. These 330 patches were unfolded in Grasshopper with 3824 small holes scripted along their edges. Then the flattened patches were laser cut using polypropylene material. Finally, the designers used 1566 rivet joints to connect 3824 openings. The fabrication and construction process of this artifact expanded on the notion of skin and structure in architecture and created a catalog of assembling possibilities. The architectural tectonic operations such as paneling, folding, and joining were used to create a new expression of the coral form.

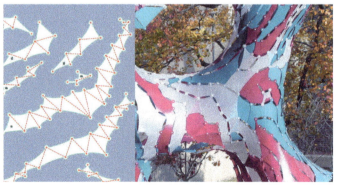

4   **330** laser cut patches. Photograph by Ming Tang. 2017.

Augmented Coral Tang, Marcu

5   Screen shot of the animated form through Microsoft HoloLens.

Physical Transcendence. Method: Augmented Reality

First, the digital coral was reconstructed using the marching-cube algorithm to simulate the skeletal structure of a coral. Free from the "essential copy" mindset, the new coral model is a symbolic simulation of the reality. The same 330 paths from the pathfinding algorithm were used again to generate an imaginary coral skeleton with the intention of blurring the real and the virtual. The 330 paths were translated into the Autodesk Maya program to construct a bone system. The skeleton was then animated with the Maya animation tools. After transferring the skeleton model into the Unity game engine and HoloLens, the animation was controlled by the user's gesture and voice. Through the HoloLens spectator system and its semi-transparent "optical see-through" screen, the designers combined computer-generated images with a view of the real world.

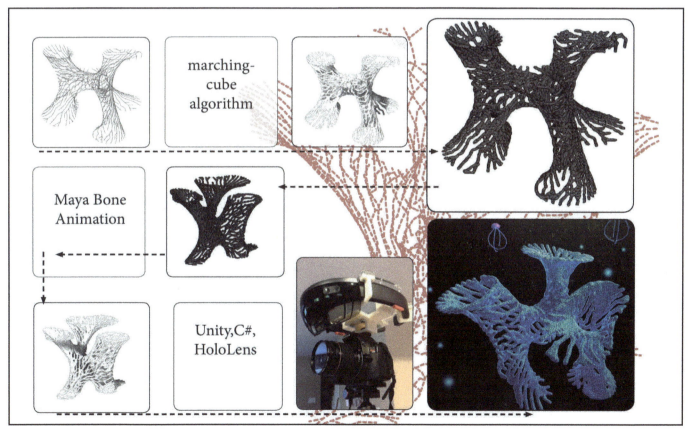

6   Process of making mixed reality.

7   The installation has two components. Physical polypropylene prototypes speculate on the role of architectural pleats and the metamorphosis of two-dimensional material to three-dimensional form. Holographic coral created an illusory presentation of the same shape through augmented reality. Photograph by Ming Tang. 2016.

Exhibition

The project was exhibited at the 2016 Sculptural Objects Functional Art and Design (SOFA) international fair in Chicago. The installation consisted of an animated hologram projected through the Microsoft HoloLens space-mapping technology and recorded onto live video. The mixed reality environment acted as an imaginary undersea space to host other real sculptures during the SOFA exhibition. The holographic animated coral and other water effects were superimposed on the real sculpture to create an illusion of a marine environment. The HoloLens allowed the public to observe, navigate and manipulate the virtual coral through gestures and voices.

ACKNOWLEDGMENTS

We thank the Third Century grant, the Communication Urban Environment (CUE) grant, and the FDC Department & Interdisciplinary Grant at the school of architecture and interior design, University of Cincinnati.

More information on the project is available at http://ming3d.com/VR
Faculty: Ming Tang, Mara Marcu
Graduate assistant and teaching assistant: Han Shen, Nolan Loh, Muhammed Bahcetepe, Andrew Watson, Mathew Klump, Kevin Goldstein, Austin Gehman, Jiajing Xie, Weiqi Chu
Students: Architecture and interior design students in SAID 2013, fall semester. 2016, University of Cincinnati.

REFERENCES

Biocca, Frank, Taeyong Kim, and Mark R. Levy. 1995. "The Vision of Virtual Reality." In *Communication in the Age of Virtual Reality*, edited by Frank Biocca and Mark R. Levy, 3–14. Hillsdale, NJ: Lawrence Erlbaum Associates.

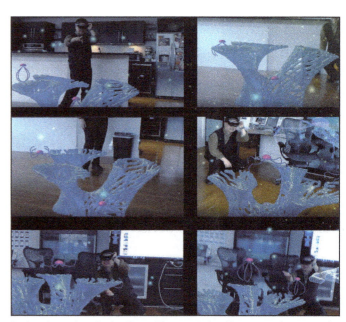

8   In an immersive mixed reality world, augmented reality supports the spectator's perception, decision, and action looped through various sensorial and motor interfaces.

9   2017 Sculptural Objects Functional Art and Design (SOFA) international fair.
    Photograph by Ming Tang. 2016.

Ming Tang is a tenured Associate Professor at School of Architecture and Interior Design, University of Cincinnati. He is a registered architect and the founding partner of TYA Design. Before he taught at the University of Cincinnati, he led the Electronic Design program at the Savannah College of Art and Design and was a professor in the Architecture Department. He has worked with Michigan State University's M.I.N.D Lab, University of Southern California's Institute for Creative Technologies, and China Architecture Design & Research Group. He is the author of the book, *Parametric Building Design with Autodesk Maya*, published by Routledge in 2014. http://ming3d.com

Mara Marcu is an Assistant Professor at the University of Cincinnati and founder of MM13. Mara studied at Harvard University Graduate School of Design and trained with Pritzker Prize Laureate Glenn Murcutt. Prior to her academic career, she worked for Rafael Vinoly Architects and Ghost Lab 7 directed by Brian MacKay-Lyons. Marcu exhibited at WUHO Gallery in Los Angeles, Universidad de Monterrey in Mexico, Saintes Art Institute in France, SOFA Chicago, and Eloise Gallery in Charlottesville. Mara is the founder of ECHOS with the first upcoming volume published with Actar.

Motivational Rock: Entropy in Architecture

Filip Tejchman
University of Wisconsin
Milwaukee

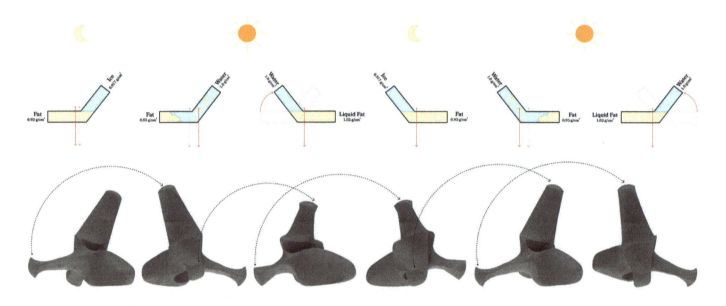

1   Motivational Rock movement related to diurnal temperature changes.

Introduction

In *Patterns of Intention*, Michael Baxandall (1985) states that "to live in a culture is synonymous with a specific education of the senses," an idea that Antoin Picon (2003) described as "the cultural construction of perception." Considering the breadth of virtual simulation and visualization modalities currently available to designers, how can it be that our "vision" of energy is still rooted to a range of anachronistic attitudes? Is the volume of rhetoric emerging from the "green-noise" movement so overwhelming that any mention of energy and architecture is automatically relegated to negotiating between climate and buildings, performance and sustainability? Perhaps the underlying reason for this limited scope of vision is not our tools or instruments, but the culture of perception we have cultivated? Thus it is hardly surprising that the contemporary relationship between architecture and energy is defined by the discipline's compulsion to optimize the late-twentieth-century architectural project for the crisis of the twenty-first century.

Site

Motivational Rock is a project engaged in the design of a series of artificial rocks intended for placement within the Racetrack Playa in Death Valley, CA. This particular site is already home to a phenomenon commonly referred to as the "sailing stones." The movement of these rocks is caused by "ice shove," a process through which the rainwater run-off from the surrounding mountains freezes into a thin layer on the playa floor. Due to the extreme diurnal temperature swings in Death

PRODUCTION NOTES

Architect:	Filip Tejchman
Status:	In Process
Site Area:	7 sq. km.
Location:	Death Valley, CA
Date:	2017-2018

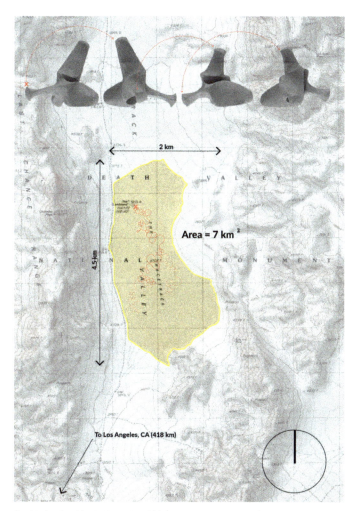

2   Motivational Rock site and path(s) (Filip Tejchman, © 2017).

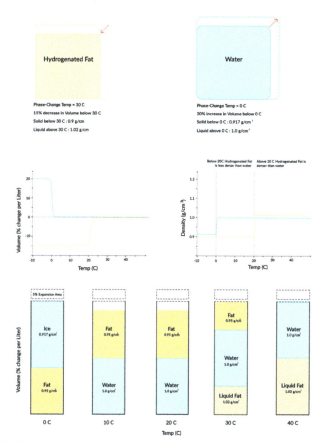

3   (Above) As the temperature varies throughout the day/night/year, the density, volume and distribution of the phase-change materials (PCM) inside the Motivational Rocks will cause the centroid, or center of mass, to shift and cause the rocks to reposition themselves. By using a proprietary combination of hydrogenated fats, we achieve a change in density that acts in reciprocity and opposition to similar transformations present in water.

Valley, this sheet of ice breaks apart and temporarily creates mini-glaciers of ice that push the surrounding rocks. The sailing stones demonstrate an alternative architectural agenda with regards to energy, one in which form and material are configured to organize and intensify ambient thermodynamic flows with the express purpose of cultivating the generation of new orders of structure and pattern.

Energy, Entropy, and Patterns

While the motion of the sailing stones is driven by external factors, the Motivational Rocks are instead powered by their internal transformation. This is achieved by a combination of factors. First, the external geometry of the rock is configured so that each edge/surface cannot lay flat on a surface. This, coupled with a centroid that is outside of the mass, leads to a form that is inherently unstable. This instability is then leveraged by making the rocks hollow and filling them with a combination of phase change materials (PCM). The selected materials are water and a proprietary blend of hydrogenated fat. In the case of the

latter, the unique properties exhibited are an ability to withstand an almost infinite number of freeze-thaw cycles, as well as a temperature dependent shift in both volume and density in reciprocity to water. This means that at temperatures above 30°C, the fat will be denser and heavier than water, while at temperatures below this, the fat will be less dense and float. Thus as the temperature changes throughout the day/night and year, the interior composition of the Motivational Rock will constantly be reconfigured and the center of mass will shift, causing the rocks to move.

Conclusion

In his book, *Energy Flow in Biology*, the biophysicist Harold Morowitz (1968) famously stated that "the flow of energy through a system acts to organize that system." The patterns, forms and structures that we observe, whether geological, political, economic or architectural, are shaped in direct reciprocity to the exchange of energy, to the pervasive force of entropy. While the grooves that trail the movements of the sailing stones are a

4   Motivational Rocks

Motivational Rock: Entropy in Architecture Tejchman

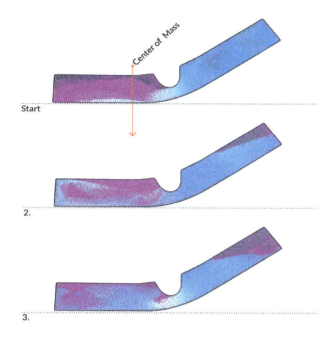

5   (Above) The distribution of mass was simulated using the RealFlow Dyverso multiphase particle physics engine. This example shows a combination of a granular and fluid particle interaction that is characteristic of the mixing that occurs between the solidified fat and liquid water at approximately 30°C. The mass used for both particle sets corresponds to those values listed on the left: (fat = 0.95g/cm³; water = 1.0g/cm³)

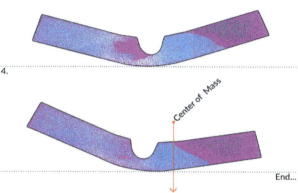

6   (Right) As the temperature varies throughout the day/night/year, the density, volume and distribution of the phase-change materials (PCM) inside the Motivational Rocks will cause the centroid, or center of mass, to shift and cause the rocks to reposition themselves. By using a proprietary combination of hydrogenated fats, we achieve a change in density that acts in reciprocity and opposition to similar transformation present in water.

material calculation of the convergence of matter and force, the traces left behind by the Motivational Rock represent the convergence of culture and nature. The intent is to index and make visible an unexplored vantage point from which to cast entropy in architecture as a mechanism through which energy can be manifested as real rather than as a reductive abstraction often utilized to delineate energy as just another resource.

REFERENCES

Arnheim, Rudolf. 1971. *Entropy and Art: An Essay on Order and Disorder* Berkeley, CA: University of California Press.

Baxandall, Michael. 1985. *Patterns of Intention: On the Historical Explanation of Pictures*. New Haven, CT: Yale University Press.

Messina, Paula and Phil Stoffer. 2005. "Differential GPS/GIS Analyis of the Sliding Rock Phenomenon of Racetrack Playa, Death Valley National Park." United States Geological Survey.

Morowitz, Harold. 1968. *Energy Flow in Biology*. Cambridge, MA: Academic Press.

Picon, Antoine. 2003. "Architecture, Science, Technology, and the Virtual Realm." In *Architecture and the Sciences: Exchanging Metaphors*, edited by Antoin Picon and Alessandra Ponte, 292–313. New York, NY: Princeton Architectural Press.

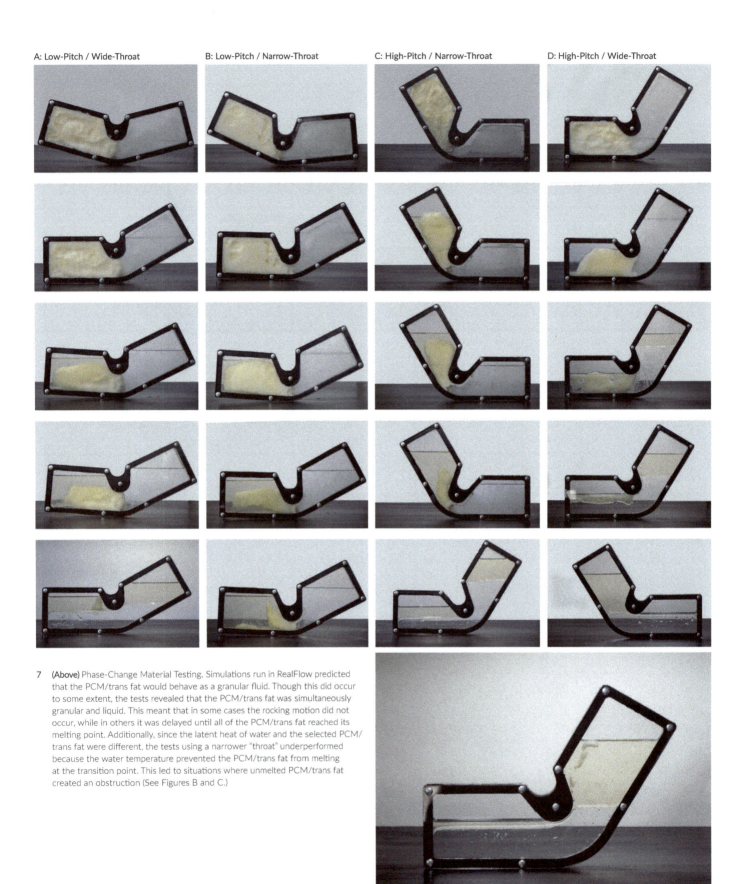

A: Low-Pitch / Wide-Throat   B: Low-Pitch / Narrow-Throat   C: High-Pitch / Narrow-Throat   D: High-Pitch / Wide-Throat

7   (Above) Phase-Change Material Testing. Simulations run in RealFlow predicted
    that the PCM/trans fat would behave as a granular fluid. Though this did occur
    to some extent, the tests revealed that the PCM/trans fat was simultaneously
    granular and liquid. This meant that in some cases the rocking motion did not
    occur, while in others it was delayed until all of the PCM/trans fat reached its
    melting point. Additionally, since the latent heat of water and the selected PCM/
    trans fat were different, the tests using a narrower "throat" underperformed
    because the water temperature prevented the PCM/trans fat from melting
    at the transition point. This led to situations where unmelted PCM/trans fat
    created an obstruction (See Figures B and C.)

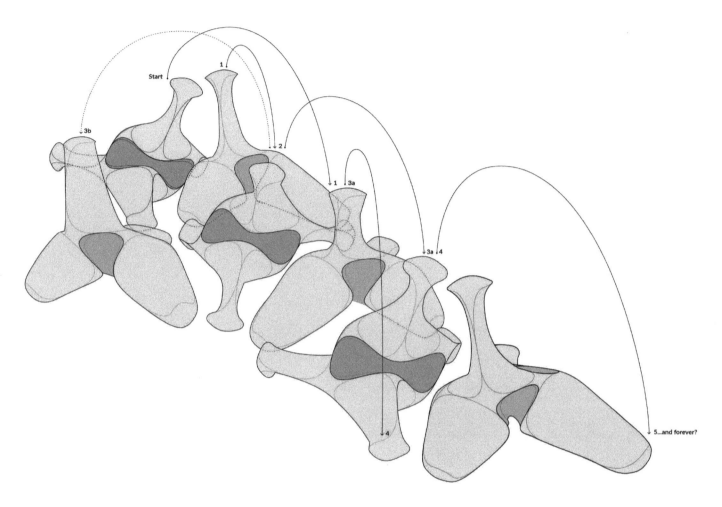

8   Motivational Rock movement diagram

Filip Tejchman is assistant professor in the School of Architecture and
Urban Planning at the University of Wisconsin–Milwaukee. He is the
founder of Untitled Office and **Work and Research**, a design practice that
explores the intersection of building, culture, and thermodynamics. His
writing has appeared in Volume, the Journal of Architectural Education,
MUSEO, and the Praxis Journal of Writing + Building and his research
has been awarded a Graham Foundation Grant. Tejchman has previously
practiced at the offices of Diller Scofidio + Renfro and Joel Sanders
Architects.

Latitudo Borealis

Daniel Tish
University of Michigan / RVTR

Dr. Lars Junghans
University of Michigan

Dustin Brugmann
University of Michigan

Geoffrey Thün
University of Michigan / RVTR

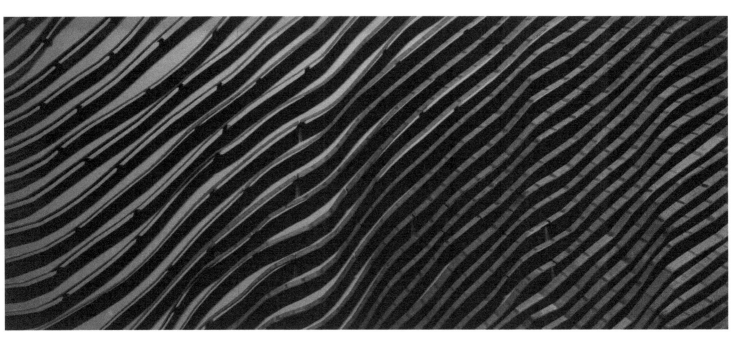

1   Latitudo Borealis: Hyper-Localized Robotically Fabrciated Shading System. 2017 RTM Exhibition, Ann Arbor, MI (RVTR, 2017)

Design and Fabrication of Hyper-Localized Shading Systems

Latitudo Borealis explores passive timber-based building envelopes that have the capacity to reverse the normative winter heat flow in order to increase building performance and decrease operational energy demand, intended for application in northern climates. Rather than heat flowing from inside to outside during the winter, the project has developed a series of experimental wall assemblies that passively store and transfer solar energy through the wall assembly from *outside* to inside. This is developed through physical prototyping and testing of layered combinations of wood slat shading systems, heat absorbers, and phase change materials (PCM) coupled with structural insulated panels (SIP) and cross-laminated timber (CLT) panels. In northern climate contexts, timber is a widely available renewable resource and the prioritization of the mass-timber assemblies can assist in reducing the need for chemically derived insulation materials. By tracking the temperature gradient through assembly samples over a simulated day-night cycle in a thermal chamber, physical testing indicated that the combination of solar absorbers and thermal storage by way of phase change material or thermal timber mass could effectively produce a reverse heat flow during the winter months. However, these assemblies were prone to overheating in the summer and thus required the addition of an external shading system. The team developed a prototypical assembly for application on a speculative pavilion located in Feldkirch, Austria, where climatic conditions and available solar resources are ideal to take advantage of the thermal storage capacities identified in early physical wall assembly studies.

2　Seasonal surface radiation maps, annual differential and resultant genetically optimized shading configuration developed for the Feldkirch Pavilion. (RVTR, 2017)

The specific geometry of the pavilion produces an extensive envelope perimeter with 29 unique orientations and self-shading conditions requiring multiple shading variations and configurations across each surface.

The design of the shading system necessitated the development of optimization protocols capable of delivering the maximum amount of winter radiation to drive the reverse heat flow, while minimizing the amount of summer radiation that results in overheating across all surficial variations. The project developed genetically optimized processes within accessible computational design environments (Manzan et al. 2009; Bechthold et al. 2011) that use highly detailed solar radiation data to produce hyper-localized shading configurations in order to account for the various solar orientations and partial shading conditions from other elements in the immediate environment. Radiation maps of the summer and winter conditions are generated first by the DIVA 4 Grasshopper plug-in (Lagois et al. 2010), then a differential map of the two seasons' radiation is constructed to expose areas of opportunity for winter radiation. The spacing

of the shades and their angle relative to the wall surface are determined in relation to the differential radiation data, allowing for a high degree of variability across each surface while minimizing the number of variables to optimize for.

Shading configurations are optimized through the use of a genetic algorithm in the Galapagos component in Grasshopper (Rutten 2013). The genetic algorithm produces a series of randomized individuals and evaluates them against a fitness function in order to determine the best performing individuals to be bred for future generations. The fitness function for this process once again uses the DIVA 4 plug-in to test the amount of radiation reaching the surface through the shading system in the winter and the summer. The final fitness factor is then determined by weighting these radiation values to take into account the average length and intensity of the cooling and heating season to accurately balance the positive effects that the solar radiation has in the winter as compared to the negative effects it can have in the summer. The highest performing individuals are carried over to the next generation and this

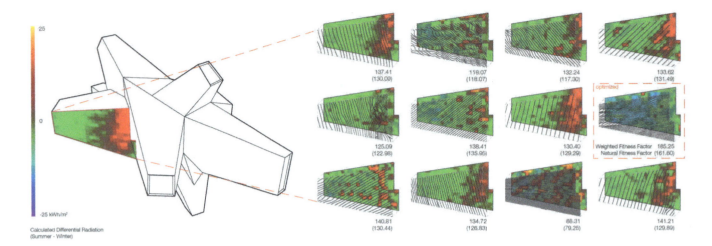

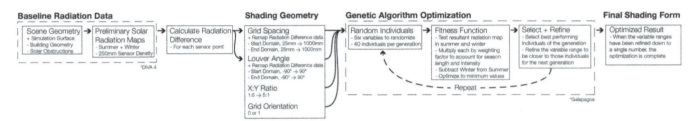

3   Computational Design Workflow and selected configurations of individual surface solution space developed through GA optimization process, (RVTR, 2017)

4   A selection of timber-based wall assembly types evaluated through phsyical testing process (L to R): SIP + Heat Absorber + Custom Shading, SIP + PCM + Heat Absorber + Custom Shading, Voided CLT + Wood Heat Absorber, Voided CLT. (Junghans, 2017)

process is repeated over many generations, successively narrowing the range of possible values, while allowing for the occasional opportunity for mutation, until the algorithm converges on a single optimized result. This process is carried out separately for each surface of the proposed building to produce highly customized optimal shading configurations throughout.

Within this context of high differentiation, the team developed a standard process for delivering unique geometries required for each shade through a replicable file-to-fabrication process that

would minimize waste. Robotic hot pipe bending builds upon previous digital steam bending technologies (Menges 2011; Mankouche et al. 2012) while eliminating the need for jigs or formwork and delivering heat locally at the moment of bending. The robotic tooling is configured with a pneumatic gripper that holds the wood at the end of the stock while feeding it into the pneumatic hot pipes incrementally. Quartersawn red oak with a cross section of 63 x 6 mm was chosen for prototyping as a locally sourced product with consistency of grain, flexibility, and desirable structural characteristics. The fabrication process

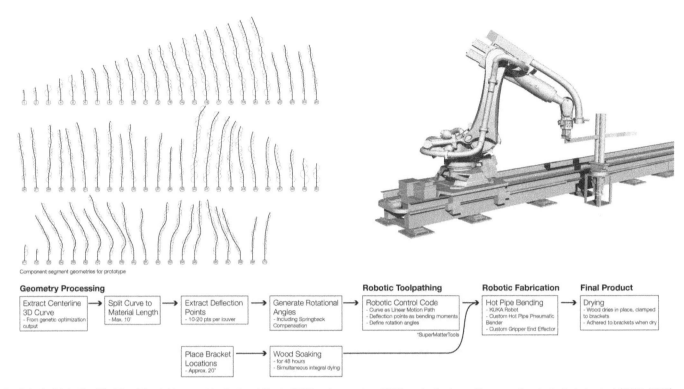

Component segment geometries for prototype

Geometry Processing				Robotic Toolpathing	Robotic Fabrication	Final Product

Geometry Processing

Extract Centerline 3D Curve
- From genetic optimization output

→ Split Curve to Material Length
- Max. 10'

→ Extract Deflection Points
- 10-20 pts per louver

→ Generate Rotational Angles
- Including Springback Compensation

Robotic Toolpathing

Robotic Control Code
- Curve as Linear Motion Path
- Deflection points as bending moments
- Define rotation angles

*SuperMatterTools

Robotic Fabrication

Hot Pipe Bending
- KUKA Robot
- Custom Hot Pipe Pneumatic Bender
- Custom Gripper End Effector

Final Product

Drying
- Wood dries in place, clamped to brackets
- Adhered to brackets when dry

Place Bracket Locations
- Approx. 20"

→ Wood Soaking
- for 48 hours
- Simultaneous integral dying

5   Robotic Fabrication Workflow, Wood slat geometries for translation to SMT input parameters, KUKA workcell set up with pneumatic actuated hot pipe tool. (RVTR, 2017)

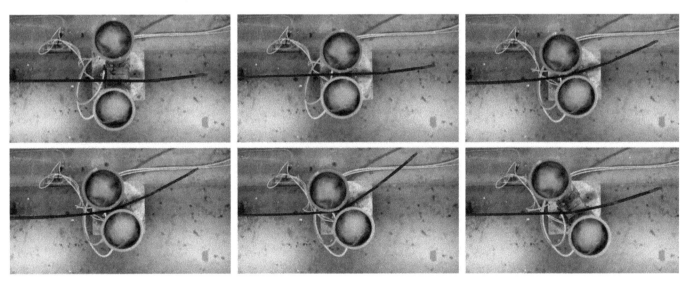

6   Sequenced plan images of the robotic bending process with pneumatic hot pipe tool. (D. Brugmann, 2017)

depends on the high moisture content and elasticity of the wood, after it has soaked in a black fabric dye bath for at least 48 hours, as well as its local conductive heat transfer of approximately 180°C. The translation from digital model to robotic fabrication (Pigram et al. 2012) begins by generating NURBs curves from the optimized shading solution, which are then divided into segments and converted to polylines depending on their overall length. The angle of bending between each segment of the polyline is used to calculate degrees of rotation of the hot pipe tool while also compensating for springback. The polyline length, number of divisions, and Cartesian position of the parts are input parameters for the SuperMatterTools (SMT) KUKA robotic toolpathing software, which produces the pneumatic actuated sequence. The robotic sequence is entirely automated for each shade part with the hot pipe tool gripping the wood tangentially and pulling the wood around the arc of the pipe as it rotates, making variable radii and multipitch helical bending moments possible.

As part of project development, documentation and assessment

7 Rendering of the Feldkirch Pavillion depicting application of the shading system over long span CLT panel assemblies. (RVTR, 2017)

a 9 m² shading prototype was produced for testing and exhibition as part of the 2017 Research Through Making program at the University of Michigan.

Detailed project description: https://vimeo.com/210950031

ACKNOWLEDGMENTS

Latitudo Borealis was undertaken with financial support from a Taubman College of Architecture and Urban Planning 2017 Research Through Making grant. The authors wish to thank the following project team members for their contributions to the work: Deokoh Woo, Isabelle Leysens, Rachael Henry, Karen Toomasian, Travis Crabtree, Kallie Sternburgh, Mark Krecic and Kathy Velikov.

REFERENCES

Bechthold, Martin, Jonathan King, Anthony Kane, Jeffrey Niemasz, and Christoph Reinhart. 2011. "Integrated Environmental Design and Robotic Fabrication Workflow for Ceramic Shading Systems." In *Proceedings of the 28th International Symposium on Automation and Robotics in Construction*, 70–5. Seoul, Korea: ISARC.

Lagios, Kera, Jeff Niemasz, and Christoph Reinhart. 2010. "Animated Building Performance Simulation (ABPS): Linking Rhinoceros/Grasshopper with Radiance/Daysim." in *SIMBUILD 2010: Fourth National Conference of the International Building Performance Simulation Association USA*, 321–7. New York: IBPSA-USA.

Mankouche, Steven, Matthew Schulte, and Joshua Bard. 2012. "Digital Steam Bending: Recasting Thonet Through Digital Techniques." In *Synthetic Digital Ecologies: Proceedings of the 32nd Annual Conference of the Association for Computer Aided Design in Architecture*, edited by Jason Kelly Johnson, Mark Cabrinha, and Kyle Steinfeld, 116–26. San Francisco: ACADIA.

Manzan, Marco, and Francesco Pinto. 2009. "Genetic Optimization of External Shading Devices." In *Building Simulation 2009: Eleventh International International Building Performance Simulation Association Conference.*, 180-7. Glasgow: IBPSA.

Menges, Achim. 2011. "Integrative Design Computation: Integrating Material Behavior and Robotic Manufacturing Processes in Computational Design for Performative Wood Constructions." In *Integration Through Computation: Proceedings of the 31st Annual Conference of the Association for Computer Aided Design in Architecture*, edited by by Joshua Taron, Vera Parlac, Branko Kolarevic and Jason Johnson, 72–81. Banff/Calgary, Canada: ACADIA.

Pigram, David, Iain Maxwell, Wes McGee, Ben Hagenhoffer-Daniell, and Lauren Vasey. 2012. "Protocols, Pathways, and Production." In *Rob | Arch 2012: Robotic Fabrication in Architecture, Art, and Design*, edited by Sigrid Brell-Cokcan and Johannes Braumann, 143–8. Vienna: Springer-Verlag.

Rutten, David. 2013. "Galapagos: On the Logic and Limitations of Generic Solvers." *Architectural Design* 83 (2): 132–5.

8   Latitudo Borealis, exhibition view with pavillion model and shading system sample installed. Liberty Research Annex, March 15–April 9, 2017. (RVTR, 2017)

Daniel Tish is a PhD student at the University of Technology Sydney, a Lecturer at the University of Michigan and an Associate at RVTR. He received his M.Arch with distinction from the University of Michigan in 2015. He was a 2014 Dow Sustainability Fellow, and his thesis was awarded an honorable mention in the 2015 Jacques Rougerie Innovation and Architecture for Space international competition. His interests lie in the computational investigations of complex systems and geometries, especially those pertaining to responsive and interactive architectural environments.

Dustin Brugmann is a FABLab Research Associate and Lecturer at the University of Michigan. He received his M.Arch from the University of Michigan in 2015 and Bachelor of Arts in Architecture from Miami University of Ohio in 2010. He worked for the Danish Institute for Study Abroad from 2010–11, Bernard Tschumi Architects as a Junior Designer from 2011–13, and was also awarded the Quarra Stone / Matter Design Research Fellowship in 2015. His research interests span digital and craft methods of making towards hybrid and novel methods of architectural production.

Lars Junghans PhD is Associate Professor at University of Michigan Taubman College of Architecture and Urban Planning. His research interests focus on innovative building automation systems, the development of building optimization algorithms and the improvement of building envelopes for high performance buildings. Dr. Junghans was lead engineer for the award winning "Concept 22/26" building with Baumschlager-Eberle in Lustenau, Austria, a high performance office building without any active systems for heating, cooling or ventilation. Ongoing research focuses on the integration of artificial intelligence in building automation technology.

Geoffrey Thün is Associate Dean of Research and Creative Practice and Associate Professor at the University of Michigan Taubman College of Architecture and Urban Planning. He is a founding partner of RVTR, which serves as a platform for exploration and experimentation in the agency of architecture and urban design within the context of dynamic ecological systems, infrastructures, materially and technologically mediated environments, and emerging social organizations. The work ranges in scale from regional territories and urbanities to full-scale prototypes that explore responsive and kinetic envelopes that mediate energy, atmosphere, and interaction.

Kaleidoscopic Monolith

Kenneth Tracy
Singapore University of
Technology and Design, ASD

Christine Yogiaman
Singapore University of
Technology and Design, ASD

1   Photograph of a girl interacting with installation in the evening. (Photo by Traxon Technologies, 2017)

Designed and built for iLight Marina Bay 2017, Kaleidoscopic Monolith incites curiosity from spectators through light, reflection, and form. Contradictory strategies are used to enhance the complex presence of the object. At a distance it is perceived as a single convex form that subtly changes profile from different angles of approach. On closer inspection its rippling surface contains a pattern of concavities. Filled with kaleidoscopic reflections these voids distort, repeat, and reorient the context. Light projected from the center of each dimple surrounds the piece in an ambient, glowing pool and illuminates onlookers whose own reflections become part of the spectacle. Radial geometry with multiple symmetries and faceted, reflective surfaces evoke the cylindrical kaleidoscope toys the piece is inspired by. Like the colorful patterns created by the toy, the installation resists a singular meaning and instead provokes participants to discover their own allusions through interactive play.

PRODUCTION NOTES

Client: URA, Singapore

Status: Completed

Location: Marina Bay Waterfront

Date: March 2017

Tiling Pattern

To create Kaleidoscopic Monolith digital tools were created to discretize the form into radial patterns, output the structural frame, optimize the distribution of lights, and to articulate the surfaces of the installation's skin. A method of freeform discretization (Pottmann 150) was developed that allows hierarchical geometric relationships and patterning to be overlaid onto a freeform surface with positive Gaussian curvature (Schwinn and Menges 95). The Grasshopper 3D definition

2   Close-up photographs of installation in the day and evening.

3   Kaleidoscopic Monolith installation in Singapore Marina Bay Waterfront.

combines the use of plane regions and patterns of UV-mapped points derived from non-periodic tiling to achieve a continuously varied but recognizable pattern. Starting from a 2D pattern of points interpolated from the centroids of pentagonal Penrose tiles, the script then maps the points onto a radially lofted NURBS surface. Surface points and their respective normal are then used to define a set of plane regions, which are trimmed to generate a polyhedral mesh made up of planar, n-gon tiles. These planar, straight-edged panels are the base geometry for the surface articulation, lighting distribution, and horizontal frame members.

Frame and Skin

Layers of parts fabricated from a variety of different machines were integrated to accommodate the structure, skin, sensors, and lighting (Figure 4). A bespoke, 3D-printed lighting mount connects the LED lighting modules and tiled skin to either side of tabs folded from the horizontal aluminum frame members. CNC

routed from 3 mm aluminum, the slotted frame consists of radial vertical members supporting horizontal members with tabs that are hand-bent to angles normal to the tile faces (Figure 7).

CNC knife-cut panels made from .014'' thick metalized BoPET (Biaxially oriented polyethylene terephthalate) rest on the outside of the frame, supported at their centers by light bezels. Characterized by inflected profile curves that transition from convex to concave, the ruled-surface form of the tiles creates greater rigidity and captures reflections. Individual ruled surfaces are stitched together using hand-assembled tabs creating tightly connected, rigid seams. Even using .014'' film this assembly type allows for a high degree of surface fidelity and stiffness. Planar perimeter bezels support the outer edges of the tiles where adjacent tiles are stapled together via tabs tucked inside the skin (Figure 5). Six vertical "peals" were used to organize groups of preassembled tiles for mounting and to group the LED light strips.

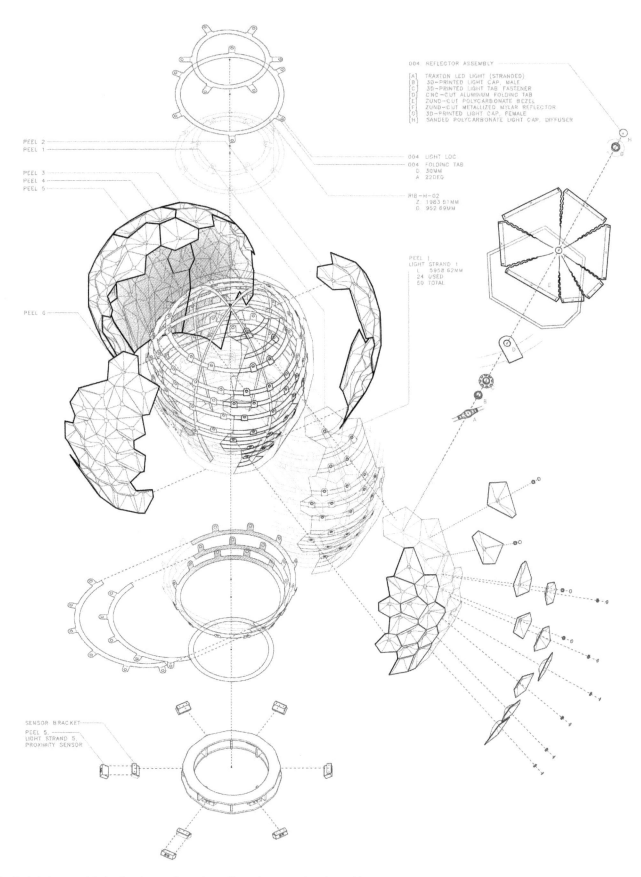

004 REFLECTOR ASSEMBLY

[A] TRAXTON LED LIGHT (STRANDED)
[B] 3D-PRINTED LIGHT CAP, MALE
[C] 3D-PRINTED LIGHT TAB FASTENER
[D] CNC-CUT ALUMINUM FOLDING TAB
[E] ZUND-CUT POLYCARBONATE BEZEL
[F] ZUND-CUT METALLIZED MYLAR REFLECTOR
[G] 3D-PRINTED LIGHT CAP, FEMALE
[H] SANDED POLYCARBONATE LIGHT CAP, DIFFUSER

PEEL 2
PEEL 1

004 LIGHT LOC
004 FOLDING TAB
D 30MM
A 220EQ

PEEL 3
PEEL 4
PEEL 5

R18-H-02
Z 1983.51MM
D 952.89MM

PEEL 1
LIGHT STRAND 1
L 5958.62MM
24 USED
80 TOTAL

PEEL 6

SENSOR BRACKET
PEEL 5,
LIGHT STRAND 5,
PROXIMITY SENSOR

4   Exploded axonometric drawing, documenting systems of layered components and assembly process.

Kaleidoscopic Monolith Tracy, Yogiaman

5 Individual ruled surfaces are stitched together using hand-assembled tabs creating tightly connected, rigid seams.

6 A bespoke, 3D-printed lighting mount connects the LED lighting modules and tiled skin to either side of tabs folded from the horizontal aluminum frame members

7 In-process documentation of assembly, showing portions of the frame and skin.

8 Interior view of the lightweight structure. Assembly is done by coordination between inside and outside of the component layers.

Surface and Interactivity

Proximity information from 6 ultrasonic sensors in the base of the installation controls the 6 strips of addressed LED lights. As observers approach, the lights incrementally dim to allow ambient reflections to be observed in the concavities of the tiles. The continuously curving tiles distort figure and form into colors and patterns. Distorted, ruled reflections of sky, buildings, cars, trees, and people mix to create abstract, kinetic patterns (Figures 10, 12).

9   Kaleidoscopic Monolith installation in Singapore Marina Bay Waterfront, daytime.

10   Close up photograph of dimpled tiles in daytime, reflecting surrounding urban context.

ACKNOWLEDGMENTS

Kaleidoscopic Monolith installation is designed in collaboration with Kenneth Tracy, Christine Yogiaman and Suranga Nanayakkara, faculty at SUTD, Singapore. OSRAM Lighting Solutions both contributed to the execution and donation of lighting system, Traxon Dot XL-3 RGB connected via e:cue Butler XT2, that animated the surface of the installation.

Fabrication Team: Pamela Dychengbeng Chua, Pang Xin Hua, Tay Jing Zhi, Caroline. Lighting Team: Lai Jun Kang, Tenzin Han Wei Chan. Assembly Team: Basil Yap Ji Tsing, Eugene Kosgoron, Ho Zhi Yuan, Tracy Yee Enying, Nur Amalina Bte Md Halim, Sally Tan Jie Ying, Ong Jie Min, Kelly Yeo Jing Er, Kerine Kua

REFERENCES

Schwinn, Tobias, and Achim Menges. 2015. "Fabrication Agency: Landesgartenschau Exhibition Hall." *Architectural Design* 85 (5): 92–99. doi:10.1002/ad.1960

Pottmann, Helmut, Michael Eigensatz, Amir Vaxman, and Johannes Wallner. 2015. "Architectural Geometry." *Computers and Graphics* 47 (C): 145–164

11 Kaleidoscopic Monolith installation in Singapore Marina Bay Waterfront, early evening time

 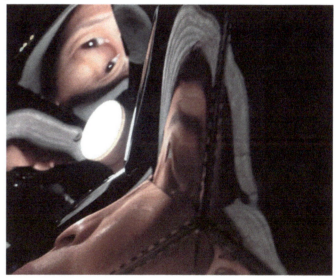

12 Close-up photograph of dimpled tiles in the evening. Lights in the center of tile dimples glow to illuminate participants, whose reflections create abstract, kinetic patterns.

Kenneth Tracy is an Assistant Professor at the Singapore University of Technology and Design, and has previously held teaching positions in American University of Sharjah, Washington University in St Louis, Pratt Institute and Columbia University. In 2010, Kenneth co-founded Yogiaman Tracy Design, an award-winning experimental firm. Formerly he was a founding partner at Associated Fabrication, Brooklyn, New York. Kenneth's investigations into the materials and processes of building borrow from industrial, artistic and traditional production techniques to expand the range of possibilities for architecture. Grounded in professional fabrication experience, his research manifests in full-scale tests, installations, and buildings.

Christine Yogiaman is an Assistant Professor at the Singapore University of Technology and Design, where she coordinates the university's signature interdisciplinary beginning design course, "Introduction to Design," which merges project and studio-based design pedagogy. She has previously held teaching positions in American University of Sharjah and Washington University in St Louis. Christine directs Yogiaman Tracy Design, an award-winning design and research practice based in Singapore. Christine's work combines labour intensive acts in traditional crafts with rule-based, digital frameworks to create culturally embedded, affective work.

HEXY
Soft Self-Organization Robot

Yuan Yao
AADRL

Yuhan Li
AADRL

Yang Hong
AADRL

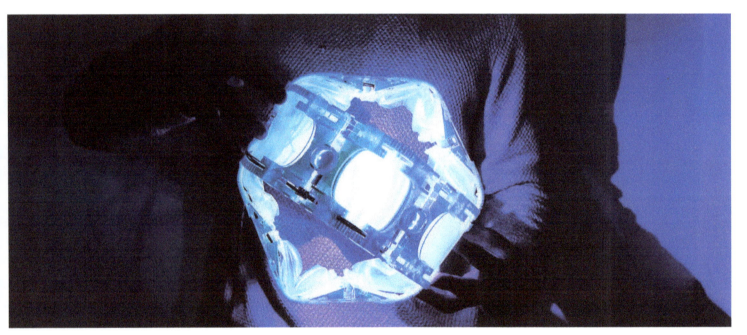

1   HEXY unit lighting up with human touch (photographer: Yihui Wu)

ARCHITECTURE VS ROBOT

Team: Yuan Yao, Yuhan Li, Yang
         Hong

Tutor: Theodore Spyropoulos

Status: Unbuilt

Date: 2016-2017

In the contemporary realm of technology, cybernetic research, AI, and robotic research are defining the near future of human society. In the future, robots with artificial intelligence will be able to participate in social life and fundamentally change humans' lifestyle. Now, many researchers are focusing on servant-like robots or androids that can serve human beings. However, this kind of robot has little influence in architecture because its behavior is detached from architectural space, structure, and function. So what is the kind of robot that can be integrated into architecture and deeply influence people's lifestyles and architectural space?

HEXY is a research project investigating the possibility of applying a self-organization unit system into a residential house to create adaptive architectural space. The aim is to provide an alternative solution for adaptive living in the near future when the unit agents are able to create organizations for architectural and human usage. The research explores self-organization of mobile robotic agents that define architecture beyond the fixed and finite towards the reconfigurable and infinite. The robots become architectural material, structure, and even texture.

2   HEXY is another species living in Case Study House #4 to become the "Functional Landscape" (photographer: Yihui Wu)

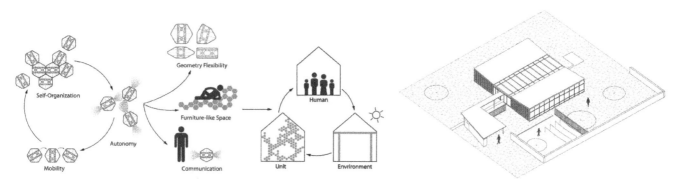

3   Diagram showing the concept of "Adaptive House System"   4   Case Study House 4 "Greenbelt House" for HEXY dwelling

HOUSING SOLUTION

Housing is a critical problem in cities nowadays. On one hand, the increasing population requires more living space while the buildable area is limited. On the other hand, dwelling narrowness is prevalent in contemporary society in mega cities. A bed, a table, and a wardrobe will take most of the space in a room. What if we design a self-organization system that can replace the role of conventional furniture and lighting devices? What if the system can create different types of space at different times of the day, the week, the month, or even over years? It is a chance to introduce robot agents in the house to create a symbiotic life with humans so that people can have a changeable living environment within the limited house space.

UNITS: FROM LOW TO HIGH POPULATION

From low to high population, this research explores prototype design, unit behavior, unit aggregation, and unit transformation to explore the potential of the self-organization system and its behavior. On the house level, the research focused on functional landscape, lighting systems, and reconfigurable space to visualize how the units are able to create functional space in the house and live within human residences. The robotic agent is a new species in the house, not only part of the original house but also its extension.

On the unit level, HEXY is a transformable hexagon geometry unit which can change from hexagon to rectangle, triangle, and more, showing the flexibility of a single unit through its multiple transformations. By using membrane material and distributing the control systems on the outer skin of the unit, HEXY is able to show a lightweight and transparent prototype. A single unit is integrated with actuators, sensors, skins, air bags, structural bones, and a micro-processor so that a single unit is able to sense the surrounding information and make autonomous decision about its movement.

With more than one unit, units can communicate and collaborate to create more complex organization such as the "linear cluster".

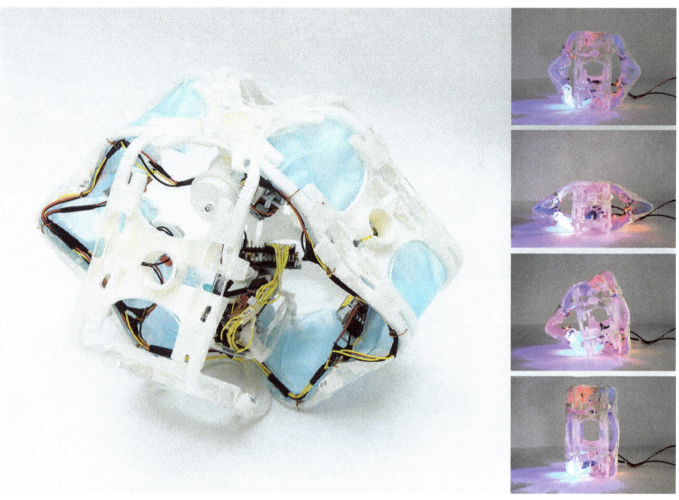

5 **Left:** HEXY Prototype with soft body and air actuation system. **Right:** HEXY Transformation

6 HEXY's collaborate movement as linear organization

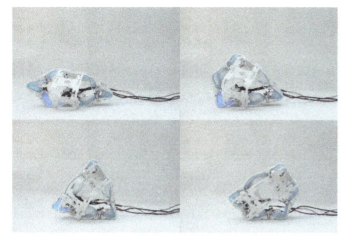

7   HEXY's rolling movement

8   HEXY climbing onto other units to create a larger organization

9   HEXY occupies the house and reconfigures into different organizations from morning to night (from energy collection cluster to bed-like organization)

The linear cluster behaves like a swarm to crawl forward. Multiple units can also form clusters to help other units climb onto each other.

When hundreds and thousands of units get together, the system is able to create different taxonomies of functional landscape as a combination of furniture, structures, and lighting systems. Each unit is imbued with the capability of transformation which enables the whole system to be either rigid or soft and elastic. The softness makes the organization suitable for humans to sit and touch. Individual unit transformations enable the overall transformation of the cluster. So HEXY is not only able to reconfigure the space by moving, but also to change the function of the cluster by transformation.

24 HOURS—1 YEAR

The project sets up several scenarios to visualize how HEXY can live in the house with human beings within different time periods. Two typical life scenarios are 24 hours and 1 year. In 24 hours,

HEXY needs to react to human activity and reconstruct the space with fast speed which will consume more energy. So the units need an efficient organization to collect energy. In the 1 year time period, HEXY's organization in the house is mainly affected by the sun angle. During the summer, the units will create shading structures and get closer to the glass to collect more solar power. During the winter, the units will create more smooth and flat organization for humans and themselves to enjoy the sunshine.

FUTURE

The reality of technology is not yet able to create perfect self-organizing robots because of many reasons, such as the precision of movement, failure of mechanical and electrical devices, data processing, and material stability. However, in the near future, those problems might be solved with more mature technology such as nano technology to reduce the size and weight of the unit. We should be optimistic about the future of self-organizing robots and foresee the potential of the system to create dynamic and adaptive architecture.

10 A birds-eye view of HEXY forming different parts of the house as the extension of house structure and replacement of furniture

11 HEXY can create lighting for illumination and create "Functional Landscape" for humans such as dining, sleeping, and entertaining

12 1 year house life: HEXY creates adaptive house strutcures changing the house environment and residence's lifestyle

13 House at night: HEXY creates dynamic interior lighting to hold different house activities such as reading, party, rest, and chatting.

ACKNOWLEDGMENTS

We want to take this chance to thanks to our AADRL tutor Theodore Spyropoulos, the director of AADRL, who has been devoted to this topic for many years, and provided valuable insights to our project. We also need express our thanks to other AADRL tutors including Rob Stuart Smith, Shajay Bhooshan, Patrik Schumacher, Mustafa Elsayed, and Apostolos Despotidis, who have been tutoring and reviewing our project during the research. Second, we need to thank our helpers Yihui Wu, Ruilin Yang, and Ziqian Wang, who helped us in the final production stage to take photos, make models, and other assistance. Last, we need to thank AKT London for their structural consultation and advice in the cluster structures.

Yuan Yao graduated from University of Southern California in Los Angeles in 2015 and Architecture Association Design Research Lab in London in 2017. He is interested in parametric design, prototyping, and digital fabrication. In AADRL, he was on team HEXY and was responsible for the prototype.

Yuhan Li graduated from AADRL in 2017. He was on team HEXY and mainly worked on digital modeling and animation.

Yang Hong graduated from AADRL in 2017. He was on team HEXY and contributed to the code simulation.

Arachne
A 3D-Printed Building Façade

Lei Yu
Tsinghua University
Archi-Solution Workshiop

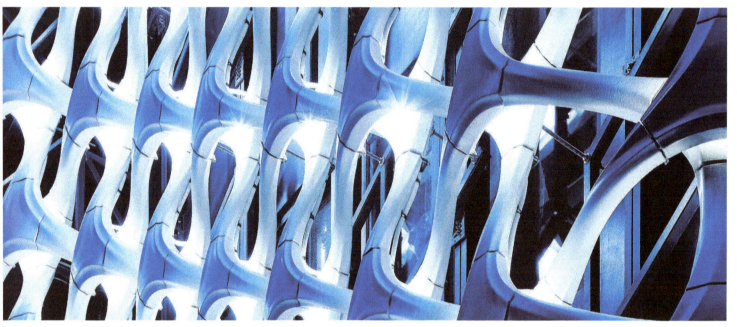

1   Arachne: Night view in detail (photographer Xing Fu, 04.01 2017, © Fuxing Photograph Studio).

Arachne is a digital architectural endeavor to redefine an ordinary building with 3D-printed components. To reflect its literal title, Arachne is designed and installed by the spatially intertwined lattices that hung on the building in the curtain wall mechanism.

The mass gift-wrapped by Arachne is a three-story building, 10 meters high and 12 meters wide. This assignment was contracted to cover the main façades, which face an important public square, with a strong iconic articulation to collect attention. 3D-printing technology was selected to meet this requirement, owing to its fabulous capacity to adopt the design concept. There are two major considerations:

- Give the building a stand-out interface by applying a special screen that presents a spatial and non-uniformed network.
- Pursue the subtle variations in detail during the form transformation by naturally following the internal forces.

Geometrically, a hexagon was chosen to develop the form. Three groups of threads are braided to create an interwoven network. This network is forced to deform in the location that have intersections with the building masses, such as the balcony and the rain roof. The density of the network is also carefully managed for an optimized appearance. Those threads disappear when turning the building's corner and end up with a simpler formation. The whole network, based on

PRODUCTION NOTES

Architect:	Lei Yu
Client:	Yuexiu Group
Status:	Completed
Site Area:	3888 sq. ft.
Location:	Foshan, China
Date:	2017

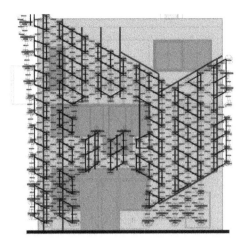

2   Facade components with the installation codes.

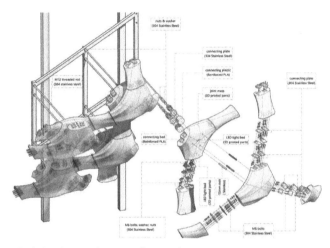

3   Explosive diagram of curtain wall connection.

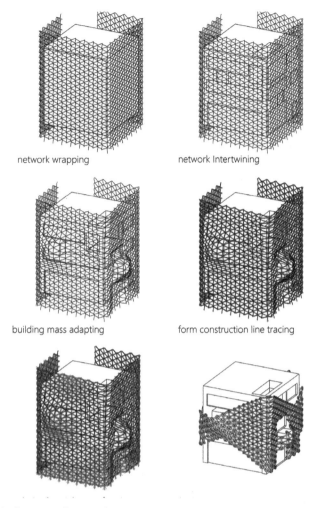

network wrapping   network Intertwining

building mass adapting   form construction line tracing

4   Form generation procedure.

3D-printed components, stays in an adaptive manner like a silky wrap.

There are over 2,000 components that could be categorized into two types: hexagon joints and connecting struts, which collectively weigh over 5 tons and took 50 large FDM printers more than 4 months to fabricate. Each component is different from the others, requiring a specific tag system for inventory during the production and position mapping during the installation. The mullion grid is formatted by the surface's hexagonal layout. Every part enrolls the system either by bolts or screws. The particle lights are located on the second layer for a backlit illustration. All information is outputted from a digital pipeline programmed in Grasshopper and C#, and visually investigated in Rhinoceros.

To increase the durability of an outdoor installation in PLA, a plastic 3D-printed filament, there are mainly two important issues to deal with: fire resistance and sun irradiance aging. An inflammable additive was mixed during the manufacture of the printable filament to satisfy the fire code. But the anti-aging solution was more complicated. Unlike ABS, PLA is not friendly to most paints. A kind of fluorocarbon gel was brushed before adding a prime layer of the white paint, and coated with a glazing paint to finalize the cosmetics. This treatment process prevents the plastic from being oxidized and increases its durability.

The installation was completed in three weeks. It is such a unique experience for the team to give every single piece a designated location; if there are any human errors, the contingent zone must be stopped to restore accuracy. There is an 8 mm gap between every two pieces, and a 4 mm silicon cushion pad is used to adjust the bias in case its deviation accumulates.

It took one year to finish this 3D-printed façade from concept to installation. During this year, our design team had to overcome many problems for which we had neither reference to nor experience in when taking 3D-printing technology up to building

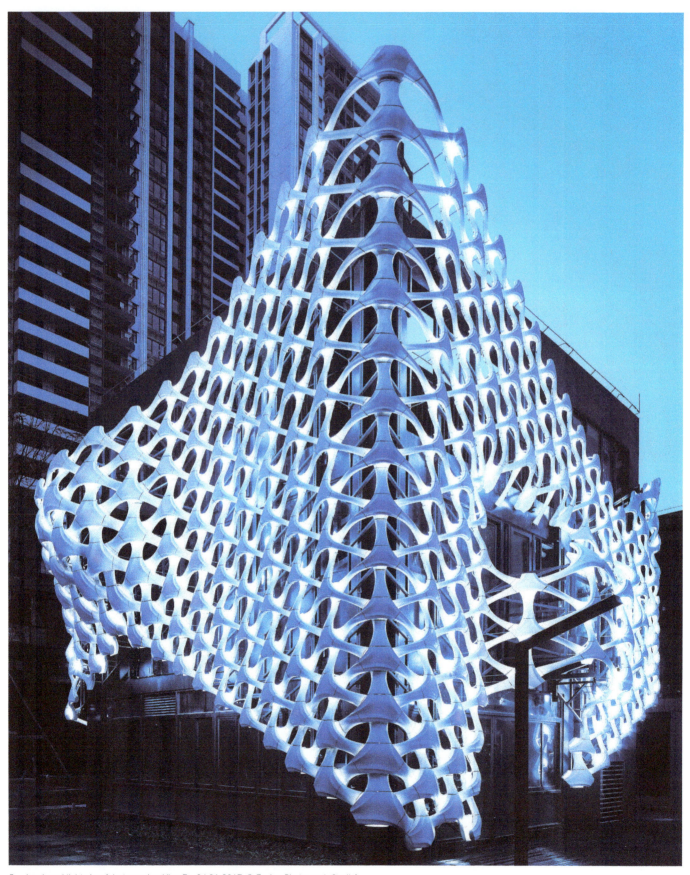

5   Arachne: Night view (photographer Xing Fu, 04.01 2017, © Fuxing Photograph Studio).

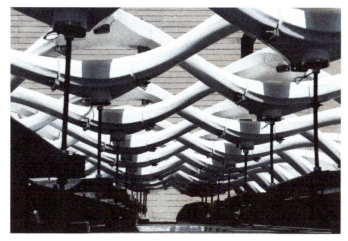

6 Curtain wall connection (photographer Guan Wang).

7 Embeded lighting wire (photographer Guan Wang)

8 3D-printed components in detail (photographer Lei Yu, 04.01 2017)

9 Facade Detail: Day view (photographer Xing Fu, 04.01 2017, © Fuxing)

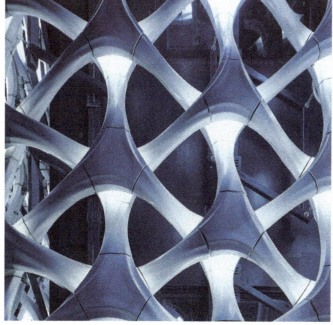

10 Facade Detail: Night view (photographer Xing Fu, 04.01 2017, © Fuxing)

11 Arachne: Day view (photographer Xing Fu, 04.01 2017, © Fuxing Studio).

12 Arachne: Day view (photographer Xing Fu, 04.01 2017, © Fuxing Studio)

13 Arachne: Day view (photographer Xing Fu, 04.01 2017, © Fuxing Studio).

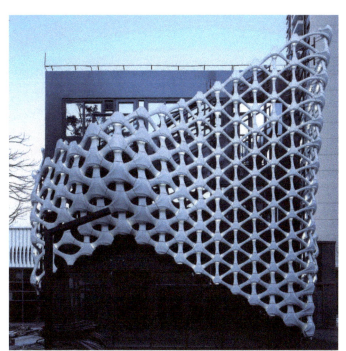

14 Arachne: Night view (photographer Xing Fu, 04.01 2017, © Fuxing Studio)

scale. Fixing the last component in place was an impressive moment, in that the physical installation was identical to the digital model and renderings, a fact only made possible by the new design and fabrication methodology.

ACKNOWLEDGEMENTS

Curtain wall consultant: Weijie Wang, Centry Star Group

Installation team: Aa Wu construction team.

Photograph: Fuxing © Fuxing Photograph Studio

Lei Yu is a Ph.D Candidate at Tsinghua University. He got his MArch from Harvard's GSD in 2004. He is the founder of Archi-solution Workshop (ASW), and the co-founder of DADA (Digital Architecture Design Association). His teaching experience includes ETH Zurich, Tsinghua University, and Tongji University. He was featured as Beijing Design Week Elite of 2015. For ACADIA 2016, VULCAN PAVILION was selected as runner-up of the jury selected projects.

ACADIA 2017

CREDITS

288   ACADIA ORGANIZATION

290   CONFERENCE MANAGEMENT & PRODUCTION CREDITS

292   PEER REVIEW COMMITTEE

294   ACADIA 2017 SPONSORS

ACADIA ORGANIZATION

The Association for Computer Aided Design in Architecture (ACADIA) is an international network of digital design researchers and professionals that facilitates critical investigations into the role of computation in architecture, planning, and building science, encouraging innovation in design creativity, sustainability and education.

ACADIA was founded in 1981 by some of the pioneers in the field of design computation including Bill Mitchell, Chuck Eastman, and Chris Yessios. Since then, ACADIA has hosted over 30 conferences across North America and has grown into a strong network of academics and professionals in the design computation field.

Incorporated in the state of Delaware as a not-for-profit corporation, ACADIA is an all-volunteer organization governed by elected officers, an elected Board of Directors, and appointed ex-officio officers.

PRESIDENT
Jason Kelly Johnson California College of the Arts
pres@acadia.org

VICE-PRESIDENT
Michael Fox Cal Poly Pomona
vp@acadia.org

SECRETARY
Mara Marcu American University of Sharjah
secretary@acadia.org

TREASURER
Mike Christenson North Dakota State University
treasurer@acadia.org

MEMBERSHIP OFFICER
Phillip Anzalone New York City College of Technology
membership@acadia.org

TECHNOLOGY OFFICER
Andrew Kudless California College of the Arts
webmaster@acadia.org

DEVELOPMENT OFFICER
Shane Burger Woods Bagot, Smartgeometry
development@acadia.org

COMMUNICATION OFFICER
Adam Marcus California College of the Arts
communications@acadia.org

BOARD OF DIRECTORS

2016 Election (Term: Jan 2017 - Dec 2018)

Dana Cupkova, Carnegie Mellon University
Jose Sanchez, USC
Phillip Anzalone, Columbia University
Mara Marcu, American University of Sharjah
Lauren Vasey, ICD University of Stuttgart
Mike Christenson (alternate), North Dakota State University
Andrew John Wit (alternate), Temple University
Marcella Del Signore (alternate), Tulane University

Conference Management & Production Credits

CONFERENCE CHAIRS
Takehiko Nagakura Associate Professor, MIT / Director, Computation Group, MIT
Skylar Tibbits Assistant Professor, MIT / Co-director and Founder, Self-Assembly Lab, MIT

GENERAL COORDINATOR
Skylar Tibbits Assistant Professor, MIT / Co-director and Founder, Self-Assembly Lab, MIT

CONFERENCE ADVISOR
Dennis Shelden Director, Digital Building Lab, Georgia Tech

PAPER SESSIONS CO-CHAIRS
Mariana Ibañez Assistant Professor, Department of Architecture, MIT / Principal, Ibañez Kim Studio
Caitlin Mueller Assistant Professor, MIT / Co-director, Structural Design Lab, MIT

PROJECTS CO-CHAIRS
Joel Lamere Assistant Professor, Department of Architecture, MIT / Principal, GLD Architecture
Cristina Parreño Alonso Belluschi Lecturer, Department of Architecture, MIT / Cristina Parreño Architecture

WORKSHOP CO-CHAIRS
Brandon Clifford Assistant Professor, Department of Architecture, MIT / Co-founder, Matter Design
Justin Lavallee Technical Instructor / Director, MIT Architecture Shops

EXHIBITION CO-CHAIRS
Azra Aksamija Associate Professor, Art, Culture and Technology Program, MIT
William O'Brien Jr. Associate Professor, Department of Architecture, MIT / Principal, WOJR / Co-Founder, CLOK

HACKATHON CO-CHAIRS
Federico Casalegno Associate Professor of the Practice, MIT / Director, MIT Design Lab, Mobile Experience Lab, MIT
Greg Demchak Director of Product Management, Synchro Software Ltd.

REGIONAL EVENT CO-CHAIRS
Carl Lostritto Assistant Professor, Department of Architecture, RISD
Dimitris Papanikolaou Assistant Professor, School of Architecture and Department of Software & Information

ADMINISTRATIVE MANAGEMENT
Andreea O'Connell MIT Department of Architecture

PLANNING AND ORGANIZATION
Patricia Driscoll MIT Department of Architecture
Inala Locke MIT Department of Architecture
Maroula Bacharidou MIT Department of Architecture
Jesica Dunaway Nishibun MIT Department of Architecture

WEBSITE
Maroula Bacharidou MIT Department of Architecture

COVER IMAGERY
Maroula Bacharidou, MIT Department of Architecture

COPY EDITING FOR PUBLICATIONS
Pascal Massinon, Ph.D.
Mary O'Malley

GRAPHIC DESIGN
Rebekka Kuhn Principal, Rebekka Kuhn Communications Design

PUBLICATION EDITOR
Anastasia Hiller

CONFERENCE ASSISTANTS
Paloma Francisca Gonzalez Roja MIT Department of Architecture, Poster Production/ Tour Coordination TA
Cagri Hakan Zaman MIT Department of Architecture, Hackathon TA
Joshuah Jest MIT Department of Architecture, Exhibition Production TA
Chang Liu MIT Department of Architecture, App Development/ Poster Production TA
Sarah Wagner MIT Department of Architecture, Workshop TA

EDUCATION ROUND TABLE SESSION
Ruairi Glynn Director, Interactive Architecture Lab / Lecturer, The Bartlett School of Architecture, UCL
Jason Kelly Johnson Associate Professor, California College of the Arts / Founding Design Principal, Future Cities Lab/ President, Association for Computer Aided Design in Architecture
Carl Lostritto (moderator) Assistant Professor, Department of Architecture, Rhode Island School of Design
Dan O'Sullivan Associate Professor, Associate Dean for Emerging Media, Tisch School of the Arts, Tokyo Broadcasting System Chair, Interactive Telecommunications Program (ITP), New York University (NYU)
Dimitris Papanikolaou (moderator) Assistant Professor, School of Architecture and Department of Software & Information Systems, UNCC
Heather Roberge Associate Vice Chair and Director of the Undergraduate Program in Architectural Studies, , UCLA Department of Architecture and Urban Design / Founder, Murmur design
Meejin Yoon Professor and Head of the Department of Architecture, Massachusetts Institute of Technology / Founding Design Principal, Höweler + Yoon Architecture LLP and MY Studio

PEER REVIEW COMMITTEE

Mania Aghaei Meibodi   ETH Zurich

Ana Anton   ETH Zurich

German Aparicio   Gehry Technologies

David Benjamin   The Living

Kory Bieg   The University of Texas at Austin

Brennan Buck   Yale University

Brandon Clifford   Massachusetts Institute of Technology

Oliver David   University of Stuttgart

Matias del Campo   University of Michigan

Christian Derix   Woods Bagot

Tomas Diez Ladera   Institute of Advanced Architecture Catalonia

Benjamin Dillenburger   ETH Zurich

Frederico Fialho Teixeira   The University of Queensland

Michael Fox   Cal Poly Pomona

Adam Fure   The University of Michigan

David Gerber   The University of Southern California

Kimo Griggs   The University of Washington

Cynthia Gunadi   GLD Architecture

Hua Hao   Southeast University

Alvin Huang   The University of Southern California

Chikara Inamura   Massachusetts Institute of Technology

Andrej Jipa   ETH Zurich

Steven Keating   Massachusetts Institute of Technology

Omar Khan   The University of Buffalo

Simon Kim   The University of Pennsylvania

John Klein   Massachusetts Institute of Technology

Chris Knapp   Bond University

Gabriel Kozlowski   Massachusetts Institute of Technology

Jared Laucks   Massachusetts Institute of Technology

Joel Lamere   Massachusetts Institute of Technology

Carl Lostritto   Rhode Island School of Design

Gregory Luhan   The University of Kentucky

Adam Marcus   California College of the Arts

Bob Martens   Technische Universität Wien

Mania Meibodi   ETH Zurich

Constantinos Miltiadis   Graz University of Technology

Jonathan Nelson   Bond University

Catie Newell   The University of Michigan

Cristina Parreño Alonso   Massachusetts Institute of Technology

Andy Payne   Harvard University

Chris Perry   Rensselaer Polytechnic Institute

Benjamin Rice   The University of Texas at Austin

Penn Ruderman   Office of Penn Ruderman Architects

Roi Salgueiro Barrio   Massachusetts Institute of Technology

Christoph Schindler   SchindlerSalmeron

Jason Scott Johnson   The University of Calgary

Amin Tadjsoleiman   NADAAA, VAVStudio

Josh Taron   The University of Calgary

Michael Weinstock   The Architectural Association

Huang Weixin   Tsinghua University

Andrew Witt   Harvard University

Achilleas Xydis   ETH Zurich

ACADIA 2017 SPONSORS

PLATINUM SPONSOR

SILVER SPONSOR

BRONZE SPONSOR

proving ground

 WALTER P MOORE

SPONSOR

iris

cbt

HACKATHON SPONSOR

COMMUNICATION SPONSOR

EVENT SPONSOR

www.ingramcontent.com/pod-product-compliance
Lightning Source LLC
Chambersburg PA
CBHW041006050326
40689CB00030B/4993